MAINE AL FRESCO

The Fifty Finest Outdoor Adventures in Maine

by

Ron Chase

North Country Press
Unity, Maine

Copyright © 2021 by Ron Chase

All rights reserved. No part of this book may be reproduced or transmitted in any form or by any means without written permission of the author.

Back cover photo: Skiing Mount Blue State Park
(Photo by Bill Blauvelt)

ISBN 978-1-943424-70-2

LCCN 2021950929

North Country Press
Unity, Maine

To my beautiful granddaughters
Raina and Freya

In memory of outdoor companions who have passed:

Kelly Bentz
Lloyd Brown
Ed Collins
Alice Douglas
Audrey Ingersoll
Bill "grampy" Kaiser
Ted Lombard
Eric Lougee
Bill McKenna
Taylor Pelotte
Jo Pendleton
Skip Pendleton
Rodney Reed
Mickey Stultz
Terry Tzavarrus
Ed Webb
Marie Webb

Acknowledgments

This book would not have been possible without my outdoor companions. The camaraderie we've shared and the support they've provided has been invaluable and perhaps the foremost aspect of my outdoor experiences. I dare not attempt to name them as I would undoubtedly forget someone. Many of their names are included in the narratives. I do want to thank two outdoor friends who made direct contributions to the book. Carolyn Welch shared personal journals of the Kenduskeag Stream Canoe Race and the St. John River Canoe Trip. Dave Lanman, who along with Carolyn was co-leader of the St. John trip, also shared his files related to the trip. Their help was very much appreciated.

Special thanks to my wife Nancy who continues to be supportive of my quixotic writing endeavors. She also completed the first edit of every chapter which was indispensable.

Foreword

For the past forty-five years, I've had the good fortune to explore and experience Maine's finest outdoor adventures with my wife and sons and a large group of exceptionally capable friends who have become extended family. We've climbed the highest, most scenic mountains, many in winter, canoed the iconic tripping rivers, hiked trails in the Camden Hills and Acadia National Park, cycled coastal islands and the best bike paths, sea kayaked to remote islands and along the Bold Coast, canoed and kayaked the most challenging whitewater, paddled the large lakes, cross country skied the finest trails, backpacked some of the Appalachian Trail and mountainous routes in Baxter State Park, and participated in the spring downriver races. In short, it's been a wonderful journey and this book is an attempt to share the best of it.

How does one determine what constitutes the fifty finest outdoor adventures in Maine is a fair question. The obvious answer is it's subjective. Some, such as climbing Mount Katahdin, sea kayaking the Bold Coast, exploring Acadia National Park, navigating Moosehead Lake, canoeing the Allagash, and paddling the intimidating rapids in the Kennebec Gorge are apparent. I submit that deciding on the remainder is a function of personal life experiences. My selections are an attempt to include a combination of mountain hiking with an emphasis on winter outings, biking, sea kayaking, whitewater paddling, Nordic skiing, lake paddling, canoe tripping, backpacking, and downriver racing. Every region of the state is represented and, purely by happenstance, fifteen of the sixteen counties are included. I encourage readers to consider their preferences when reading my choices.

I believe this book is unique in that it is a collection of narratives relating actual outdoor adventures, yet there is an addendum with each chapter that provides fundamental guidebook information. With one exception, I actually participated in the described adventures and the renditions reflect my views or recollections of what transpired. Since some of the events happened many years ago and I'm now an old man, a senior perspective is inherent. Many of the most memorable occurrences in life result when calamity occurs, so there is no shortage of misadventures depicted. While sometimes failing, I try not to take myself too seriously so humor is often an anecdotal part of the escapades.

The chapter that chronicles the Kenduskeag Stream Canoe Race is the one episode that I didn't actually participate in. Although I competed in the 1984 and 1989 races, my recollection of both events was fragmented. Fortuitously, my longtime friend Carolyn Welch has been a contestant in twenty-four Kenduskeag races and kept a detailed written account of each. She graciously shared her journal along with some videos and I selected my favorite to relate. I'm confident readers will find it an entertaining compelling story.

Probably the greatest danger encountered on an outdoor adventure is the drive to and from the activity. However, as with almost any endeavor, potential hazards exist. Adventurers are encouraged to carry sufficient safety equipment, gear, and supplies to address the issues unique to that particular pursuit and anticipated weather conditions. Some undertakings, such as whitewater boating, sea kayaking, and skiing require proper instruction from a qualified instructor and acquiring proficiency entails a significant learning curve. While impossible to anticipate all of the potential risks, each chapter addendum includes a discussion of the unique potential hazards for that particular exploit.

Severe weather is probably the most common cause of death and injury while participating in outdoor activities. Always obtain a reliable weather forecast prior to a trip. If bad weather is predicted, don't go. Carry a GPS, map, and compass and know how to use them. Never go alone.

Enjoy wildlife without disturbing it. Always protect the environment. Practice a carry-in and carry-out policy and never leave litter and trash behind. Respect the rights of private landowners.

I hope you find the book enjoyable and informative and that it inspires you to new adventures of your own.

Table of Contents

SECTION I. MOUNTAIN HIKES

Chapter 1 - Mount Katahdin in Winter 1
Chapter 2 - Cadillac Mountain 9
Chapter 3 - Tumbledown and Little Jackson Mountains 14
Chapter 4 - North Brother, South Brother, Fort Mountain, and Mount Coe in Winter 18
Chapter 5 - Traveler Mountain Loop Trip in Baxter State Park in Winter 25
Chapter 6 - Bigelow Mountain 32
Chapter 7 - Puzzle Mountain 37
Chapter 8 - Mounts Megunticook and Battie 42
Chapter 9 - Pleasant Mountain 47

SECTION II. BIKE TRAILS

Chapter 10 - Sebago to the Sea 54
Chapter 11 - Kennebec River Rail Trail 59
Chapter 12 - Eastern Trails 63
Chapter 13 - Carriage Trails of Acadia National Park 67
Chapter 14 - Narrow Gauge Pathway in Carrabassett Valley 72

SECTION III. ISLAND BIKE RIDES

Chapter 15 - Islesboro 77
Chapter 16 - North Haven 81

Chapter 17 - Isle au Haut 85

SECTION IV. SEA KAYAKING

Chapter 18 - Damariscove Island.. 91

Chapter 19 - Eastern Egg Rock... 96

Chapter 20 - Isle au Haut 100

Chapter 21 - Mussell Ridge 105

Chapter 22 - Jewell and Eagle Islands 110

Chapter 23 - Bold Coast 115

Chapter 24 - Mount Desert Island: Frenchman Bay and Otter Cliffs 121

Chapter 25 - Mount Desert Island:Cranberry & Baker Islands 126

SECTION V. WHITEWATER KAYAKING AND CANOEING

Chapter 26 - Dead River.. 131

Chapter 27 - Kennebec Gorge 137

Chapter 28 - West Branch of the Penobscot................................. 142

Chapter 29 - Canada Falls on South Branch of the Penobscot 149

Chapter 30 - Orbeton Stream 154

Chapter 31 - Webb River.. 162

Chapter 32 - Ducktrap River 167

Chapter 33 - Gulf Hagas on W. Branch of the Pleasant River 172

Chapter 34 - Cathance River... 177

SECTION VI. NORDIC SKIING

Chapter 35 - Mount Blue State Park... 183

Chapter 36 - Harris Farm 188

Chapter 37 - Rangeley Lakes Trails Center 192

SECTION VII. LAKE PADDLING

Chapter 38 - Moosehead Lake 198

Chapter 39 - Mooselookmeguntic, Cupsuptic, and Richardson Lakes 203

Chapter 40 - Donnell Pond 207

SECTION VIII. CANOE TRIPS

Chapter 41 - Machias River 212

Chapter 42 - Allagash River and Tributaries 221

Chapter 43 - West Branch of Penobscot & Chesuncook Lake 227

Chapter 44 - St. John River 232

Chapter 45 - Moose River Bow Trip 237

Chapter 46 - Webster Stream and East Branch of Penobscot 242

SECTION IX. BACKPACK TRIPS

Chapter 47 - Appalachian Trail over Saddleback Range 250

Chapter 48 - Baxter State Park – Nesowadnehunk Field to Roaring Brook 254

SECTION X. DOWNRIVER CANOE AND KAYAK RACES

Chapter 49 - Kenduskeag Stream 260

Chapter 50 - Souadabscook Stream 265

SECTION I. MOUNTAIN HIKES

A hiker enjoys the view on Mount Katahdin's Hamlin Ridge.
(Photo – Ron Chase)

Chapter 1 - Mount Katahdin in Winter

A Peak Too Far

Nine of us slowly ascended snow- and ice-covered Hamlin Ridge in one of Maine's most remote and rugged regions, the Mount Katahdin massif in Baxter State Park. Probably the only realistic opportunity to achieve our collective goal to scale the two highest points in Maine, Baxter and Hamlin Peaks, the summits forecast was marginal at best.

On the third day of our quest, several of us veterans of previous winter climbs on Mount Katahdin were surprised with the conditions on that gray, intimidating February morning. Expecting to remove our snowshoes and affix crampons once reaching the normally ice-dominated above tree line ridge, instead we were progressing gradually on a predominantly snow-covered surface still wearing our cumbersome footgear. Sporadic patches of ice, exposed boulders, and deep snow drifts dictated tedious time-consuming maneuvering. Dark ominous clouds were forming above and already moderate winds were increasing in strength.

Our odyssey began the previous fall when trip organizer, Julia Richmond, made park hut reservations and assembled an international team of five Mainers and four Quebecers. Unlike global relations in too much of the world, this was a friendly, conflict-free endeavor. Consider our venture a microscopic contribution to a happier, more serene planet. Varying in age from 35 to 70, this weathering arthritic old man represented the top end of the maturation spectrum.

On the first day of our expedition, we skied or bare booted twelve miles from Abol Bridge on the Golden Road to Roaring Brook Hut, pulling our gear and supplies on heavily laden specially designed sleds. Traveling on an essentially hard-packed snow surface on a cold breezy day, we encountered excellent sledding during the primarily uphill tow.

The following day, sleds were hauled steeply up Chimney Pond Trail for 3.3 miles to a hut at the breathtakingly spectacular mountain tarn using micro spikes or crampons for traction. Except for a fleeting respite crossing picturesque frozen Basin Pond with magnificent views of the massif, the almost continuously precipitous path entailed an exhausting 1,425 feet of elevation gain. The luxury of the hut notwithstanding, chores such as fetching water with sleds from a hole in the ice at the far end of Chimney Pond were an immediate necessity. Hearing my perpetual whining about sore hips, the ambitious younger folks temporarily excused me from water duty. One quickly learns to appreciate the benefits of indoor plumbing when an hour is necessary to acquire water that must still be purified.

Since day three was our only full day at Chimney Pond, the intent was to summit both Baxter and Hamlin Peaks. As we knew we would be principally above tree line and relentlessly exposed to the elements, a strenuous daylong trek was anticipated. Park reports indicated both Cathedral and Saddle Trails, the shortest approaches to Baxter Peak, had greater climbing dangers and high avalanche risks. The consensus decision was for an out-and-back journey via the much longer but safer Hamlin Ridge Trail. We obtained the latest summits forecast from the park ranger stationed at the pond prior to departing. Possible light precipitation, moderate to high winds, and some cloud cover were his best estimate of likely conditions. If that prediction held, our mission had a reasonable chance of success. The entire group enthusiastically joined in the quest.

Entering a realm of portentous thickening clouds about halfway up attenuated Hamlin Ridge, our intrepid band labored on despite declining visibility. Angling right on the shoulder of Hamlin Peak, we encountered harsh winds and driving snow. Estimated at over forty miles per hour, the potent gusts menacingly threatened our stability and safety near the rim of North Basin. Approaching whiteout conditions, we slowly progressed from one cairn to the next, struggling to differentiate ice- and snow-covered cairns from similar sized rocks and boulders.

Shortly after passing a snow-encrusted sign for North Peaks Trail, we arrived at slightly rounded barren Hamlin Peak. After celebrating attainment of the first half of our objective, it was crunch time for decision making amidst the inhospitable surroundings where it was difficult to hear one another over the howling wind. Our choices were to continue for over two miles to Baxter Peak, possibly descending the potentially hazardous Saddle Trail as a bailout option if serious difficulties were confronted, or return without reaching our ultimate destination. As we hurriedly contemplated alternatives in the blustery claustrophobic environment, the prospects of additional exposure to the treacherous elements with a genuine threat of becoming disoriented and lost were too great. Halfway down the ridge some unnecessary second guessing occurred. In fact, the higher elevations remained socked in throughout the day and the winds didn't diminish.

Park rules required us to pull sleds down to Roaring Brook on our final day at Chimney Pond. Since that was a relatively brief straightforward undertaking, we had one final limited opportunity to reach elusive Baxter Peak. Believing it to be our only realistic option, six of us sanguinely decided to ascend the winter Saddle Trail with another problematic forecast. Deep snow slowed progress when time was of the essence. Accepting that success was a dubious possibility, several in our stouthearted group persevered close to the rim before formidable winds and an expired turnaround time ended the attempt. Alas, Baxter was a peak too far. After a rapid descent to Roaring Brook Hut, we returned to Abol Bridge the following day in glorious weather that would have provided a superb climbing opportunity.

Our mountaineering disappointment doesn't tell the entire story. Cheerful banter, a willingness by all to assist one another, and everyone joining in to complete the more mundane tasks typified the trip. Ski and snowshoe explorations were numerous at Roaring Brook, Chimney Pond, and isolated North Basin. Despite

Chapter 1 - Mount Katahdin in Winter

the climbing setback, I departed the park with new friends and positive feelings about the ability of a very disparate group of people to work effectively together for a common purpose...and very sore hips.

This failed attempt to summit Baxter Peak was my sixth winter trip to Chimney Pond. The previous five had resulted in successful ascents. On each occasion, we were very fortunate. Harsh potentially hazardous conditions are common in that consequential milieu frequently forcing climbers to turn back.

The most exciting and challenging winter mountaineering in Maine can be found in Baxter State Park. Fortuitously, I've experienced several winter expeditions to various locations. Summiting Baxter and Hamlin Peaks on Mount Katahdin in the winter is probably Maine's most significant mountaineering accomplishment. Four thousand foot North Brother and fellow peaks South Brother, Coe, and Fort dominate northwest of the Katahdin massif. Imposing Knife Edge offers a windswept technical traverse connecting Baxter and Pamola Peaks. Arguably the state's most exceptional ice climbing and backcountry skiing are found in the Chimney Pond/North Basin area. Numerous three thousand foot mountains are scattered throughout the park.

Many of the winter mountaineers who enter Baxter State Park are in a quest to climb the New England 100 Highest Peaks in the winter, a list established by the Appalachian Mountain Club (AMC). Baxter and Hamlin are two of the most difficult and elusive to attain. Despite a significant commitment of time, money, and energy several members of our group had failed to realize their goal. Nothing better defines why achieving that lofty objective is a substantial accomplishment.

Except for snowmobiles on the Perimeter Road and Park Rangers, no motorized traffic is allowed in the park during winter. Access to the mountains is by snowshoes, skis, crampons, or bare hiking boots. Traditionally, pulling sleds has been the principal means of transporting food and gear. While it's possible to summit some of the peaks via a long day trip, most successful climbs are the result of multi-day expeditions. Overnight shelter options are tents, lean-tos, and a handful of huts strategically situated in the park.

The primary mountaineering destinations are Chimney Pond to ascend the Katahdin peaks, Nesowadnehunk Field to climb the Brothers and nearby mountains in the northwestern sector of the park, and South Branch Pond to scale the Traveler Range in the northeast. Huts at other locations such as Daicey and Kidney Ponds also attract winter visitors but do not provide practical access to the high summits.

Every trip into Baxter in the winter includes its own unique adversities, circumstances, adventures, and misadventures. The accumulated exploits of my friends and I could easily fill a book. Frigid ascents, major storms, whiteouts on the high peaks, a near fatal fall, conflicts with park officials, and more are memories that consume my mind when thinking of Baxter.

My first winter trip into the park in February 1991 was perhaps the most memorable. Accompanied by friends John Stokinger, Tom Homsted, and the late Bill Kaiser, we were intent on climbing to the pinnacle of mile high Mount Katahdin from Chimney Pond. Ascending in bitter cold gusty conditions, Tom had a diabetic attack part way up Cathedral Ridge and Bill escorted him back to the hut at Chimney Pond. Assessing our dilemma, John and I decided to forge ahead. Chill factors worsened near the top. Both of John's crampons cracked and broke. Unable to repair them and recognizing dire signs of hypothermia, we quickly summited and survived a hazardous but successful icy descent.

On subsequent expeditions, my youngest son Adam, Bill, Tom, and many other valued friends joined me for successful winter climbs to the crown of Maine. Baxter Peak isn't going anywhere but I'm growing old. Arthritis-related problems are worsening and pulling a sled is particularly problematic. Whether or not I return in winter is uncertain. Call it avarice, narcissism, compulsive behavior, you name it, I want to be at the top of Maine in the winter one more time.

Chapter 1 - Mount Katahdin in Winter

THINGS TO KNOW

Location: Piscataquis County, north-central Maine

Rules, regulations, reservations, and access to Baxter State Park in winter: While winter regulations have been modified and streamlined in recent years, they are still extensive. Would-be users should thoroughly familiarize themselves with the winter specific guidelines and requirements on the park website: http://www.mainerec.com/baxter.asp?Category=102&PageNum=102

Elevation of high points: Hamlin Peak 4,756 feet, Pamola Peak 4,919 feet, and Baxter Peak 5,267 feet. Note: Since there is insufficient elevation loss and gain between Baxter and Pamola Peaks, Pamola is not considered a separate summit by most peak-baggers and does not meet the AMC criteria for inclusion on their list of the 100 highest.

Elevation Gains:
Abol Bridge to Chimney Pond: 2,422 feet
Chimney Pond to Hamlin Peak: 1,763 feet
Chimney Pond via Saddle or Cathedral Trails to Baxter Peak: 2,274 feet
Chimney Pond via Hamlin Ridge to Baxter Peak (descending Cathedral or Saddle): 2,632 feet
Chimney Pond via Hamlin Ridge to Baxter Peak and return over Hamlin Ridge: 3,090 feet

Distances:
Abol Bridge to Roaring Brook: 12 miles
Roaring Brook to Chimney Pond: 3.3 miles
Chimney Pond to Hamlin Peak: 2.2 miles
Chimney Pond to Baxter Peak via Hamlin Peak: 4.4 miles, 8.8 miles round-trip

Chimney Pond to Baxter Peak via Cathedral Trail: 1.7 miles

Chimney Pond to Baxter Peak via Saddle Trail: 2.2 miles

Difficulty: Strenuous

Views: Incredible

Unique Potential Hazards: Cold weather can result in hypothermia and frostbite. There is extended above tree line exposure to the elements. Long sections of steep boulder and rock scrambling on ice and snow substantially increase the risk of serious falls. Whiteout conditions can result in getting disoriented and lost. Remote locations and high elevations make rescue problematic and may result in long delays. Hikers, skiers, and climbers should not expect immediate assistance. Carrying a map, compass, GPS, and avalanche rescue equipment are recommended. Most important, all park rules, regulations, danger warnings, and guidelines should be scrupulously followed and obeyed. Park guidelines should be consulted concerning the necessary equipment, clothing, and food for a winter expedition.

Directions to Abol Bridge parking area and trailhead: From the junction of Routes 11 and 157 in Millinocket, turn right onto Katahdin Avenue, keep straight at .2 mile on Bates Street, at .8 mile the road changes to Millinocket Lake Road, at 6.4 miles road changes to Millinocket Road, at 1.2 miles road changes to Millinocket Lake Road, at 5.7 miles turn left onto Golden Road, at .7 mile turn right on Golden Road, at 4.5 miles turn left into parking area. To reach the trailhead, cross Golden Road, turn right onto Baxter Park Road, go .1 mile, and turn left onto marked trail.

Additional Recommendation: Carry a shovel in your vehicle as plows will clear open sections of the parking area, sometimes blocking vehicles.

Chapter 1 - Mount Katahdin in Winter

An alternative to winter in Baxter State Park: For those interested in a warmer Katahdin experience, the park is open from May 15 to October 15. Instead of pulling sleds to Roaring Brook, visitors can drive to the parking area. Visit their website for information on rules, access, and camping reservations: https://baxterstatepark.org/#/

Climbers ascend Cathedral Ridge on Mount Katahdin. (Photo – Nancy Chase)

Chapter 2 - Cadillac Mountain

A Cadillac of a Mountain

Cadillac Mountain in Acadia National Park is the source of many superlatives. At an elevation of 1,532 feet, it is the tallest mountain along the eastern seaboard of the United States. According to Wikipedia, the commanding prominence is the highest point within 25 miles of the shoreline of the North American continent between Cape Breton Island in Nova Scotia and Mexican peaks south of the Texas border. During fall and winter, the crest of Cadillac is the first location to experience the nation's sunrise.

Native Americans who lived along the shores of Mount Desert Island at least 5,000 years ago were most likely the earliest people to ascend Cadillac. The first reliable record of European contact was by explorer Samuel Champlain in 1604. He named the island Isle des Monts Desert or Island of Barren Mountains. Formerly known as Green Mountain, Cadillac was renamed for another French explorer Antoine Laumet de La Mothe Sieur de Cadillac in 1918. No, I wasn't hiking there when it was called Green Mountain.

Rugged majestic beauty and incredible views make Cadillac one of the premiere New England mountain hikes. However, for mountaineering purists there is a dark side; a paved road to the top. After an arduous ascent, weary hikers are often greeted with a carnival-like atmosphere when completing the climb. If one wants to avoid the incongruous environment, a winter expedition when the road is closed is an alternative. An interesting snippet of Cadillac history: a cog railway took visitors to a hotel at the summit in the late 19th century. After the hotel burned, the train was sold and transported to another consequential New England peak, Mount Washington.

Chapter 2 - Cadillac Mountain

Four primary hiking routes lead to the crown of Cadillac: North and South Ridge Trails, Gorge Path, and West Face Trail. Numerous additional passageways interconnect with these. All provide remarkable panoramic vistas of the 16 nearby granite dominated peaks, surrounding islands, and the glaciated coastal landscape.

I was part of a contingent of four retired Chowderheads with the Penobscot Paddle and Chowder Society who met for an autumn climb on Cadillac. Veterans of the usual approaches, we decided on something different, an extended trek from the east over Dorr Mountain.

Our excursion began in the parking area for Sieur de Monts Spring near Bar Harbor, a significant park attraction. An area bustling with activity, hiking trails seemingly blend with walkways used for various other recreational diversions. In short, it's confusing. After some exploration, Emery Path was located—a new route for everyone in the group. Climbing steeply on a remarkably well-designed and constructed path with almost constant views of the Porcupine Islands in outer Frenchman Bay, I was reminded of the truly prodigious accomplishments of those youngsters in the Civilian Conservation Corps who built many park trails during the Great Depression.

After persevering steadily uphill for a half mile, we joined with Schiff Path, which continued for another mile to the summit of Dorr Mountain. As we gazed expectantly west towards Cadillac, we noted the higher elevations were enveloped in clouds. A climb without views seemed probable.

Departing from Dorr, we dropped abruptly to a junction with Gorge Path situated deep in an attenuated ravine between Dorr and Cadillac. The subsequent ascent on Gorge Path entailed considerable boulder scrambling. Fortuitously, clouds diminished arriving at the chaotic, congested summit offering a plethora of exceptional views that only Cadillac can provide. The contrast between a handful of tired pack-laden hikers and a multitude of well-dressed tourists was abundantly obvious. Hurriedly escaping the pandemonium, we descended to a location sheltered from the wind and away from the teeming crowd on South Ridge Trail for a tranquil lunch break.

We continued downhill for a mile on the completely exposed South Ridge Trail. Perpetual views of the offshore Cranberry Isles was an aesthetic delight. Linking with Canon Brook Trail, we turned east. My first experience on Canon, I was impressed with the precipitous, unrelenting character of the trail that parallels and often intersects with Canon Brook in what could be described as a lengthy multi-staged waterfall. I suspect Canon would be a hazardous environment during high water or icy conditions.

Leaving the brook behind, the trail descended more gradually, connecting with Kane Path before reaching The Tarn, an idyllic pond situated in a col between Dorr and Champlain Mountains. Known to early explorers as People of the Dawn, prehistoric Wabanaki Indians could have easily chosen the eastern shore to build their temporary summer shelters protected from frequent onshore winds. Skirting The Tarn, we returned to Sieur de Monts Spring, completing a seven-mile journey replete with breathtaking views, challenging mountaineering, and a new perspective of a Cadillac of a mountain.

Ours was just one of the many exceptional hikes to the summit of Cadillac Mountain. Gorge Path begins on the Park Loop Road and climbs precipitously along Kebo Brook passing a series of small waterfalls and cataracts before reaching a trail junction that leads to the summit from a narrow notch between Cadillac and Dorr Mountains. The predominantly above-tree-line North Ridge Trail also departs from the Loop Road and offers remarkable views of Frenchman Bay. Beginning near Blackwoods Campground, the longer South Ridge Trail is mostly exposed with phenomenal views of the Cranberry Isles and eastern Penobscot Bay. Rugged, demanding West Wall Trail climbs steeply from a trailhead near Bubble Pond joining South Ridge Trail a short distance from the summit. Any choice you make is a great one!

Chapter 2 - Cadillac Mountain

THINGS TO KNOW

Location: Hancock County, Down East Maine
Length of the loop hike: Approximately 7 miles for the described trek
Elevation gain on loop hike: Approximately 1,750 feet
Difficulty: Moderately strenuous
Unique potential hazards: Extended above-tree-line exposure to the elements. Several sections require boulder and rock scrambling increasing the risk of serious falls. Due to proximity to the ocean, the weather can change quickly and become more severe. High winds and fog are often a problem. Carrying a map, compass, and GPS are recommended.
Views: Phenomenal
Directions to Sieur de Monts Spring: From the junction of Routes 1 and 3 in Ellsworth, turn right onto Route 3 and drive 18.5 miles to Kebo Street in Bar Harbor. Turn right onto Kebo and travel 1.1 miles to Park Loop Road on the left. After .9 mile turn right onto Sieur de Monts Road. Go 440 feet and bear right onto Sweet Water Circle. Travel .2 mile to Sieur de Mont Spring.
Another recommended loop hike on Cadillac Mountain: Combine Gorge Path and North Ridge Trail into a scenic loop hike. Ascend either trail from the Park Loop Road and descend the other from the summit. Enjoy the contrast of a steep, narrow canyon hike on Gorge Path coupled with a glorious, exposed jaunt on North Ridge Trail. The distance between the Loop Road Trailheads is .9 mile.
Other hiking options in the area: Acadia National Park and Mount Desert Island probably have more exceptional mountain hikes than any other area in Maine. There are no bad choices. The following additional excursions are my favorites:
Champlain Mountain: The eastern most peak on Mount Desert Island, unparalleled views of Frenchman Bay, the Porcupine Islands, and Schoodic Peninsula can be enjoyed from the summit. An easy short hike on the Beechcroft Trail begins on Route 3 a few miles south of Bar Harbor opposite the Tarn and

climbs from the west. Perhaps the steepest hiking trail in Acadia National Park, The Precipice, ascends from the east. Other trails converge at the summit, offering opportunities for a traverse.

Parkman and Bald Mountains: A short loop hike that begins near Hadlock Pond north of Northeast Harbor, there are spectacular views from both summits. This is a great choice when hikers only have a half day to play.

Sargent and Penobscot Mountains: There are numerous approaches to these exceptional barren peaks. I generally begin at Jordan Pond House and climb Jordan and East Cliffs Trails to Sargent, traverse Sargent South Ridge Trail to Penobscot, and descend Penobscot Mountain and Spring Trails back to Jordan Pond House, completing an outstanding loop trip.

Pemetic Mountain: Again, there are many trails that access the summit. A favorite for me is a traverse south from Bubble Pond on the North and South Ridge Trails to Jordan Pond.

Hikers nearing the summit of Cadillac Mountain. (Photo – Ron Chase)

Chapter 3 - Tumbledown and Little Jackson Mountains

The Second-Best Mountain Hike in Maine

What's the most spectacular mountain hike in Maine? I suspect most people believe Mount Katahdin claims that distinction. In my opinion, a close second are the peaks of Tumbledown and Little Jackson Mountains.

While the ragged, alpine summits and sheer cliffs of Tumbledown dominate the skyline northwest of Webb Lake near Weld, adjacent taller more remote Little Jackson is substantially hidden from view. Tumbledown is one of Maine's most well-known and popular mountain hikes. Given its relative anonymity, Little Jackson is much less frequently climbed—usually the destination of more seasoned hikers. Combining the two imposing mountains into one expedition is a rare exceptional endeavor.

Cool brisk days, radiant autumn colors, and the absence of black flies make fall prime time for an ascent of Little Jackson. Two retired friends agreed to join me on a proposed Penobscot Paddle and Chowder Society club hike. Don't be misled by the name, we do much more than paddle while devouring copious amounts of delicious chowder. The club has a year-round trip schedule that includes whitewater and flat water paddling, canoe trips, sea kayaking, biking, skiing, hiking, and winter mountaineering. We love all things outdoors.

Although John and Brent are both retired, over 20 years separate them. John is a youthful 79 while Brent a recent retiree. Consider me the difficult middle child in this elderly triad. Their ages notwithstanding, both are very strong hikers so I anticipated a strenuous workout. Having recently received another cortisone injection for my arthritic hips, I was at least theoretically prepared for the challenge. Readers be warned, whining is an all too frequent theme in my writings and should be summarily disregarded.

The three of us met in front of an ancient cemetery on the gravel Byron Road a few miles west of Weld early on a chilly, sunny morning. Just beyond the cemetery, the rough, poorly maintained Morgan Road turned right and traveled for about a mile to Little Jackson Trailhead, also the start of Tumbledown Mountain's Parker Ridge Trail.

Based on various reports I've read, the distance to the summit of Little Jackson is in dispute. The following represents my educated estimate, so a healthy level of skepticism is advisable. Passing Pond Link Trail on the left just a little beyond the halfway point, the rocky path ascends steadily in a densely wooded environment along a twisting mountain freshet for what I calculate to be about 2.5 miles before scaling a boulder-strewn pitch and arriving on exposed ledges. For our trek, the remaining distance approximating one mile to the summit was essentially above tree line and glorious.

A forecast predicting light breezes was badly flawed. Instead, cold gusty winds blew out of the northwest necessitating mittens, parkas, and stocking caps. A continuum of massive boulder-strewn ledges ensued. Arriving at the blustery mountain top at an elevation of 3,470 feet, we joined others seeking shelter in a stone windbreak built by hikers past.

After some discussion, the consensus was to descend an unofficial but fairly obvious trail that drops dramatically off the southwest slope of Little Jackson to Tumbledown Pond. An immediate benefit of the decision was protection from the turbulent winds. Views below of the pond and the trio of Tumbledown Peaks were phenomenal.

Approaching the remarkably picturesque mountain tarn, we turned right onto another unofficial trail sporadically marked with cairns that crosses barren, infrequently climbed North Peak, Tumbledown highpoint at 3,090 feet. While sometimes difficult to follow, the serpentine path continued down into a thick conifer forest and then rose abruptly up rugged West Peak.

Emblematic of the entire day, views were extraordinary. Numerous hikers could be observed negotiating the cliffs of our next objective, East Peak. Passing the Loop Trail junction which arrives from Byron Road, two large parties joined us. Unlike Little

Chapter 3 - Tumbledown and Little Jackson Mountains

Jackson and North Peak, the remainder of our journey was teeming with alpine travelers. The precipitous scramble up East Peak was shared with numerous enthusiastic trekkers. From the bald rounded crest, more incredible views of Tumbledown Pond along with Webb Lake and Mount Blue in the east were savored.

The blue blazed route plummeted steeply down a succession of expansive ledges to the shore of the distinctive pond. Just beyond, a junction for Brook and Parker Ridge Trails was achieved. Brook Trail descends right to Byron Road. Dozens of hikers had assembled at the pond, resting and celebrating their mountaineering accomplishment.

Tumbledown Pond warrants an expression of concern. The exceptionally majestic beauty of the location attracts large numbers of hikers and some overnight campers. Dog and human waste are a sanitation problem. Garbage often accumulates. If visitors don't learn to exercise self-discipline, draconian rules and regulations will undoubtedly follow, diminishing a truly outstanding wilderness experience.

As we departed the pond on Parker Ridge Trail and passed the western terminus of Pond Link Trail, our splendid above-treeline experience continued as we finished our expedition navigating over the impressive escarpment before returning to Little Jackson Trailhead. Completing a unique, unplanned, circuitous loop was most assuredly one of Maine's most exceptional mountain excursions—arguably second best.

What's the verdict on the hips? I see more whining in my future.

THINGS TO KNOW

Location: Franklin County, western Maine
Length of the loop hike: Approximately 8.5 miles
Elevation gain on the loop hike: Approximately 3,000 feet
Difficulty: Moderately strenuous

Unique potential hazards: Extended above tree line exposure to the elements. Several sections require boulder and rock scrambling, increasing the risk of serious falls. The section of the loop trip from the summit of Little Jackson to West Peak on Tumbledown is poorly marked and arguably a bush whack that presents a greater danger of getting disoriented or lost. Carrying a map, compass, and GPS is recommended.

Views: Phenomenal

Directions to Little Jackson and Parker Ridge Trailheads: From the junction of Routes 156 and 142 in Weld, travel 2.4 miles on Route 142 and turn left onto Byron Road. Take an immediate right on the dirt road that is normally in good condition and drive 2.5 miles to narrow Morgan Road on the right just beyond an old cemetery. Follow this rough poorly maintained road to the end. High clearance vehicles are recommended.

Other Tumbledown hiking options: The Brook Trail begins on Byron Road approximately 2 miles west of Morgan Road and ascends for about 2.5 miles to Tumbledown Pond. The Loop Trail starts about 2 miles west of Brook Trail on Byron Road and climbs for 2 miles to a col between West and East Peaks. In order to reach Tumbledown Pond hikers must then traverse East Peak. From there, many choose to descend Brook Trail completing a loop hike. Leaving a shuttle vehicle avoids a 2-mile walk on Byron Road.

A hiker descends East Peak on Tumbledown Mountain. (Photo – Ron Chase)

Chapter 4 - North Brother, South Brother, Fort Mountain, and Mount Coe in Winter

The Mother of All Storms

In early March 1993, a large cyclonic depression formed in the Gulf of Mexico. Shortly after, a substantial storm began its passage northeast. Ultimately stretching from Honduras to Canada, the powerful blizzard was unique due to its severity, massive size, and far-reaching effect. Revisionists now call it The Great Blizzard of 1993. At the time the media dubbed it The Mother of All Storms and that shall ever be its name in my mind.

Months earlier, mountaineering friends Steve Ward and the late Lloyd Brown had encouraged me to join them and several peak baggers for a planned winter climb of four mountains in the northwestern sector of Baxter State Park: North Brother, South Brother, Fort Mountain, and Mount Coe. The allure of those particular summits was that they were on the Appalachian Mountain Club (AMC) list of the one hundred highest peaks in New England. Completing them in winter is considered by many to be the holy grail of New England mountaineering. Quest of the list seemed a quixotic endeavor to me, but the proposed expedition sounded like a great adventure so I signed on.

When ten of us met at the now closed Pamola Motor Lodge in East Millinocket on the evening of March 12th, a Bangor television station reported a major storm was developing in the southeastern United States. The weather was fine in northern Maine and no one in our single-minded cabal was concerned. The following morning, the same news outlet reported several southern states were being clobbered by a blizzard they called The Mother of All Storms. It was moving up the eastern seaboard. Insouciantly confident that our weather radio would keep us apprised of developments, the dire reports were largely ignored.

Traveling in a caravan of vehicles carrying hikers, expedition sleds, winter mountaineering gear, and food, we drove through Millinocket onto the Golden Road, crossed north over the Penobscot River, and continued deep into the remote northern Maine woods on Telos Road along the west side of Baxter State Park. AMC peak bagging rules prohibited use of motorized assistance such as snowmobiles to reach qualifying peaks in the park. The plan was to haul sleds from Telos Road into the park on a network of old tote roads. After shoveling out space beside the road for our vehicles at a location near Harrington Pond, we departed east towards the park.

Sledding conditions were excellent. Partly sunny skies, light winds, seasonal temperatures, and hard-packed snow facilitated hauling our heavy loads, wearing snowshoes or skis to the park boundary. Entering the park, we soon passed through the closed Nesowadnehunk Field Campground consisting of a ranger cabin, a few park buildings, and a plethora of snow-covered picnic tables. The remainder of our journey was a three-mile trek south on the park Perimeter Road to Slide Dam Picnic Area. Tents were erected opposite the Marston Trailhead which led to the coveted peaks.

A few early arrivals broke trail on Marston with snowshoes in foot-deep snow for a long mile to the Mount Coe Trail junction. That night, Team Stormy retired to their tents, satisfied they had successfully completed an arduous haul with sleds, established a secure camp, cleared part of the trail, and were primed to accomplish their mission to ascend all four peaks the following day.

The weather changed dramatically during the night. It turned cold, very cold. Winds began blowing and trees were cracking. Awakening early, someone had a thermometer that registered twenty below zero Fahrenheit. We couldn't get reception on the weather radio. When cooking breakfast in my tent, heat from the stove combined with the frigid air resulted in a unique encounter with a whiteout inside the tent.

Undaunted, packs were loaded, snowshoes donned, and our trek up Marston Trail began. Making excellent progress on the

Chapter 4 - North Brother, South Brother, Fort Mountain, and Mount Coe in Winter

packed route, the junction with Mount Coe Trail was quickly attained. Since two members of the group, Tim Kennedy and Frank Laak, needed only Mount Coe and South Brother to finish the 100 highest, those were first on the agenda. Alternating the lead while breaking trail in very deep snow, trail markings were buried and the path vanished. Navigating by map and compass, snow was sometimes waist deep in the narrow col between Mounts OJI and Coe.

After several exhausting hours, the bottom of steep, elongated Coe Slide was located. Emitting a collective sigh of relief, we were back on the trail. Crampons were necessary for the precipitous incline on a hardened snow and ice surface. Frank had forgotten his. He perilously ascended on snowshoes while I pulled him up and Sue Johnston held his lower snowshoe in place on each step of the climb. Dark clouds were approaching from the west and winds were gusting when Team Stormy arrived at the exposed Mount Coe pinnacle.

As we negotiated our way towards South Brother on a sloping ridge, we found the snow was the deepest of the day. Trail finding continued to be problematic resulting in more long delays. One member, Jay Spenciner, collapsed into a gaping spruce trap. A collective effort was required to extricate him from his cavernous predicament. Persevering to a spur trail leading to the top of South Brother, we wearily scaled the barren summit where a frigid abbreviated ceremony was held recognizing Frank and Tim's accomplishment. To officially count, they still had to make it back. Frank was in his sixties. I remember thinking it was truly remarkable someone so old was still able to climb mountains.

As we descended from the top, limited weather radio reception was finally acquired. The garbled report indicated a major blizzard was imminent. Shortly after, a junction with the Marston Trail was reached. A right turn led to North Brother and Fort Mountains while left returned to the tents. Remarkably, our intrepid band stopped to debate whether or not the remaining peaks should be attempted. Already late afternoon, several additional hours would be necessary to complete the entire journey. Following a close vote, a disheartened descent began.

By the time we arrived at our tents, heavy snow was falling, powerful winds were howling up the valley, and it was dark. Park rangers had snowmobiled to our site leaving a written message in a tent stating, "The Park is closed. Extremely severe blizzard level winds and snow will arrive tonight. When you return, go to Nesowadnehunk Campground and break into a cabin. It is too dangerous for you to stay in tents at Slide Dam."

Within minutes, sleds were being towed up the Perimeter Road using headlights to find our way in the dark and driving snow. Steve and I were first to reach the campground. After a brief discussion, we agreed the ranger's message had not specified what cabin, so the ranger cabin was our selection. Unquestionably the right choice, the upscale facility provided firewood, a woodstove, gas lights, and a gas range. Six of us filled the beds in that cabin and the last four commandeered a nearby bunkhouse unflatteringly called "Lower House."

There we lingered—secure, warm, and well fed through the stormiest winter night I've experienced. During the evening, one member of the group kept furtively looking out the window. Bewildered, as it was so dark there was nothing to see, he was nicknamed "The Fugitive." I didn't know him well and don't remember his real name. So to me he will always remain The Fugitive.

The blizzard continued through the following morning. When it ended midday, more than two feet of fresh snow had accumulated, but the winds had died and the sun came out. We had a dilemma. Situated a long six miles from our vehicles on Telos Road, everyone agreed pulling sleds out of the park in deep snow would be an exhausting undertaking. Someone mentioned park rangers would eventually come searching for us in snowmobiles and there was plenty of food. Another observed that leaving the park with snowmobile assistance would disqualify South Brother and Mount Coe. A unanimous decision was made to start breaking trail.

Chapter 4 - North Brother, South Brother, Fort Mountain, and Mount Coe in Winter

That afternoon, snowshoes were employed to clear a wide swath for about three miles. The following day, Team Stormy left early, reaching the vehicles around noon. Our tiring efforts hadn't ended as snowplows had buried the vehicles in a massive snowbank. Another two hours of shoveling was required, but the peaks counted!

In the ensuing years, Baxter State Park opened a winter hut at the Nesowadnehunk Campground, perhaps in part to protect the ranger cabin from misguided trekkers. Initially, Lower House was used. Later, a small log cabin was built near Nesowadnehunk Stream. Friends and I have stayed there numerous times.

Using the hut as base camp, my wife Nancy, son Adam, Steve, Lloyd, and many friends have climbed the four high peaks in winter including the formidable bush whack to Fort Mountain. Of the original group, Steve, Sue, Dick Boisvert, and I completed the 100 highest in winter. Shortly after finishing in 1997, I entered a twelve-step program vowing to kick the addiction. I'm still clean. Two members of Team Stormy, Sue and Wayne "Fig" Newton have completed the Appalachian Trail multiple times but not in winter. Now, most of us are in our sixties and seventies, older than Frank during The Mother of All Storms. Amazingly, many of us are still hiking mountains. I lost touch with The Fugitive after the expedition. Steve mentioned seeing him at the L.L. Bean flagship store in Freeport, reputedly peering out the window. My great friend Lloyd Brown died of a rare heart ailment at a young age without realizing his peak bagging mountaineering dream. His cheerful companionship is sorely missed.

THINGS TO KNOW

Location: Piscataquis County, north-central Maine

For pertinent Baxter State Park winter information and unique potential hazards: See "Things to Know" at the end of Chapter 1.

Elevation of high points: Mount Coe 3,795 feet, South Brother 3,970 feet, North Brother 4,151 feet, and Fort Mountain 3,887 feet

Elevation Gains:
Telos Road to Nesowadnehunk Campground: 309 feet
Nesowadnehunk Campground to Slide Dam: Lose 109 feet
Slide Dam to Mount Coe: 2,562 feet
Slide Dam via Mount Coe to South Brother: 3,165 feet
South Brother to North Brother: 775 feet
North Brother to Fort Mountain: 229 feet (493 feet more for the return over North Brother)
Slide Dam to South Brother: 2,737 feet
Slide Dam to North Brother: 2,918 feet
Slide Dam via North Brother to Fort Mountain: 3,147 feet

Distances:
Telos Road to Nesowadnehunk Campgroud: About 6 miles
Nesowadnehunk Campground to Slide Dam (Marston Trail): 3.1 miles
Slide Dam via Mount Coe Trail to Mount Coe: 3 miles
Mount Coe to South Brother: 1.8 miles
South Brother to North Brother: 1.6 miles
North Brother to Fort Mountain: About 1 mile (bush whack)
Slide Dam via Marston Trail to North Brother: 3.8 miles
Slide Dam via Marston Trail and North Brother to Fort Mountain: About 4.8 miles

Difficulty: Strenuous
Views: Excellent from the summits of Mount Coe, South Brother, North Brother, and Fort Mountains.

Chapter 4 - North Brother, South Brother, Fort Mountain, and Mount Coe in Winter

Directions to the Telos Road point of departure: Follow Chapter 1 directions to Abol Bridge. Continue on Golden Road for 8 miles to Telos Road. Turn right, cross bridge over Penobscot River, and drive about 9 miles past Harrington Lake on the right. Shortly after, find a small turnoff on the right at the beginning of an old tote road.

Directions to Nesowadnehunk Campground in Baxter State Park: Carefully navigate east on old tote roads using a map, compass, and GPS. Recommend plotting a course on a map or GPS in advance. Some exploration may be necessary. Just before entering the park, several berms designed to prevent vehicular traffic will be encountered.

Additional Recommendation: Carry a sturdy shovel in your vehicle. Plows on Telos Road leave massive snowbanks.

An alternative to winter in Baxter State Park: For those interested in a warmer hike to the Brothers region, the park is open from May 15 to October 15. Instead of pulling sleds to Slide Dam Picnic Area, visitors can drive there. See the park website for information on rules, access, and camping reservations: https://baxterstatepark.org/#/

Advice: Never assume that you can break into any park facility without permission.

Winter mountaineers haul sleds into Baxter State Park. (Photo – Ron Chase)

Chapter 5 - Traveler Mountain Loop Trip in Baxter State Park in Winter

A Winter Expedition to South Branch Pond

Perhaps the best kept winter mountaineering secret in Baxter State Park is South Branch Pond. Most skiers, ice climbers, and mountaineers focus on Chimney Pond with their sights set squarely on Mount Katahdin's Hamlin and Baxter Peaks. Many peak baggers trek into the hut at Nesowadnehunk Field to access the four high mountains located in the northwestern part of the park. Few are attracted to South Branch Pond.

The South Branch Pond region is very unique and appealing. There are two quite distinct ponds: Upper and Lower South Branch Ponds. Although its name implies the opposite, the South Branch Pond Campground is actually located in the far northeast corner of the park. Bordered by mountains on the east and west, the ponds have the character of an inland fjord. The campground features a roomy cabin with splendid views providing an outstanding winter destination. Because other areas of the park are more popular, obtaining hut reservations at South Branch is comparatively easy.

Three peaks near South Branch have a special attraction for mountaineers: Peak of the Ridges, North Traveler, and a rarely climbed mountain called The Traveler. All over 3000 feet in elevation, The Traveler is highest at 3,541 feet. The allure is not their altitude but rather the remote location, difficulty of access, and their majestic beauty.

In February 2010, a group of seven assembled just west of the East Branch of the Penobscot River, adjacent to the northeast entrance to Baxter State Park. Our primary intent was to complete the Traveler Loop in winter. Five of us were veterans of prior excursions to South Branch Pond while two were debutants.

Chapter 5 - Traveler Mountain Loop Trip in Baxter State Park in Winter

To prepare for a winter mountaineering trip into Baxter, climbers need to take skis with poles and boots, snowshoes with climbing claws, and winter mountaineering boots with micro spikes or crampons. For hiking, poles or ice axes are suitable but most choose poles. Surface conditions will dictate the appropriate footgear in any given circumstance. Bedding, food, cook stoves, lanterns, fuel, cooking gear, eating utensils, and emergency equipment and supplies must also be transported.

Homemade expedition sleds were used to haul our gear in water resistant duffel bags. Some trekkers also carried mountaineering packs on their backs. The combination allowed for loads as heavy as 80 to 100 pounds, more substantial than most people can tote in a backpack.

Wearing skis, we began our trek, towing sleds west on the rolling Park Perimeter Road for nine miles to South Branch Road. Turning left, the road climbed for much of the remaining two miles before ending with an exhilarating downhill ski to the campground.

The hut is quite spacious. Included are a large kitchen/dining area with a woodstove, table, plenty of cupboard space, and gas lamps that sometimes work. Two bunkrooms provide four beds in each. Some in our group slept outside leaving lots of space for us sissies remaining indoors. Natural refrigeration is readily available on the porch. The park provides firewood stored in a nearby shed. Water is available at the nearby pond outlet but should be purified. An outhouse is located about one hundred feet away, entailing a frigid inconvenient walk at night. Most of us carried a pee jar. Facing south, the hut provides excellent views of Lower South Branch Pond and surrounding mountains.

The Traveler Range is considered one of the premiere loop hikes in New England. Rugged, consequential, and remotely situated, rarely is it traversed in winter. Three years prior, three members of the group, Brent Elwell, Brad Fox, and I had fortuitously finished the arduous trek. A previous attempt had failed. The successful expedition had been counterclockwise beginning with Peak of the Ridges, followed by The Traveler, and ending with

North Traveler. This time, we would proceed in the opposite direction. Because we anticipated a very challenging ten-mile journey with snow and ice conditions a mystery, a start before sunrise was planned.

Early the following morning, six of us began breaking trail with snowshoes on North Traveler Trail. The snow was deep and no signs of previous winter hikers were observed ascending the precipitous path. Despite painfully slow progress negotiating through drifted snow and over several treacherous ledges, glorious vistas of the Katahdin massif were observed from south facing cliffs. After losing the trail several times, the open summit was finally achieved shortly before noon.

With about six hours of light left and seventy percent of the trip remaining, this was the point of no return. Everyone was carrying a headlight. Since it was a clear calm day with seasonal temperatures, the optimistic decision was to continue.

An elongated open ridge leading southwest towards The Traveler afforded spectacular 360-degree panoramic views. However, prodigious amounts of snow had accumulated in a wooded col resulting in again losing the trail; further impeding headway. Seldom conquered in winter, scaling icy, barren Traveler was a rewarding triumph for the entire group. Ominously, almost half of the outing remained. It was apparent we'd finish in the dark. Crossing the perilous boulder-strewn Peak of the Ridges before sunset was imperative.

The top of Traveler provided an unhindered view of distinctive Peak of the Ridges. Since another thickly forested saddle was located between the two, a compass bearing was taken. A wise decision—the trail vanished in drifted snow almost immediately. We assiduously followed the plotted course in a congested conifer forest and accomplished the bewildering bush whack to Peak of the Ridges. After a short respite on the craggy summit surrounded by phenomenal mountain views, a compass bearing to South Branch Pond was taken just before sundown. We then navigated abruptly down the harsh terrain by headlight, and it was

Chapter 5 - Traveler Mountain Loop Trip in Baxter State Park in Winter

completely dark when we finally reached the south shore of South Branch Pond.

One member of Team South Branch, Allen Gaskell, had chosen not to participate in the loop trip. A light in the cabin could be seen an icy mile away. Finishing the excursion, our intrepid band arrived to find a fire in the woodstove and dinner waiting.

The South Branch area provides numerous opportunities for winter recreation. South Branch Road can be skied when fresh snow is present. A ski trail leads to Fowler Pond and another on the Pogy Notch Trail to Russell Pond. Hiking the South Branch Mountain Loop is also a challenging alternative. South Branch Campground can be used as the first or last stop on a traverse of the park.

On day three, skiing was the activity of choice. Since park rangers had broken Pogy Notch Trail to Russell Pond with snowmobiles, several of us skied part way. A skiing machine, Brent finished the entire roundtrip. On the following day, everyone hiked the South Branch Mountain Loop, a five-mile outing. The journey entailed a traverse of scenic South Branch and Black Cat Mountains followed by a return on ice-covered Upper and Lower South Branch Ponds. While most skied on the final full day at South Branch, Brent and I decided on another climb of Peak of the Ridges. The views were again superlative and the climb far easier in daylight.

Lighter sleds and a fast surface facilitated a speedy return to Matagamon Winter Trailhead. We had completed a memorable expedition. Remarkably, the entire trip had been storm-free, a first for us South Branch veterans.

THINGS TO KNOW

Location: Piscataquis County, north-central Maine

For pertinent Baxter State Park winter information and unique potential hazards: See "Things to Know" at the end of Chapter 1.

Elevation of high points: North Traveler 3,152 feet, The Traveler 3,541, Peak of the Ridges 3,254, South Branch Mountain 2,630, and Black Cat Mountain 2,611

Elevation Gains:
Matagamon Winter Trailhead to South Branch Campground: 321 feet
South Branch Campground to North Traveler: 2,175 feet
North Traveler to The Traveler: 989 feet
The Traveler to Peak of the Ridges: 364 feet
Total elevation gain on Traveler Loop: 3,528 feet

Distances:
Matagamon Winter Trailhead to South Branch Road: 9 miles
Park Perimeter Road to South Branch Campground: 2 miles
South Branch Campground to North Traveler: 3 miles
North Traveler to The Traveler: 2.5 miles
The Traveler to Peak of the Ridges: 1.2 miles
Peak of the Ridges to Lower South Branch Pond: Approximately 2 miles
Lower South Branch Pond to South Branch Campground: Approximately 1.2 miles
Total Loop Distance: Approximately 10 miles
Difficulty: Strenuous
Views: Phenomenal on North Traveler, Traveler Ridge, The Traveler, and Peak of the Ridges
Directions to Matagamon Winter Trailhead: From Route 11 in Patten, turn left on the Shin Pond Road and travel about 12 miles to the village of Shin Pond. Continue west on the unpaved Grand Lake Road for about 15 miles until crossing the East Branch of the Penobscot River. The winter trailhead is just west of the bridge and about 1.5 miles before the summer park

Chapter 5 - Traveler Mountain Loop Trip in Baxter State Park in Winter

entrance at Matagamon Gate. A fairly large parking area on the right is plowed periodically.

Additional Relevant Information: Matagamon Wilderness Campground is located on the right just before crossing the bridge over the East Branch of the Penobscot: https://matagamon.com/. The campground has a small restaurant, cabins, and a store that sells some supplies. It may be possible to make arrangements to have sleds and gear shuttled on the Perimeter Road to South Branch Road. Except for Park Rangers, snowmobiles are prohibited on the South Branch Road.

Additional Recommendation: Carry a sturdy shovel in your vehicle. Plows leave massive snowbanks in the parking area.

An alternative to winter in Baxter State Park: For those interested in warmer hiking in the Travelers, the park is open from May 15 to October 15. Instead of pulling sleds to South Branch Pond Campground, visitors can drive there. Canoeing and kayaking is an option on the ponds when they're free of ice. See the park website for information on rules, access, and camping reservations: https://baxterstatepark.org/#/

Another nearby destination: Katahdin Woods and Waters National Monument is located on the east side of Baxter State Park. It provides excellent opportunities for winter skiing and snowshoeing. Hiking and mountain biking are options in the other three seasons. Cabins, lean-tos, and campsites are located around the monument facilitating multi-day expeditions. For more information, visit their website:
https://www.nps.gov/kaww/planyourvisit/outdooractivities.htm

Climbers reach the summit of Traveler Mountain in Baxter State Park. (Photo – Ron Chase)

Chapter 6 - Bigelow Mountain

Racing Against the Storm

Except for three years in the Army, I've lived my entire life in Maine. One would surmise that after seven decades experiencing Maine winters, they wouldn't come as a surprise. However, for some inexplicable reason the first significant winter storm always seems to catch me unprepared.

I'm not alone. A few inches of white stuff finds savvy long-time Mainers slip sliding away on highways acting as if they're out on a sunny, summer excursion with dry roads. For too many of us, winter doesn't truly arrive until we're startled back to reality by a rash of snow-related automobile accidents.

The Penobscot Paddle and Chowder Society had scheduled a hike on Bigelow Mountain for a second Saturday in December. Undeterred by the first forecasted winter storm, Chowderheads were intent on climbing the mountain despite the inclement prediction. Actually, not that reckless; our goal was to complete the trek before the storm arrived.

Located in the Carrabassett Valley area of western Maine, the Bigelow Mountain Range is one of the state's premier mountaineering venues. Paralleling the south shore of picturesque Flagstaff Lake, Bigelow has six significant peaks. Our mission was to scale two of them, South and North Horns.

Bigelow Mountain also has the distinction of possessing three of the Appalachian Mountain Club (AMC)-designated one hundred highest peaks in New England; South Horn at 3,805 feet and two four-thousand footers, Avery and West Peaks. As a result, it's a must climb for peak baggers in pursuit of four-thousand footers or the one hundred highest. The Appalachian Trail traverses much of the mountain, seductively lending itself to some excellent backpacking options.

Friends and I have experienced multiple adventures on Bigelow spanning several decades. An early encounter was a backpacking trip with my wife Nancy and longtime friends John and Diane Stokinger. Spending nights at Horns Pond and Bigelow Col (some call it Avery Col) in wonderful autumn weather, we found it to be the perfect overnight introduction. Motivated by that exceptional endeavor, another friend and I decided on a winter trip a few years later that wasn't quite as accommodating. Inadequately equipped for extreme cold, a near sleepless night was spent in a tent at Horns Pond with temperatures dropping to 25 below zero Fahrenheit. Many valuable lessons were learned without serious consequence on that misadventure. Among them, since we had no need for arctic expedition training, a repeat performance was deemed unnecessary.

In January of 1995, the summits of Bigelow were the objective of a large group of peak baggers on a quest to climb the one hundred highest peaks in New England in winter. Since the Stratton Brook Road was buried in snow, the journey began on Route 27 near Stratton. An epic 18-mile alpine day ensued climbing the four high Bigelow peaks using skis, snowshoes, and crampons. Two memories stand out: an under cast at higher elevations allowed us to hike the summits in sunshine while a freezing rainstorm raged below, and late mountaineering friend Lloyd Brown was a major player on the trip.

For many years, Lloyd was a fun-loving mainstay in the Maine winter mountaineering community. Almost always accompanied by his beloved dog Kito, he fell short of his alpine goals due to an untimely death. Sadly missed, Lloyd passed away at much too young an age.

Our recent trek began with four Chowderheads, my wife Nancy, Julia Richmond, Brent Elwell, and me, meeting at the Stratton Brook Trailhead approximately 2.5 miles east of Route 27. The storm was scheduled to arrive late afternoon. Our goal was to complete the hike and exit the potentially treacherous unplowed Stratton Brook Road before significant snow accumulated.

Chapter 6 - Bigelow Mountain

Crossing a sturdy hiking bridge over Stratton Brook outlet, the enthusiastic band of chowder lovers vigorously rambled up Fire Warden's Trail to a junction with Horns Pond Trail. Ascending north on Horns Pond Trail for 2.5 miles to the Appalachian Trail, we lingered briefly for lunch at Horns Pond lean-to. We affixed micro spikes before negotiating a steep, icy half mile scramble to South Horn. Magnificent views of West and Avery Peaks in the east were observed on arrival at the barren pinnacle. Sugarloaf Mountain dominated the skyline with nearby Crocker and Saddleback Ranges seemingly junior alpine accomplices.

Descending towards the pond, a short, attenuated spur trail led to North Horn where there were breathtaking panoramic vistas of Flagstaff Lake. Two late arriving Chowderheads, Suzanne and Gary Cole, joined us at the summit. They had hiked the Appalachian Trail from Stratton Brook Road, a shorter more demanding alternative approach.

Remarkably calm at the top, the storm could be discerned advancing from the southwest. Realizing it would soon envelop the entire mountain, we hurriedly descended to our vehicles, ending an 11.5-mile expedition. It was snowing on arrival, but difficulties were avoided as we cautiously negotiated the slippery Stratton Brook Road to Route 27.

Then the most dangerous challenges of the day began: navigating on dark, snowy highways trying to avoid collisions with drivers careening along slippery roads as if it were a clear sunny August afternoon. Dodging the kamikazes, we safely reached our destinations satisfied with another remarkable adventure on Bigelow.

THINGS TO KNOW

Location: Franklin and Somerset Counties, western Maine
Distances:
Stratton Brook Trailhead to Fire Warden's Trail: .4 mile
Fire Warden's Trail to Horns Pond Trail: 2.1 miles

Horn's Pond Trail to Appalachian Trail near Horns Pond: 2.5 miles
Horns Pond to South Horn summit: .5 mile
Appalachian Trail to North Horn: .2 mile out
Total Stratton Brook Trailhead to Horns and back: Approximately 11.5 miles
Stratton Brook Trailhead via Fire Warden's Trail to Bigelow Col: 4.6 miles
Bigelow Col to Avery Peak: .4 mile
Avery Peak to West Peak: .7 mile
West Peak to South Horn: 2.1 miles
Stratton Brook Road Appalachian Trailhead to Bigelow Range Trail: 3.2 miles
Bigelow Range Trail Junction to Horns Pond: 1.7 miles
Elevation of high points: West Peak 4,150 feet, Avery Peak 4,090 feet, South Horn 3,805 feet, and North Horn 3,704 feet. Note: North Horn was originally designated a 100 highest peak in New England by the AMC. It has subsequently been removed.
Elevations Gains:
    Stratton Brook Road to Horns Pond: 1,893 feet
    Horns Pond to South Horn: 639 feet
    Stratton Brook Road to Bigelow Col: 2,509 feet
    Bigelow Col to Avery Peak: 308 feet
    Bigelow Col to West Peak: 368 feet
    West Peak to South Horn: Approximately 650 feet
Difficulty: Strenuous

Unique potential hazards: There is periodic above tree line exposure to the elements. Substantial boulder and rock scrambling will be encountered increasing the risk of serious falls. Remote locations and high elevations make rescue problematic and may result in long delays. Hikers and climbers should not expect immediate assistance. Carrying a map, compass, and GPS is recommended.

Views: Exceptional on the summits of Avery and West Peaks, and North and South Horns

Chapter 6 - Bigelow Mountain

Directions: From the village of Carrabassett Valley drive north on Route 27 for 9.1 miles to an unmarked dirt road on the right (Stratton Brook Road). Travel east on this rough road for .9 mile to the Appalachian Trailhead. Continue east on the Stratton Brook Road for approximately 1.5 miles to the Stratton Brook Trailhead.

Other Bigelow hiking options: Alpine bookends on the Bigelow Range are Cranberry Peak (elevation 3,213 feet) and Little Bigelow Mountain (elevation 3,040 feet). From the village of Stratton on the west side of the Bigelow Range, the Range Trail climbs 3.3 miles to the summit of Cranberry Peak. From the east side of the Bigelow Range on the East Flagstaff Road, the Appalachian Trail ascends 2.9 miles to the summit of Little Bigelow Mountain. A traverse of the entire Bigelow Range from Stratton to East Flagstaff Road is approximately 18.5 miles

A hiker enjoys a view of Flagstaff Lake from North Horn on Bigelow Mountain. (Photo – Ron Chase)

Chapter 7 - Puzzle Mountain

Puzzling Avian Encounters

Being semi-retired has benefits. Old age is not one of them. Perhaps the most significant advantage is time flexibility, at least what little is left. I try to write and operate my tax consulting business on bad weather days and play on nice ones. In short, my goal is to work a little and play a lot.

I'm privileged to have numerous retired friends who enjoy outdoor adventures. Gary, Suzanne, and Brent are three of the closest. The late Skip Pendleton labeled our geriatric group AARPIES. Whatever the moniker, we're constantly studying the weather in search of suitable circumstances for a wilderness excursion.

A stormy December weather pattern comprising of rain, snow, sleet, and persistently gusty winds had challenged our planning acumen. A pause in precipitation resulted in a flurry of emails with my three frequent companions. The conclusion was a favored endeavor and one of the most popular hikes in western Maine, a climb of Puzzle Mountain in North Newry.

A relatively new trail network, the Grafton Notch Loop Trail, which opened in 2003, passes over Puzzle Mountain's southwest peak. The 38.2-mile circuit through Mahoosuc Land Trust property traverses seven summits. The strenuous journey has become one of Maine's premiere backpack expeditions. Prior to my knee replacement, it would have been a goal for me. Alas, old age dictates foregoing the challenge. Carrying a full pack for that distance would risk the longevity of my prosthetic knee. I'm far too much of a sissy to endure the thoroughly unpleasant rehabilitation process a second time unless absolutely unavoidable. I admit pangs of envy whenever the usually young multiday trekkers are encountered.

Chapter 7 - Puzzle Mountain

My three friends were already assembling their gear when I arrived at the Route 26 trailhead. A recent rainstorm had washed away much of the snow, but beginning near Bethel there was a surviving accumulation. After greetings, my immediate concern was whether or not micro spikes were necessary. An inspection indicated the surface was marginal so two of us elected to wear them from the outset. As we confronted periodic spans of ice at higher elevations, everyone was employing them before the outing ended.

The Puzzle Mountain portion of the path is a 3.2 mile trek to the distinctive open 3,133 foot summit. While the weather was sunny and dry, conditions were imperfect as it was cold and breezy. A crusty layer of snow and patchy ice punctuated much of the trail. Initially crossing a dirt road and scaling a pitch, the route then ascended gradually in an open hardwood forest. After about two miles, the path turned left and the gradient increased.

I consider myself a promising birder. Devoting years of diligent study, I've learned to quickly identify pigeons, sea gulls, and robins. Gary and Suzanne are more advanced. While climbing, Suzanne spotted a mysterious gray and white bird soaring above us. My visceral observation was a sea gull. Doubting the veracity of my pronouncement, she speculated we might have experienced the rare sighting of a goshawk, confirming the same on her bird app. The outing had barely begun and my bird tally was expanding geometrically.

The prolonged steep section completed, the passage narrowed as it wrapped westerly around an abrupt incline before ascending some short switchbacks in a dense stand of conifers. Emerging onto an expansive open ledge with spectacular views of Grafton Notch and the Mahoosuc Range, we had to endure penetrating blustery winds from the northwest.

Entering a sheltered wooded section, we navigated an aggregation of immense boulders with lengthy stretches of hard ice. At 2.6 miles, a junction for Woodsum Spur was encountered on an elongated sloping ledge. Signage indicated the partially visible rugged summit was another six-tenths of a mile. After scrambling over several complex rocky inclines, we negotiated up a consequential icy slide.

Persisting through sparse stunted growth, we observed a tiny bird fluttering beyond a nearby tree. When it landed on a limb, Gary astutely identified our feathered friend as a white-winged crossbill. Since I had never heard of a cross billed whatchamacallit my bird count had blossomed to an impressive five.

Winds were howling as we approached a precipitous ledge beneath the summit. Everyone huddled below donning parkas prior to completing the final ascent. No photos from the top for me—my camera battery froze despite being enclosed in an insulated container. From there, Grafton Notch Loop Trail continues its meandering odyssey north while Woodsum Spur begins a circuitous decline. Given the frigid conditions, Puzzle pinnacle was the extent of our expedition.

Following a brief respite in a protected area on the east side of the summit cone, we began our descent. The views of Sunday River White Cap and the White Mountains beyond from west facing ledges were breathtaking. Finishing the journey, I wallowed in self-satisfaction knowing I had migrated from promising to fledgling birder status. The sky is the limit!

THINGS TO KNOW

Location: Oxford County, western Maine
Length of out and back hike: 6.4 miles
Elevation gain: Approximately 2,350 feet
Difficulty: Moderate
Unique potential hazards: Some exposure to the elements when nearing the summit. Substantial boulder and rock scrambling in the last mile increases the risk of serious falls. Carrying a map, compass, and GPS is recommended.
Views: Outstanding from a west facing open ledge at about 2.5 miles and exceptional on the summit cone.

Chapter 7 - Puzzle Mountain

Directions: From the junction of US Route 2 and Maine Route 26 in Newry, drive north on Route 26 for 4.7 miles to the Grafton Notch Loop Trailhead. A sizeable parking area is on the right.

Other hiking options in the area: The Grafton Notch Region is one of Maine's premiere hiking venues. The following additional excursions are recommended:

Woodsum Spur: This is an adjunct to the Puzzle Mountain out and back hike. Leaving east at the 2.6-mile trail junction, the path travels over a series of scenic ledges for approximately 2.1 miles to the summit. Many trekkers add the spur for an 8.6 mile out and back hike.

Sunday River Whitecap: A 3,335-foot open summit with spectacular views, it can be reached by traveling west from the Route 26 Grafton Notch Loop Trailhead for about 7 miles. The 14-mile roundtrip can be shortened to about 6 miles by following the itinerary recounted in the March 16, 2018, Times Record newspaper article, The Other Sunday River: https://www.pressherald.com/2018/03/16/the-other-sunday-river/.

Old Speck Mountain: At an elevation of 4,180 feet, Maine's fourth tallest mountain can be ascended from the Grafton Notch State Park Trailhead by following the Appalachian Trail west for about 4 miles to the summit. For details of a winter climb, see the Bangor Daily News Blog Network article, Old Man on Old Speck: http://rchase.bangordailynews.com/2019/02/18/old-man-on-old-speck/

Table Rock, West Baldpate, and East Baldpate Mountains: Follow the Appalachian Trail east from Grafton Notch State Park for three great hikes in one. Picturesque Table Rock can be a short 2.4-mile roundtrip trek. At 2.8 miles, arrive at partially exposed 3,662-foot West Baldpate with excellent views of the surrounding mountains. Travel another mile to rugged, barren East Baldpate; at an elevation of 3,812 feet one of the New England 100 highest. Completing all three entails a 7.6-mile roundtrip.

Backpacking Grafton Notch Loop Trail: For information on this strenuous exceptional trip, visit: https://www.mainetrail-finder.com/trails/trail/grafton-loop-trail

Hikers descend Puzzle Mountain. (Photo – Ron Chase)

Chapter 8 - Mounts Megunticook and Battie

Poetic Mount Megunticook

"Where the mountains meet the sea," is an oft-quoted phrase attributed to poet Edna St. Vincent Millay to describe the Camden Hills. Located in Camden Hills State Park, Mount Megunticook is the tallest of the Camden Hills at an elevation of 1,385 feet. According to park literature, the prominent summit is also the highest mainland mountain on the Atlantic coast. Cadillac Mountain is preeminent but situated on Mount Desert Island.

Arguably the most scenic location in Maine, Megunticook's Ocean Overlook provides some of the most phenomenal ocean vistas found anywhere. Atop the sheer Megunticook Cliffs facing southwest, hikers can look directly down into picturesque Camden Harbor with Curtis Island Lighthouse guarding the entrance. Beyond, dozens of islands decorate spectacular Penobscot Bay.

Poet and playwright Edna St. Vincent Millay spent much of her youth living in Camden within sight of majestic Mount Megunticook. She is reputed to have enjoyed hiking its trails and those of nearby Mount Battie. In 1912, a young Millay catapulted to fame with her poem *Renascence*, capturing the essence of the charm and beauty of those mountains looming over the rugged shore of Penobscot Bay. She went on to become the first woman to receive the Pulitzer Prize for Poetry and one of the most famous literary figures of the 20th century.

My Megunticook hiking experiences began when I moved to the mid-coast area in the 1970s. In the intervening decades, I've summited the lofty peak at least two or three times a year, qualifying for the century club if there was one. Since there isn't, obsessive compulsive Megunticook disorder might be the appropriate diagnosis.

A favorite personal endeavor is what I call the "Megunticook Hike and Bike." Leaving the parking lot at park headquarters, I bike up Mount Battie Road for about a mile to the Tablelands

Trail. Cabling my bike to a tree, I hike for another mile to Ocean Overlook then an additional half mile to the wooded Megunticook high point. Backtracking to the bike, the outing is completed by cycling to the top of Mount Battie followed by an exhilarating steep downhill ride to park headquarters. For some odd reason, I've never been able to interest others in this escapade.

Over the years, I've experimented with several variations of the Megunticook hike and bike, including using cross country skis when the park didn't plow the road in winter. On a few occasions, a late cycling start meant descending the road in the dark, once nearly striking a walker with my bike. We both resolved to wear headlamps in the future. An unplowed Mount Battie Road with hard packed snow provides a stimulating descent on cross country skis. Unfortunately, they've plowed it in recent years.

I chose the first day of winter for a Megunticook climb, and found that the Mount Battie Road was plowed and partially ice-covered. I decided to limit my activity to just hiking, so micro spikes appeared to be the best option for ensuring traction. Beginning on Megunticook Trail just beyond the campground, I ascended the east side of the mountain on a packed snow surface to Adam's Lookout Trail. Turning left, it ambles over some ledges with excellent views of Penobscot Bay before arriving at the Ridge Trail in a narrow boulder strewn junction. From there the path climbs precipitously along Megunticook Cliffs to Ocean Overlook.

Don't forget to take a camera on this hike as you're almost guaranteed some wonderful photo ops from that picturesque location. Stop to visualize a passionate Edna St. Vincent Millay sitting at the edge of the precipice contemplating the beauty of her surroundings. She almost assuredly visited this spot many times.

Donning my parka for protection against frigid northwest winds, I skirted along the cliffs and persisted in a predominantly conifer forest to the true summit where a large cairn marks the pinnacle. Returning on the panoramic Ridge Trail then descending Tablelands Trail to Mount Battie Road, I was surprised to encounter a couple sliding the icy road on plastic coasters. After years of varied Megunticook capers, this was a novel alternative to contemplate.

Continuing what has become an obligatory extension of the trek for me, I hiked to the summit of Mount Battie where the stone tower was festively adorned with Christmas lights. At an elevation of 780 feet, more outstanding views of Camden Harbor and Penobscot Bay were the reward. Securely dropping rapidly down the icy Mount Battie Road on micro spikes, another Megunticook excursion was completed. No bikes or skis this time but I'll take a lightweight flying saucer on my next winter Megunticook adventure.

Did I mention that if you are a Maine resident over 64 years of age there is no entrance fee? If you're a fellow senior who can walk, hike, bike, ski, or slide, enjoy a free day in beautiful Camden Hills State Park and save your pension income for prescriptions. If these activities don't appeal or exceed your limitations, drive to the top of Mount Battie when the road is open and experience some of the same views that inspired Edna St. Vincent Millay over a century ago.

THINGS TO KNOW

Location: Knox County, mid-coast Maine

Length of the described Megunticook and Battie loop hike: Approximately 5 miles

Elevation gain: Approximately 1,300 feet

Difficulty: Easy to moderate

Unique potential hazards: Some boulder and rock scrambling along Megunticook Cliffs increases the risk of serious falls. Recommend obtaining a free park map at the tollhouse and carrying a compass and GPS.

Fees: Camden Hills State Park charges entrance and camping fees. Maine residents 65 and older are not required to pay entrance fees.

Views: Exceptional at Ocean Overlook and the summit of Mount Battie

Directions: From Camden, travel north on US Route 1 for two miles to Camden Hills State Park on the left. Immediately after entering the park, bear left to a large parking area across the road from the park gate and tollhouse. The Megunticook Trailhead is .2 mile straight up the park road beyond the tollhouse and through the campground.

Other hiking options in Camden Hills State Park: There is a network of over 30 miles of hiking trails in the state park. Visit their website for more information: https://www.state-parks.com/camden_hills.html. Some recommended treks are:

Maiden Cliff: Beginning on Route 52 in Camden, complete a 2.5-mile loop with exceptional views from the cliff and the ridge above.

Bald Rock: From the junction of Youngtown Road and Maine Route 173 in Lincolnville, a parking area is the start of a 3-mile roundtrip out and back hike with outstanding views of Penobscot Bay. The trek can be lengthened with side hikes to Derry and Frohock Mountains. See the Times Record newspaper article dated January 26, 2018, entitled Leaky Capers on Bald Rock Mountain for more information on this hike:
 https://www.pressherald.com/2018/01/26/leaky-capers-on-bald-rock-mountain/

Mount Battie: An easy three-mile roundtrip from State Park Headquarters, views at the top rival Ocean Overlook. Hiking trails parallel Mount Battie Road or walkers can use the road. Watch out for traffic when the road is open and beware of errant cyclists when walking at night. Two short trails to the summit begin outside of the park in Camden.

Other hiking options in the Camden Hills: The Camden Hills is a mecca for easy day-hikes. The Georges River Land Trust maintains a system of trails in the southern sector of the Camden Hills Range: http://www.georgesriver.org/. Two recommended hikes are:

Chapter 8 - Mounts Megunticook and Battie

Ragged Mountain: Beginning on Maine Route 17 near Mirror Lake in Rockport, the Georges Highland Path winds circuitously for 2.5 miles to the 1,288-foot open summit. Other trails to the top of Ragged begin on Hope St., Barnstown Road, and the Camden Snow Bowl. For details on two hikes on Ragged Mountain, see the *Bangor Daily News* Blog Network article, A Fiery Tale on Ragged Mountain: http://rchase.bangordailynews.com/2017/12/25/a-fiery-tale-on-ragged-mountain/

Bald Mountain: This easy 2.4 mile out and back hike starts on Barnstown Road. The exposed summit provides exceptional views of the surrounding mountains and Penobscot Bay.

A hiker on Mount Megunticook's Ocean Overlook. (Photo – Ron Chase)

Chapter 9 - Pleasant Mountain

A Pleasant Traverse

Snow had arrived early in Maine, leaving a frosty layer of white stuff covering most of the prominent peaks during the first week of December. Pleasant Mountain near Denmark was no exception with an accumulation of several inches at higher elevations.

The closest substantial mountain to my home in Topsham, Pleasant is a long one-hour drive. The two-thousand-foot monadnock is the tallest peak in southern Maine and probably the most popular mountain hike in the region. Also the site of Shawnee Peak Ski Area, a network of trails offer a multitude of hiking alternatives—most including exceptional views of surrounding lakes and more distant mountains.

Consisting of a ten-mile trail system managed by Loon Echo Land Trust, four trailheads ultimately lead to the highest summit where there is a closed fire tower and truly phenomenal views from cliffs facing west towards the White Mountains in New Hampshire. The Fire Warden's Trail begins on Wilton Warren Road and rises 2.3 miles from the west. Slightly shorter Bald Peak Trail originates on the Mountain Road not far from the ski area and ascends northeast. They have a common imperfection: no truly exceptional views until hikers reach the top.

My preferred trails are Ledges and Southwest Ridge, also known as Mackay Pasture Trail. At a distance of 1.8 miles and climbing from the southeast, Ledges offers the shortest route to the summit while Southwest Ridge is the longest but most scenic. An abundance of trails approaching from substantially different directions provide several opportunities for planning an appealing traverse.

I volunteered to lead the first scheduled Penobscot Paddle & Chowder Society trip of the winter season. After learning the high

Chapter 9 - Pleasant Mountain

peaks in western Maine and the White Mountains had been clobbered with a progression of storms dumping copious amounts of snow and with wind chills predicted to approach 30 below zero Fahrenheit at lofty altitudes; I decided on a more benign Pleasant Mountain challenge.

Perhaps discouraged by the early arrival of winter, only three Chowderheads signed up for the trip: my wife Nancy and longtime outdoor friends Suzanne and Gary Cole. No, I didn't exert undue pressure on Nancy unless a generous bribe meets that standard.

After exchanging emails, a consensus was reached to attempt a traverse. Addicted to scenic trails, I successfully lobbied for a climb of Southwest Ridge and descent of the Ledges. The proposed itinerary included virtually every impressive view on the trail complex with the exception of those on a spur path leaving Bald Peak Trail and Bald Peak itself.

Meeting in the almost full parking area at the Ledges Trail on Mountain Road, we left a vehicle and shuttled to the Southwest Ridge Trailhead on the opposite side of the mountain. Concerned with the prospect of high winds and possibly icy footing, we packed parkas, warm mittens, and micro spikes. Because snow-covered trails would be compacted by the large turnout of hikers, snowshoes were left behind. Ten years ago, I would have carried snowshoes to train for the upcoming more strenuous winter mountaineering. At my age, I'm functioning one hike at a time – no unnecessary weight to be inflicted on the ancient joints.

Beginning on a thin blanket of snow, we ascended gradually in a sparse predominantly deciduous forest. As we emerged on a rocky bluff after hiking less than a mile, a panoramic vista of Beaver and Moose Ponds appeared—a delightful reward. Persevering up a series of open ledges to Southwest Peak, we were provided wonderful glimpses of the spectacular snow-capped Presidential Range in New Hampshire.

Proceeding from Southwest Peak in four to six inches of crusty snow, we reached a junction with Ledges Trail after 2.7 miles. Turning left and climbing steeply for a short distance, we were met with gusty but manageable winds at the summit. After donning parkas, we savored breathtaking views before seeking shelter from the frigid breezes below. Rejoining Ledges Trail, we rapidly descended to a unique sequence of precipitous ledges, source of the trail's name.

Stopping at a distinctive location on the ledges called Overlook, we celebrated Gary's birthday with delicious cake baked by Suzanne. Without disclosing his age, I can report that although younger than I, he definitely qualifies for senior citizen status. It doesn't seem that long ago I was often the youngest person on an endeavor. Alas, those halcyon days are gone.

Departing the ledges, we negotiated down a succession of switchbacks and navigated through a wet slippery section before passing a trail kiosk and reaching Mountain Road. Completing the journey in about four hours, ours had been perhaps the finest most picturesque mountain trek in southwestern Maine on a glorious winter day.

Land trusts have positively impacted my life for many years, yet I've lacked a clear understanding of the important role they play in Maine and the breadth of benefits provided. An accidental encounter on Pleasant Mountain changed that. While hiking on Southwest Ridge Trail, I met Jon Evans busy on a trail maintenance project. After learning he was Stewardship Manager for Loon Echo Land Trust, a very stimulating conversation about the land trust, its history and relationship with Pleasant Mountain followed. While familiar with Loon Echo as a result of the trailhead information kiosks, I didn't realize the extent of their mountain preservation holdings or the scope of labor required to maintain the trail network.

Later, I visited Jon at Loon Echo's headquarters on Depot Street in Bridgton also meeting Executive Director, Matt Markot. What ensued was for me a very informative conversation. The cookies were great, too!

Contrary to what many suspect, we old dogs can still learn new tricks. I now know that Loon Echo conserves numerous properties in the Northern Sebago Lake region totaling almost 7,000

Chapter 9 - Pleasant Mountain

acres. Besides preserving the land and maintaining multi-use trail systems that I regularly use, they also protect water resources, wildlife habitats, and working farms and forests. I mistakenly assumed that as a 501(c)(3) non-profit organization they were exempt from paying real estate taxes, but just the opposite is true. They remit them on a significant majority of their properties including a consequential annual tax payment for the Pleasant Mountain lands.

Regularly hiking, biking, paddling, and skiing on land trust properties, I now have a much greater appreciation for their efforts. Education is a wonderful thing, even for us old folks.

THINGS TO KNOW

Location: Oxford County, southwestern Maine
Length of traverse: 4.7 miles
Elevation Gain: 1,169 feet
Elevation: 2,006 feet
Difficulty: Easy to moderate
Unique potential hazards: Some exposure to the elements on sections of Southwest Ridge and Ledges Trails, and at the summit. Carrying a map, compass, and GPS is recommended. Pleasant Mountain trail maps are sometimes available at trailhead kiosks.
Views: Exceptional on Southwest Ridge and Ledges Trails, and at the summit.
Directions for the Traverse:
Ledges Trailhead: From Bridgton, follow US Route 302 west for about 5 miles. Turn left onto Mountain Road and continue past Bald Peak Trailhead on the right at one mile to a parking area on the left for Ledges Trail at 3 miles.
Southwest Ridge Trail: From the junction of Mountain Road and US Route 302, continue west on 302 for 4.1 miles to Denmark Road in Fryeburg. Turn left onto Denmark Road and drive 1.9 miles through an intersection with Harnden and Wilton

Warren Roads. Continue straight for .9 mile to a small, unmarked parking lot on the left. The trailhead is located in the far left rear corner of the parking area.

Other hikes on Pleasant Mountain:
Fire Warden's Trail: Beginning on Wilton Warren Road, this 2.3-mile trail joins Bald Peak Trail near the summit.

Bald Peak Trail: Starting on the Mountain Road, this path ascends for 2.2 miles before connecting with the Fire Warden's Trail. At .4 mile, a short side hike on the left visits impressive Needles Eye where a small stream plunges through a precipitous narrow gorge.

Sue's Way and North Ridge Trail: At the .7-mile junction on Bald Peak Trail, Sue's Way turns right and ascends for .5 mile to North Ridge Trail. From there, the loop angles south, climbs over a rocky scenic peak, and reconnects with Bald Peak Trail after .8 mile.

Other recommended hikes on Loon Echo Land Trust properties: Visit their website at: https://www.loonecholandtrust.org/

Bald Pate Mountain Preserve: Located on the east side of Route 107 in Bridgton, this preserve includes 6.7 miles of scenic trails. Connecting with Five Field Farm ski trails, there is an option for a combined hike and ski in the winter.

Raymond Community Forest: This new preserve has about 4 miles of trails open to hiking, snowshoeing, and skiing. Located near Crescent Lake in Raymond, Pismire Bluff provides exceptional views of Crescent Lake, Rattlesnake Mountain, and the Presidential Range in New Hampshire. Mountain biking is permitted on the trails west of Conesca Road.

Chapter 9 - Pleasant Mountain

Hikers enjoy a view on Pleasant Mountain's Southwest Ridge Trail. (Photo – Ron Chase)

SECTION II. BIKE TRAILS

A cyclist passes Jordan Pond on Acadia National Park Carriage Roads. (Photo – Ron Chase)

Chapter 10 - Sebago to the Sea

Exploring Sebago to the Sea

At my age, I've reluctantly come to the realization that I'm not going to be able to continue my current level of athletic involvement indefinitely. I can envision a time when my outdoor activities will be limited to cross country skiing in the winter and biking during the remaining three seasons. They're the only two sports that don't cause discomfort or aggravate something. Running and Telemark skiing are already in the past. Make no mistake I'm not surrendering, but my inner realist acknowledges the truth. There is an upside, I love skiing and biking.

My biking preferences have also evolved as I've aged. Steep single track trail riding has lost its glitter. When looking down a narrow, twisting precipitous decline, my first thought is the longevity of my plastic knee quickly followed by a decision to dismount and walk. Enthusiasm for muddy trails departed about a decade ago. Mud and I are no longer compatible. While continuing a fair amount of road riding, the seeming increase in distracted and reckless drivers substantially detracts from the experience.

Enough about what I don't like. I love well-maintained bike trails that are completely separated from traffic. Some of my favorite Maine rides are the Kennebec River Rail, Narrow Gauge, and Eastern Trails. The Carriage Roads in Acadia National Park are in my opinion the finest trail rides in Maine. I find myself returning to them on a regular basis because they provide safe exhilarating scenic cycling experiences away from noisy congested highways.

While the number of high caliber trails is growing, Maine is not a particularly bike friendly place. We have a paucity of quality trails compared to many states and most roads lack safe marked bike shoulders. Recognizing there are many important competing interests for finite tax dollars, Mainers would be well-advised to complete a comprehensive analysis of the health and quality of life benefits of expanding biking choices.

A preferred bike ride is Sebago to the Sea Trail. Located in the towns of South Windham, Gorham, and Standish, the trail system offers an interesting combination of paved and unpaved surfaces varying in difficulty from easy to moderate.

About a one-hour drive from my home in Topsham, I make the trek to Sebago to the Sea several times a year. Probably another example of old age and creeping senility, I find their website, literature, and maps quite confusing. Whether the Mountain Division Trail and Sebago to the Sea are one and the same or separate interconnected systems is unclear to me. Regardless, I've fashioned a favored excursion incorporating all or much of Sebago to the Sea and part of the presumed Mountain Division Trail.

There are several access points. For my most recent ride, I started at Shaw Park in Gorham. Situated two miles northwest of South Windham on Route 237, this trailhead has ample parking and a toilet. A caretaker is usually present in the summer.

Beginning my ride following a short connecter path to the paved Sebago to the Sea Trail and turning left, I rode three miles on a section that parallels old railroad tracks; a scenic area that passes rural homes and old farms. The paved sector ended at what signage indicates is the Mountain Division Trail.

Continuing abruptly left on a rough gravel road, the wide trail climbs steeply for a short distance. Right after the gradient leveled off, I encountered six friendly horseback riders. Attempting to safely accommodate each other, everyone slowed and separated. Horseback riders frequent the trail system. The Mountain Division Trail proceeds for just over a mile to Route 35 in Standish where there are athletic fields, parking, and another toilet. On the return, I narrowly avoided a collision with a large doe blocking the way. After we stared at one another for several seconds, she scampered off into the woods.

Backtracking to the presumed Sebago to the Sea trail junction, a left turn led past Otter Pond on a rocky surface. Several cyclists and walkers were sunning themselves on the shore. Following Sebago to Sea signs, a moderately demanding sometimes hilly dirt trail continued north for a mile to a trailhead on Route 237. Crossing the road, a narrow route angled left for a short mile to Route 35.

Turning left onto Route 35 for a brief distance, Sebago to the Sea Trail then veered right joining the paved Pond Road for a mile to the end. The Pond Road is a narrow passageway with minimal traffic providing a pleasurable ride. At the terminus of Pond Road, a kiosk marks the beginning of a challenging segment of trail that continues for another mile to a ninety-degree left turn. The remaining .2 mile to Sebago Lake is very rugged requiring difficult maneuvering. I found myself walking around a wet section and through an accumulation of boulders that more daring riders might attempt to negotiate. The struggle was worth the effort as the path ends at a small, picturesque beach on the east shore of the lake. A sunny spring day, there was a glorious view of snow-capped Mount Washington in the distance. Alas, I had forgotten my camera.

Returning and rejoining the paved component of Sebago to the Sea Trail, a very enjoyable cruise followed to Route 202 in South Windham. Near the Shaw Park connector, a narrow railroad bridge was traversed where several kids were diving into the Presumpscot River. Ah yes, diving from bridges, those were the days!

Returning for a mile and turning left onto Gambo Road, a short jaunt past the Gambo Road Trailhead brought me to a pedestrian/bicycle bridge over the Presumpscot. A paved spur trail resumed to Shaw Park, completing a twenty-mile ride.

Sebago to the Sea Trail is very popular. If you're old like me, go on a weekday when it's less crowded.

THINGS TO KNOW

Location: Cumberland County, southern Maine
Length: Approximately 20 miles for the described trip

Surface: Paved, gravel, and dirt
Recommended bike type: Hybrid or trail
Views: Excellent at the northern end on Sebago Lake. The trail has several picturesque locations.
Difficulty: Paved portions are easy. Unpaved sections on the northern end are moderately difficult.
Unique potential hazards: Other riders, walkers, and runners will be encountered. There are some potentially dangerous potholes on the paved section. The railroad bridge over the Presumpscot is narrow, drops off on both ends, and often has people congregating on it. Cyclists should consider dismounting and walking. Care should be exercised when horseback riders are encountered. When in doubt, dismount and walk or stop and allow them to pass. Be careful at road crossings, particularly Routes 237 and 35 where the traffic is fast.
Directions to Shaw Park Trailhead: From the junction of US Route 202 and Maine Route 237 in South Windham, drive west on 237 for about 2 miles to a sign for Shaw Park on the right. Follow the park road past a residence on the left to the end where there is a parking area, athletic fields, and access to the Presumpscot River.
Trail information and additional access points: Visit Sebago to the Sea website at: https://www.sebagotothesea.org/

Chapter 10 - Sebago to the Sea

Teenagers jump off the bridge on the Sebago to the Sea Trail. (Photo – Ron Chase)

Chapter 11 - Kennebec River Rail Trail

Fractured Memories on the Kennebec River Trail

In my opinion, the Kennebec River Rail Trail is the best bike trail in central Maine. Paralleling the long inactive Maine Central Railroad tracks, it's a most excellent paved path connecting Gardiner and Augusta. Having grown up in Gardiner and the little town across the river, Randolph, it's a place with many special memories.

My 5th grade class at Randolph Grammar School (RGS) may have been one of the last student groups to take a passenger train between Gardiner and Augusta. In May 1958, our aged teacher Miss Gould led a class of about thirty awestruck kids on a field trip to the state capital. Marching us across the Gardiner-Randolph Bridge to Depot Square in Gardiner, our wide-eyed group of preadolescents boarded the train for Augusta.

It was a day of excitement and adventure for a group of ten- and eleven-year-olds as the tougher-than-nails Miss Gould escorted us in military fashion to the Blaine House, State Capitol Building, and the Augusta House where her mandated lunch of choice was baked chicken with mashed potatoes and peas. No alternative meals were considered – Miss Gould didn't do alternatives. It was a marvelous, unforgettable day.

Weighing in at about eighty pounds, Miss Gould was no lightweight, but rather a stern disciplinarian. At a time when corporal punishment was losing favor, she may have conducted the last mass strapping of students in Maine, maybe the entire country. Serial offenders, five of us boys were accused of swearing on the playground and illegally climbing to the top of the clearly unsafe fire escape. As I later told my dad, "I didn't do it." The name of the girl who ratted on us will not be disclosed.

Chapter 11 - Kennebec River Rail Trail

We were summarily tried, convicted, and sentenced, at which point Miss Gould lined us culprits up in front of the class and administered ten healthy whacks on the hand of each with a hard leather strap. As she was exhausted by the time she finished, if you had to get strapped by anyone at RGS, tiny Miss Gould was the executioner of choice. Trust me when I tell you that two of the true heavyweight educators could really lay on a mean wallop. The more draconian of the two never announced how many lashes were to be inflicted. Her MO was simple; she didn't stop until tears were drawn.

I digress. The Kennebec River Trail is a truly enjoyable and scenic ride, most of it along the river. I almost always begin in the Hannaford Supermarket parking lot in Gardiner where there is usually ample parking. My reasoning is simple. I prefer to start the ride climbing uphill and enjoying an easier descent on return. After I explained this to my late great friend Bill Kaiser a few years ago when I introduced him to the trail, he scoffed in disgust. "Ronnie," he said. "That's ridiculous. The river is flat between Gardiner and Augusta, there's no difference in elevation." According to Wikipedia, the official elevation for Augusta is 68 feet and 23 for Gardiner. I rest my case, Bill. Wish you were still with us so I could really rub it in.

A beautiful sunny day punctuated my recent ride. Leaving the Gardiner trailhead, I was one of several cyclists who rode north, enjoying views of the river and Randolph beyond. At about mile one, ancient logging booms could be observed spanning the river. The square log-ribbed rock piles were used to hold millions of tons of pulp wood floated downriver for decades before log drives ended in the late sixties. Just north is Brown's Island where three friends and I paddled a "borrowed" rowboat in search of Captain Kidd's buried treasure approximately sixty years ago. Finding no treasure, we struggled mightily against a strong unanticipated incoming tide on our return.

Shortly after, the trail left the river and traveled slightly inland to Hallowell. When I was young, Hallowell was a very poor, struggling community. Now, it's gentrified. Unfortunately, the business district is the only flaw in the trail. For about a half mile, the pathway ends. The choice is riding through congested Water Street traffic or taking unpaved Front Street behind the stores next to the river signed for private traffic only. Being a Miss Gould certified scofflaw, I usually take Front Street – she would not approve.

Once north of town, riders are back to an idyllic paved trail, much of it along the river. Typically, activity increases approaching Augusta. Proceeding to the Augusta parking area, my odometer read 6.3 miles, providing an exceptionally pleasant near thirteen-mile roundtrip ride.

Located adjacent to the Hannaford Supermarket in Gardiner, the southern trailhead begins on the northern end of the parking lot. Visualize the inimitable Miss Gould herding her class into the old train depot that's still in existence across the street. Don't underestimate her, she sometimes wields a strap.

THINGS TO KNOW

Location: Kennebec County, central Maine

Length: Approximately 13 miles roundtrip

Surface: Paved. If unpaved Front Street is used in Hallowell hard packed dirt for about 200 yards.

Recommended bike type: Road, hybrid, or trail

Views: Excellent along the river

Difficulty: Easy with a few minor hills

Unique potential hazards: Congested traffic in Hallowell. Other riders, walkers, and runners will be encountered. The trail is quite narrow near Gardiner and cyclists should slow down or dismount. Exercise caution at the Greenville Street crossing on the south side of Hallowell.

Directions to Gardiner trailhead: From the junction of US Route 201 and Maine Route 126 in Gardiner, follow Water Street east for a short distance to Main Avenue. Turn left on Main Avenue and drive a short distance to the Hannaford Supermarket parking lot on the left. The trailhead is on the immediate right.

Chapter 11 - Kennebec River Rail Trail

Trail information and additional access points: Visit Kennebec River Rail Trail website at: https://www.krrt.org/

Cyclists ride the Kennebec River Rail Trail in Gardiner. (Photo – Ron Chase)

Chapter 12 - Eastern Trails

Cruising the Eastern Trails

Cycling is one of my favorite activities and a primary source of aerobic exercise. The older I get the more I enjoy it. A runner for almost forty years, a knee replacement compelled me to quit. The knee guy said, "If you keep running, you'll be back for another one." A certified sissy, I'm not suffering that very painful rehabilitation again if I can avoid it.

Harvard Medical School reports what I've long believed. Cycling is a great exercise and a wonderful form of recreation for almost everyone, especially old people. An outstanding aerobic workout, it's much easier on the joints than walking and running. Those clever folks at Harvard say cycling is excellent for your heart, brain, blood vessels, muscles, balance, and bone density. Having just finished a bike ride, I'm already feeling smarter and tougher. Unbalanced since birth, doubt there's any cure for that. If you're a fellow geriatric, grab a bike and get out on the trails. It's good for you.

I ride a lot. The actual mileage logged in a year is confidential as I don't want to be accused of being obsessive compulsive, a rumor without merit. Safety is my biggest cycling concern. There are simply too many people driving around sexting, texting, and nipping. My preference is to get away from traffic and ride bike trails separated from motor vehicles whenever possible.

The state of Maine promotes itself as a cycling-friendly place. Unfortunately, that's not really true, at least comparatively speaking. Many states, perhaps most, have a superior network of bike trails. Traveling to Utah and back this summer, I rode 33 different trails in 13 states, most just off major highways. In Florida, there are scores of paved bike trails dispersed throughout the Sunshine State filled with gray-haired cyclists. Here in Maine, only a handful

Chapter 12 - Eastern Trails

of genuine bike trails provide a decent ride. Many cyclists consider a ten-mile round trip to be the minimum acceptable distance. The vast majority of our scenic country roads lack a safe shoulder for bike travel. The good news: things are improving.

Arguably the finest trail ride in southern Maine is the Eastern Trail. The Scarborough to Saco sector is exceptional. My wife Nancy recently joined me for a ride. She's younger than I so you'll have to consult with her on whether or not she qualifies as a senior.

Departing from Black Point Road Trailhead, we rode south on the mostly crushed stone and gravel trail for about a mile where a toilet is strategically located. This is just far enough away from the parking area to avoid most of the trashing these necessary amenities receive when the people sexting, texting, and nipping can easily drive to them. The toilet is remarkably clean—a testament to the fine work the Eastern Trail Alliance performs maintaining the trail and its facilities.

Just beyond, riders reach very scenic Scarborough Marsh. A captivating area, it's almost impossible to avoid stopping to embrace the wonderful views. I've never ridden the trail when kayakers and canoeists weren't simultaneously exploring the tidal waters. As usual, knowing waves were exchanged by people mutually enjoying a special place.

After traversing the marsh and carefully crossing Pine Point Road, cyclists enter a shaded remarkably peaceful section of trail that continues for about five miles to Saco. My bike odometer read 6.9 miles when we arrived near Interstate 195 in Saco. Deciding to avoid street crossings in the remaining mile, we returned to Black Point Road for a near fourteen-mile trek.

Three and a half words about changing flat tires – don't do it. Changing tires is a dirty, messy business and something almost always goes wrong. I'd rather clean the toilet than change a bike tire. To be clear, I'm talking about my home toilet not the typical trailhead privy. When I have a flat tire, I invoke Ron's Over 70 Rule: Only people under 71 should change flat tires. I go to extreme measures to avoid this noxious chore. I'll ride on the rim or walk the bike for miles instead.

Once back to my vehicle, I head to the nearest bike shop. This rule is also good for the economy as it helps small businesses thrive. I try to do my part.

THINGS TO KNOW

Location: Cumberland and York Counties, southern Maine

Length: Approximately 14 miles for the described ride. See below for additional cycling alternatives.

Surface: Mostly crushed stone and gravel

Recommended bike type: Hybrid or trail - road bikes are not recommended.

Views: Exceptional in Scarborough Marsh

Difficulty: Easy

Unique potential hazards: There are several potentially hazardous road crossings. Traffic is quite fast on Pine Point Road just south of Scarborough Marsh. Expect to encounter other riders, walkers (many with dogs), runners, and those hauling or pushing strollers. Congestion is greatest near trailheads, particularly Black Point and Pine Point Roads.

Directions to Black Point Road Trailhead: From the junction of US Route 1 and Maine Route 207 in Scarborough, drive east on 207 for .4 mile to a right turn opposite Eastern Road. A large parking area is .3 mile.

Additional Eastern Trail biking options:

The Scarborough to Saco sector continues for 1.2 miles beyond the described ride.

The Biddeford to Kennebunk sector is an outstanding 6.1 mile one-way ride and normally less congested than Scarborough to Saco.

Trail information and additional access points: Visit the Eastern Trail's website at: https://www.easterntrail.org/

Chapter 12 - Eastern Trails

Paddling Scarborough Marsh: For information on paddling Scarborough Marsh see the *Portland Press Herald* article, Scarborough Marsh Surf & Turf:

https://www.pressherald.com/2018/10/12/ron-chase-on-scarborough-marsh-surf-turf/

Riders cross the bridge over Scarborough Marsh on the eastern trail. (Photo – Ron Chase)

Chapter 13 - Carriage Trails of Acadia National Park

Around the Mountain and More

The Carriage Roads of Acadia National Park are the best bike trail rides in Maine. At least that's my opinion and a sentiment shared by many of my outdoor friends.

Built by John D. Rockefeller, Jr. in the early part of the 20th century, the Carriage Roads consist of 46 miles of trails on a broken stone surface. Originally intended for horse and carriage, they are reputedly the best remaining examples of broken stone roads in the United States and include sixteen architecturally remarkable stone-faced bridges that span roads, streams, and waterfalls throughout the trail system. Rockefeller's subsequent donation of these roads was instrumental in formation of Acadia National Park.

With evocative names like Witch Hole, Paradise Hill, and Aunt Betty Pond, the trails weave around lakes, ponds, and mountains, one rising to the summit of Day Mountain. There are no bad choices as each offers a serene, picturesque escape from busy Mount Desert Island roads with ubiquitous scenic vistas. My favorite is Around the Mountain Trail. Actually, Around the Mountain circumnavigates Sargent, Parkman, and Penobscot Mountains and Bald and Gilmore Peaks. The entire ride is about twelve miles in distance.

Hiking trails intersect the Carriage Roads in numerous locations. About two decades ago while completing a solo ride on Around the Mountain I found the North Sargent Trail crossing high on the northwest shoulder of Sargent Mountain. Noting that it was less than a mile to the summit, I left my bike and ascended to the top. At an elevation of 1,373 feet, Sargent is the second highest peak in Acadia and offers breathtaking 360-degree views

Chapter 13 - Carriage Trails of Acadia National Park

of the park, surrounding mountains, and offshore islands. Descending on the North Sargent Trail, hikers are compensated for their efforts with a spectacular panorama of Somes Sound.

I announced an Around the Mountain Bike and Hike Trip as part of the Penobscot Paddle and Chowder Society annual fall outdoor extravaganza on Mount Desert Island. While none of the younger members were interested in the ambitious excursion, three elderly Chowderheads signed on. Our median age was a youthful 68.

Assembling at Lower Hadlock Pond Trailhead on Route 3 near Northeast Harbor on a gorgeous sunny fall day, all of us were equipped with trail bikes. While a few cyclists use road bikes on the Carriage Trails, the rocky surface punishes thin narrow tires increasing the risk of flats. Having never met a flat tire I liked, I've converted both of my bikes to tubeless tires with sealant injected. I've been flat-free for over five thousand miles.

I chose Lower Hadlock Pond Trailhead as the starting point—the intent was to accomplish most of the climb at the beginning of the trip. Shifting into low gear, a steady ascent began on the twisting trail. A mile into the climb, a riding companion noticed something unusual clinging precariously to a tree branch above. A porcupine was hanging ominously over the trail. After the obligatory photo was taken, the prickly critter was abandoned unbothered. Our collective hope was that he wouldn't fall on an unsuspecting cyclist, resulting in a thorny encounter.

As we continued our arduous climb, distinctive Bald Peak was passed. Turning north, sporadic glimpses of Somes Sound appeared while pedaling steeply along the west side of Parkman Mountain. Soon after, the gradient moderated and we arrived at North Sargent Trail. We had biked steadily uphill for four miles, and another five hundred feet of elevation gain was required hiking to the summit. Concerned that a tired walker or runner might opt for a speedy descent, we cabled our bikes to trees.

While the hike on Sargent is precipitous, the trail quickly rises above tree line and marvelous views monopolize the senses. Lunch at the summit was a delight with calm winds and almost limitless views. We noticed a large ring of surf surrounding distant Baker Island as a result of an offshore storm, so our choice to forego sea kayaking was validated. While suffering a collective senior moment we initially bumbled down the wrong trail until someone noted the scenery was unfamiliar. Rectifying the blunder, the remainder of our descent to the Carriage Road was trouble-free with wondrous views of Somes Sound, the only fjord on the eastern shore of the United States.

The reward for our uphill bicycle trek was a glorious downhill ride for about four miles to the foot of stunning Jordan Pond. From there, the trail traveled circuitously west for another four miles to the starting point. Arriving there after several hours of cycling and hiking, we had experienced a truly exceptional day in paradise.

THINGS TO KNOW

Location: Hancock County, Down East Maine

Length: Approximately 12 miles for the described ride. See below for more rides.

Surface: Broken stone

Recommended bike type: Hybrid or trail - road bikes are not recommended.

Views: Outstanding. The Carriage Roads arguably provide the most exceptional views of any bike rides in Maine.

Difficulty: Easy to moderate. Some steep climbs and descents.

Unique potential hazards: Other riders, walkers, and runners will likely be encountered. The trails are particularly busy near trailheads. Horseback riding is permitted on some trails and cyclists are directed to yield to them.

Directions to the Lower Hadlock Pond Trailhead: From the junction of Routes 198 and 3 shortly after crossing the bridge onto Mount Desert Island from the north, follow Route 198 south for about 10 miles to the trailhead and parking area on the left.

Chapter 13 - Carriage Trails of Acadia National Park

Additional recommended Carriage Road rides:
Eagle Lake Loop: From Eagle Lake Trailhead on Route 233 about 6 miles
Witch Hole Loop: From Eagle Lake Trailhead on Route 233 about 6.5 miles
Jordan and Bubble Ponds Loop: From Jordan Pond Trailhead on Park Loop Road about 8.5 miles
Day Mountain Loop: From Jordan Pond Trailhead on Park Loop Road about 8.5 miles
Numerous longer trips can be completed by combining recommended rides.

Cycling the Park Loop Road: The approximately 18-mile ride on the Acadia National Park Loop Road is probably the most scenic paved road ride in Maine. I recommend beginning at the Jordan Pond Parking area. Ride north climbing steadily on the Park Loop Road in two-way traffic for about four miles to the Cadillac Mountain Road. Shortly after, the Loop Road becomes one-way traveling southerly along the eastern slope of Champlain Mountain. Pass through a park gate and pay the fee. From Sand Beach to Hunter's Beach, enjoy incredibly phenomenal coastal views. Ride inland and return to Jordan Pond. During the park busy season which seems to be from mid-May to mid-October be prepared for lots of traffic and many distracted drivers enjoying the scenery. Recommend avoiding weekends and holidays. Climbing the Cadillac Mountain Road to the summit adds about six very challenging miles to the ride. Normally, there is substantial traffic and the steep road frequently twists and turns. About ten years ago, I completed the entire 24-mile ride beginning at first light on a fall weekend. I was able to avoid heavy traffic throughout.

A cyclist rides around the mountain on the Carriage Roads. (Photo – Ron Chase)

Chapter 14 - Narrow Gauge Pathway in Carrabassett Valley

Riding the Narrow Gauge

One of the most unique bike trails in Maine is the historic Narrow Gauge Pathway in Carrabassett Valley. The trail follows the former Kingfield and Dead River Railroad bed used to convey logs to a sawmill situated in Bigelow at the northern terminus of the railway in the early 20th century. Two-foot narrow gauge tracks were chosen instead of the standard size because they were easier to construct and less expensive. An added benefit, the smaller locomotives were able to operate more efficiently in the rugged mountainous terrain. Passengers and freight were also transported on the once bustling train system. Floods, a sawmill fire, and disuse resulted in discontinuance of the railroad in 1927. The Town of Carrabassett Valley constructed the pathway in 2001.

Traveling next to the boulder-strewn Carrabassett River located in a deep valley between Sugarloaf Mountain and the Bigelow Mountain Range, you will agree that serene and scenic describe the bucolic crushed-stone and dirt surface trail. Wide hybrid or mountain bike tires are required on the rough surface. Motorized vehicles including ATVs and snowmobiles are prohibited. The trail is groomed for cross-country skiing in the winter, an area where snowfall is usually plentiful.

After a fifteen-year hiatus from the trail, my wife Nancy and I met with our longtime friend Dave Lanman at the Airport Trailhead on a hot, steamy summer day. Located adjacent to a small airport about a mile north of the Carrabassett Valley Town Office, spacious parking and a restroom are available.

We began the ride on a rough abbreviated multi-use connector trail that soon traverses the Carrabassett River on a relatively new well-designed bridge to a kiosk that announces the beginning of

Narrow Gauge Pathway. Immediately crossing a short footbridge over Houston Brook, the trail began climbing gradually west in a forested area. Shade from a canopy of overhanging trees during most of the ascent provided welcome relief from the sweltering heat. While never steep, the path rose steadily for much of the remaining ride to the northern end in Bigelow.

Temporarily leaving the Carrabassett River behind and persevering uphill for a short mile past a Maine Huts Trail junction on the right, the path rejoined the mountain freshet overlooking the steepest part of the river—a precipitous attenuated Class IV/V section of whitewater which my paddling companions and I refer to as Upper Carrabassett. Memories of previous descents were a significant distraction while passing the most difficult rapids called Pinnacle Rock, Don's Hole, Terry's Perch, and Triple Drop.

River views coupled with lush vegetation in this area provided an exceptional scenic contrast. Picnic tables were scattered strategically along the trail, most occupied by cyclists taking a break or enjoying a snack. Several overheated riders negotiated down the abrupt embankment for cool relief in the still chilly river water. Not this senior cold water sissy, bathtub warm is my standard.

At mile 1.75, a picnic table was positioned on the right opposite Triple Drop. With a modest effort, a clear view of the narrow twisting descent which ends with a vertical tumble into a confined frothy basin can be observed. If it looks challenging, that's because it is.

Shortly after the sixth picnic table, the path veered away from the river and crossed a long bridge over a wetlands area where moose can sometimes be seen feeding. About a half mile beyond, an ancient cabin was passed on the left where the trail briefly connects back with the river. A hunting and fishing camp built by railroad workers in 1900; the hut is privately owned and still in use. Located in an area formerly called Crockertown, the erstwhile logging community was named for early lumberman Isaac Crocker.

Proceeding to mile 4.2, a left turn leads to Campbell Field Trailhead. Our trio persisted northwesterly to a junction on the

Chapter 14 - Narrow Gauge Pathway in Carrabassett Valley

right for Stratton Brook Hut. A sign indicates the hut is 2.2 miles east. The outskirts of the old village of Bigelow was reached at 5.3 miles. Posted as private property, the former Bigelow Train Depot is situated at the far end near Route 27 and is now a private residence.

Angling left, we continued over a bridge and past a side trail to the Stratton Brook Trailhead on the right. Just beyond, the Narrow Gauge Pathway culminated at Route 27 where there is no parking. The .1-mile spur to Stratton Brook Trailhead was more difficult than the pathway. Possessing the qualities of a mountain bike trail, the approach to the parking area was steep and rocky.

Returning to the intersection leading to Campbell Field, a brief ride brought us to the trailhead where there is a picnic table, restroom, and ample parking. After a lunch break, we cycled back to the Airport Trailhead completing an exceptional 11.25-mile roundtrip that included the short excursions to Stratton Brook and Campbell Field Trailheads. The return junket was almost all downhill—what a treat for three senior riders in cycling paradise!

THINGS TO KNOW

Location: Franklin County, western Maine

Length: Approximately 11.25 miles for the described ride, the outing includes side trips to Stratton Brook and Campbell Field Trailheads

Surface: Crushed Stone and dirt

Recommended bike type: Hybrid or trail

Views: Excellent, particularly along the river

Difficulty: Moderate with steady uphill travel south to northwest

Unique potential hazards: Other riders, walkers, and runners will be encountered. Caution should be exercised traveling downhill as there are occasional potholes.

Directions:

Airport Trailhead (southern): From the junction of Routes 16, 27, and 142 in Kingfield, drive north on Routes 27/16 for about 10 miles to the Carrabassett Valley Airport on the right. Follow the sign for Narrow Gauge Pathway to the parking area.

Campbell Field Trailhead: From the Airport Trailhead turnoff, drive 4 miles north on Routes 27/16 to a right turn. The actual trailhead is an additional .1 mile.

Stratton Brook Trailhead: From the Campbell Field Trailhead turnoff, continue north on Routes 27/16 for 1.3 miles to a right turn.

Alternative Rides: A ride can be extended by joining the Maine Huts Trail system at the junctions indicated in the narrative. Several side trails provide more challenging mountain bike options.

A cyclist rides along the Carrabassett River on the Narrow Gauge Pathway. (Photo – Ron Chase)

SECTION III. ISLAND BIKE RIDES

A cyclist rides a scenic road on Islesboro. (Photo – Ron Chase)

Chapter 15 - Islesboro

Biking Islesboro on the Ritz

For several years early in my career with the Internal Revenue Service (IRS), I covered the islands along the coast of Maine. Thoroughly enjoying my many trips to the beautiful, rugged atolls, I particularly appreciated meeting the unique independent inhabitants. The fine people residing on them weren't always as fond of me and our communications were sometimes unpleasant. In fact, occasionally they were downright hostile.

Much has changed since I left the IRS behind. Nowadays, my visits to the islands are for pleasure not business—no more combative interactions and disagreeable enforcement encounters. Instead, I serenely navigate my kayak along the shores or peacefully bike their scenic roads.

Islesboro is an exceptional bicycle outing. The 14-mile-long island offers sweeping vistas, numerous picturesque coves and harbors, and lightly traveled primarily paved roads. Located three miles from Lincolnville Beach in Waldo County, it's just a twenty-minute ferry ride from the mainland with several crossings each day.

I'd been waiting for a Goldilocks day to post a Penobscot Paddle & Chowder Society club bike trip to the engaging oasis in central Penobscot Bay. Discerning what appeared to be the perfect opportunity, my longtime friend Brent Elwell was the only respondent. Both retired, we had the advantage of choosing a warm sunny weekday for our junket.

Arriving at the Lincolnville Ferry Terminal, we were surprised to find the roundtrip ticket price for an adult with a bike is actually higher than one for a vehicle and driver. Since a Mini Cooper takes up more space than about a dozen bicycles, this appears to be faulty logic in the extreme. My jaded suspicion is the ferry service

Chapter 15 - Islesboro

is compensating for cost overruns on the backs of cyclists. Anticipating a beautiful bike ride, we sucked up the monetary pain and paid the exorbitant charge.

The overpriced ferry excursion was idyllic with spectacular views of the Camden Hills and nearby islands. Arriving at Grindle Point, we followed Ferry Road past Broad Cove to a junction where the post office and several town buildings are located. Progressing north on Main Road by the architecturally unique granite and brick Alice Pendleton Memorial Library brought us to The Narrows, a panoramic restricted isthmus that connects the northern and southern sectors of the island. As we continued north through the tiny village of Pripet, we rounded the upper end of the island near Turtle Head Cove and our trek south on hilly Meadow Road ensued.

Re-entering The Narrows and angling right past the Historical Society onto West Bay Road, we proceeded along a substantial beach and returned to the Ferry Terminal. After enjoying lunch on the shore next to the Sailor's Memorial Museum adjacent the ferry landing, we recommenced traveling south through the quaint hamlet of Dark Harbor where there is a shopping area with opportunities to purchase food, ice cream, and snacks.

Persisting south past numerous Gilded Age mansions and the modern palatial homes of the rich and famous, the highway ended at Pendleton Point a scenic picnic and recreational area. A few years ago, the promontory was one of our stops on a long-distance sea kayak trip. Taking a hiatus from biking, Brent and I hiked the rocky shoreline reminiscing about sea kayak escapades past.

Islesboro is an exceptional sea kayak destination. Nearby Warren Island State Park opposite the ferry terminal offers outstanding campsites for paddlers some with phenomenal views of the mountainous mainland. The approximate boundary between East and West Penobscot Bay, Islesboro is a waypoint for trips to North Haven, Vinalhaven, Cape Rosier, and Deer Isle Archipelago. A lengthy circumnavigation of Islesboro can also be completed in a day trip from Warren Island.

Dazzled by three attractive young ladies on our jaunt back to the ferry terminal, we stopped for refreshment at their lemonade stand in Dark Harbor. The price of relief was a dollar a glass and no senior discount! My admittedly faltering recollection is the cost of a glass of lemonade was five cents when I was a kid. That's what Charlie Brown advertised. Since over sixty years have transpired since those halcyon days, maybe the current rate accurately accounts for inflation. At the price they're charging perhaps the young entrepreneurs will be able to forgo student loans when they're ready for college.

Completing a 37-mile outing, our day ended with another remarkable but expensive ferry ride back to Lincolnville Beach. We traveled home light on cash but flush with warm memories of a most excellent day of cycling without any contentious tax deliberations.

THINGS TO KNOW

Location: Waldo County, offshore mid-coast Maine

Length: 37 miles for the described trip. See below for shorter alternative trips.

Surface: Mostly paved for the described trip. The road is dirt for a short distance before reaching Pendleton Point.

Recommended bike type: Road, hybrid, or trail. I prefer a hybrid bike for island trips as they provide greater flexibility for exploration.

Views: Exceptional at several locations including the following: The Narrows, Seal Harbor, Grindle Point, and Pendleton Point

Difficulty: Easy to moderate; some steep climbs and descents

Unique potential hazards: Narrow roads with two-way traffic

Directions to Islesboro Ferry Terminal: From the junction of US Route 1 and Maine Route 173 in Lincolnville, travel a very short distance north on Route 1. Take an immediate right turn just before Lincolnville Beach.

Chapter 15 - Islesboro

Information on the Islesboro Ferry schedule and exorbitant bicycle rates: Visit their website at: https://www.maine.gov/mdot/ferry/islesboro/

Shorter alternative rides:
Northern Half of Islesboro: From the Ferry Terminal ride north to The Narrows, complete the loop and return – approximately 20 miles.
Southern half of Islesboro: From the Ferry Terminal, ride east to the Village of Islesboro and then south through Dark Harbor to Pendleton Point and back – approximately 16 miles.

A cyclist rides along the beach on Islesboro. (Photo – Ron Chase)

Chapter 16 - North Haven

Cycling Picturesque North Haven

My introduction to the Maine coastal islands came when I was a young revenue officer with the Internal Revenue Service (IRS) in 1973. Revenue officer responsibilities did not make me particularly popular with independent island fishermen. The mission was to collect seriously delinquent taxes, often using harsh enforcement measures, and conducting preliminary investigations on those perceived to have committed various other tax sins. In short, I was not loved.

Conversely, I embraced the islands and their resilient uncompromising inhabitants. Their rough and tumble hard-working lifestyle, harsh weather, and relative isolation were very appealing. Most of all, I savored the rugged majestic islands.

On an early visit to Beals Island in Washington County, the local radio station announced a warning over the airwaves that the IRS was crossing the Beals Island Bridge from Jonesport. When I traveled to North Haven and Vinalhaven Islands on the ferry from Rockland, my reluctant customers had an abundance of prior warning as advance ferry reservations were a necessity. Not surprisingly, most weren't home on my first few visits. Since many of the Maine State Ferry Service employees lived on the islands or had relatives there, I suspected a connection. Without disclosing some of the draconian realities of IRS procedures, I found ways to get their attention. Some actually became friends, especially after they learned I was a native Mainer not from away.

Working out of the IRS office in Rockland, it was common for me to have a large inventory of cases on North Haven and Vinalhaven. Driving a ridiculously conspicuous government Jeep, I usually stayed at the Tidewater Motel on Vinalhaven for two or three nights. If warranted, I took the short ferry trip across Fox

Chapter 16 - North Haven

Islands Thoroughfare to North Haven. A runner, I usually jogged the roads at the end of the day. On a couple of occasions, disenchanted fishermen gently nudged me off the road as a reminder I was an unwelcome visitor on their turf. Given the adversarial nature of my presence, I considered that acceptable island etiquette. At some point, I met cyclists transporting bikes on the ferry. My reaction was simple, "What a concept!" Exceptionally scenic rides on lightly traveled roads and I might go unrecognized wearing a helmet. I resolved to return for cycling adventures in a later life.

A few years ago, I completed solo bike trips on Islesboro, North Haven, and Chebeague Islands. This summer, I decided to schedule some Penobscot Paddle and Chowder Society weekday island trips for ancient retired Chowderheads like me. North Haven was first on the list. My wife, Nancy, and two retired friends, Bill and Sally Blauvelt, enthusiastically joined me on a gorgeous hot and sunny summer day.

Leaving from the ferry landing in Rockland, the one-hour voyage to North Haven was worth the price of admission. Quickly passing mile-long Rockland Breakwater on our left, the impressive Camden Hills loomed behind. Distinctive Owls Head lighthouse was immediately to our right. After crossing West Penobscot Bay, we ended the journey enveloped by the ragged shores of North Haven and Vinalhaven in Fox Islands Thoroughfare. The entire traverse was a succession of breathtaking views.

Our bike ride was equally exceptional. After disembarking from the ferry in the bustling village, we rode north past the airport and turned left onto Crabtree Point Road where several panoramic ocean vistas were encountered on the hilly peninsula. Returning to North Haven Shore Road, the gang stopped for lunch at a shaded picnic table next to a small market where the remainder of our itinerary was contemplated.

Deciding on a loop trip on the outer island roads, we persisted northwest on North Shore Road soon crossing a bridge over picturesque Pulpit Harbor and stopping for obligatory photos. Rounding the eastern end of the island, our sunbaked group arrived at the entrance to Mullen Head Park. Following rough dirt roads to an idyllic site overlooking Mullen Cove and outer Penobscot Bay, we lingered for a much-appreciated respite.

Departing south from the park, our intrepid band passed tranquil Cubby Harbor on the South Shore Road and returned to the village. With time to spare before the last ferry departed, we explored the busy harbor community. Connoisseurs of fine beers, Bill and Sally found an excellent microbrewery.

Our trek was a little over twenty miles in distance. Hybrid or trail bikes are recommended for the excursion as the roads in Mullen Head Park are rocky and the captivating location is a "must see." The return trip on the ferry was thoroughly stimulating with constant views of the majestic Camden Hills overlooking the bay.

As far as could be ascertained, I went unrecognized during the bike ride. It probably had something to do with the absence of a full head of black hair and decades of accumulated wrinkles. Think I'll try Vinalhaven next.

THINGS TO KNOW

Location: Knox County, offshore mid-coast Maine
Length: 20 miles for the described trip
Surface: Mostly paved but side trips are dirt and gravel, with about a mile of rough gravel road in Mullen Head Park.
Recommended bike type: Hybrid or trail. I prefer a hybrid bike for island trips as they provide greater flexibility for exploring. Road bikes are not recommended.
Views: Exceptional at several locations including Crabtree Point, Pulpit Harbor, Mullen Head Park, and South Shore Road
Difficulty: Easy to moderate; some steep climbs and descents
Unique potential hazards: Narrow roads with two-way traffic
Directions to North Haven Ferry Terminal: From the junction of US Route 1 and Maine Route 73 in Rockland, drive north on Main Street (Route 1) for a short distance. Turn right just after passing Talbot Avenue on the left where you'll find the

Chapter 16 - North Haven

ferry terminal and a large parking area. A fee is charged for parking.

Information on the North Haven Ferry Schedule and exorbitant bicycle fees: Visit their website at:
https://www.maine.gov/mdot/ferry/northhaven/

Cyclists ride Crabtree Point on North Haven. (Photo – Ron Chase)

Chapter 17 - Isle au Haut

Isle au Haut by Bike

Biking through the village on a breezy summer day, one had the sense of stepping back in time. For those of us who grew up in Maine in the fifties and sixties, it's a place reminiscent of our youth. Narrow roads with old homes cluttered close together and vintage cars from that era parked in many driveways, tiny churches, a general store, and a one room Post Office—all accentuated the similarities with that bygone period. Yet, the quaint hamlet is only a few miles off the Maine coast on beautiful and scenic Isle au Haut.

Located on the outer perimeter of Penobscot Bay, Isle au Haut is a seven-mile ferry ride from the Town of Stonington on Deer Isle. My wife Nancy and I found the cruise exceptional as we traveled through the rugged picturesque islands of the Deer Isle Archipelago before crossing an exposed channel in the outer bay. Passing the remote Merchant's Row Islands, the vessel motored in a southerly direction entering Isle au Haut Thorofare, a narrow passage between Kimball Island and Isle au Haut. The northern end of the village came into view as the ferry gained entrance into the thoroughfare. We disembarked with our bicycles at the town landing. The voyage took about forty-five minutes. Exclusively a passenger ferry, no motor vehicles are allowed. A second stop is made at Duck Harbor Campground a few miles south, but bicycles must be left at the town landing.

Isle au Haut was named by the French explorer Samuel de Champlain when he sailed along its shores in 1604. The literal English translation is "the high island." As the ferry leaves Stonington on a clear day, the reason for its name is obvious: Isle au Haut is unmistakably the highest island in Penobscot Bay. At an

Chapter 17 - Isle au Haut

elevation of 543 feet, Mount Champlain located on the northern sector of the island is the actual high point.

From the town landing, the preferred bike route is a twelve-mile loop around the island. Five miles are paved while some portions of the unpaved sections are rough and a trail bike is recommended. About half of the island is in Acadia National Park and the remainder privately owned. The roads located in the park are all unpaved and some difficult to negotiate. An excellent map of the island obtained from the National Park Service was a very helpful guide.

A small general store is located a short distance north of the town landing. Food, water, and other supplies can be obtained there. A short cycle to the store provides an excellent excuse to peruse the picturesque village that is both a working fishing community and home to a small colony of seasonal residents.

We chose to ride the loop counterclockwise. This allowed for completion of the most difficult and challenging part of the excursion first before finishing with the easier paved section. Riding south, the road traveled through the southern end of the village past the Ranger Station to the park entrance. Soon after, Duck Harbor Trail intersected. Biking is prohibited on all park hiking trails. An estimated four miles of rocky, uneven riding brought us to Western Head Road near Duck Harbor Campground.

Riders should consider a side trip on Western Head Road leading to scenic Cliff Trail on the southwestern extreme of the island. While the short jaunt is a rewarding addition to the outing, cyclists should be prepared for the most demanding maneuvering of the day.

A spring-fed water pump is situated a short distance from Western Head Road junction where cool potable drinking water can be acquired. A nearby hiking trail connects to the campground and Duck Harbor Boat Landing. An information kiosk and a public toilet are located at the intersection. Farther down the road, another hiking trail leads to the summit of Duck Harbor Mountain where phenomenal views of much of Penobscot Bay can be enjoyed. For us, completion of the Western Head Road spur was followed by an exhilarating hike to the summit of spectacular Duck Harbor Mountain.

Returning to the loop road, we climbed steeply in an easterly direction. While still unpaved, the road began to widen and surface conditions gradually improved. After about two miles the park boundary was crossed, and an abbreviated hilly paved section began. Shortly after, the road turned north paralleling the eastern shore of the island on the right and Long Pond on the left. Another unpaved stretch of road was encountered adjacent Long Pond. This sector was in good condition.

Two miles of gravel road riding ensued. Pavement followed and continued for the remainder of the tour. Approaching the northeastern terminus of the island, sporadic views of the majestic coastline were welcome compensation for our efforts. Turning abruptly west, the road headed towards the village. According to the Delorme Maine Atlas, a trail in this area leads to the summit of Mount Champlain. Unable to locate the trailhead during our ride, the journey concluded with a gradual descent into a captivating version of the mid-twentieth century.

Isle au Haut is an exceptional destination for cyclists, hikers, and sea kayakers. Not a tourist community, very little is available for overnight accommodations and eateries. No camping options were found on the privately owned portion of the island.

Completing the ride with time to enjoy a leisurely respite in pleasurable surroundings while awaiting the ferry, Nancy and I finished the excursion with another remarkable voyage through one of the most exceptional clusters of islands on the coast of Maine.

THINGS TO KNOW

Location: Knox County, offshore mid-coast Maine
Length: Approximately 15.4 miles for the described trip
Surface: Paved, gravel, rough dirt, and rock
Recommended bike type: Trail
Views: Exceptional in several locations

Chapter 17 - Isle au Haut

Difficulty: Easy to difficult. Western Head Road is particularly challenging.

Unique potential hazards: Narrow roads with two-way traffic. Cyclists should be prepared for demanding sometimes wet road and trail conditions. Helmets, foul weather clothes, and eye protection are a must. Day trippers should take a change of clothes and footwear, and plenty of food and fluids. Don't rely exclusively on the general store as it has odd hours.

Directions to the Stonington Isle au Haut Ferry Terminal: From the junction of US Route 1 and Maine Route 15 in Orland, travel south on 15 for about 22 miles to a right turn on Thurlow Hill Road in Stonington. Turn onto Thurlow Hill Road for .1 mile and then left onto Sea Breeze Avenue. Stonington Isle au Haut Ferry Terminal is at the end.

Information on Isle au Haut ferry service: Visit their website at: https://www.isleauhautferryservice.com/

Camping on Isle au Haut: Although it's a logistical challenge camping is an option for cyclists at Duck Harbor Campground in Acadia National Park. On one trip, a group brought their camping gear on a small bicycle trailer and hauled it for about 4 miles from the town landing to the campground. It is also possible to leave bicycles at the town landing, take camping gear by ferry to Duck Harbor, and hike back for the bicycles. Regardless, staying at the campground affords one the opportunity to be in the midst of a multitude of outstanding hiking trails and is well situated for some excellent island cycling or sea kayaking. To obtain information on camping at Duck Harbor, visit their website at: https://www.nps.gov/acad/planyourvisit/duckharbor.htm

To obtain a map of Isle au Haut: Go to this link and download:

http://npmaps.com/wp-content/uploads/acadia-isle-au-haut-trail-map.pdf

A cyclist rides Isle au Haut's Western Head Road. (Photo – Ron Chase)

SECTION IV. SEA KAYAKING

The mountains of Acadia National Park provide the background as a kayaker approaches Baker Island. (Photo – Nancy Chase)

Chapter 18 - Damariscove Island

Kayaking to Historic Damariscove Island

More than four centuries ago, Damariscove Island was a busy place. Before Jamestown and Plymouth Colonies were founded, the island was occupied as a commercial fishing enterprise in 1604. Abenaki Indians were even earlier intermittent residents, sporadically visiting what they called Aquahega in primitive canoes during the summer months.

Located off the coast of Boothbay, Damariscove has a rich history. Captain John Smith charted the island in 1614 and by 1622 there were more than a dozen year-round fishermen living there. They sent cod to the Pilgrims in Plymouth during the spring of that year to help prevent starvation. By 1671, it was a thriving community operated by Massachusetts Bay Colony.

In the summer of 1676, Native Americans attacked every English settlement east of the Kennebec River during the King Philip's War. Three hundred survivors fled to Damariscove for protection. Indian attacks continued for several decades and British ships raided the island during the Revolutionary War. Damariscove prospered as a farming community into the 20th Century. The site of numerous shipwrecks particularly on offshore ledges called The Motions; a lifesaving station subsequently operated by the U.S. Coast Guard was built in 1897.

The island is now uninhabited with the exception of visitors to the former Coast Guard Station that is privately owned. Boothbay Region Land Trust controls the remainder and preserves it in a "forever wild" status. A few local fishermen use the harbor and the trust retains a couple of moorings and a pier.

Damariscove Island is one of the premiere sea kayak destinations along the Maine coast. My first voyage to the island was with a friend about a dozen years ago. It was a cold windy November

Chapter 18 - Damariscove Island

day and had I known the history of shipwrecks, I would have chosen a peaceful hike on the mainland instead. After completing a three-mile open crossing from Outer Heron Island, we encountered large breaking waves and gusty winds when turning the southeastern tip of Damariscove. After finding temporary shelter in the harbor, our exit on the western end was another "white knuckle" escapade navigating between exposed ledges in turbulent seas.

One advantage of old age is the accumulation of instructive life experiences. An argument can be made for calling that wisdom; however, most of my friends would strenuously object to applying that characterization to me. Although occasionally faltering, my initial Damariscove misadventure taught me to scrupulously avoid sea kayaking in hazardous waters. Before scheduling a trip, I obtain the most reliable weather forecast possible—winds normally the most important factor. Mystifyingly, several excursions to Damariscove have established that an excellent forecast does not necessarily mean a gentle reception at the island terminus. Tides, ledges, and several thousand miles of ocean fetch seem to create a perfect storm of unstable conditions on the best of days. Despite the uncertainty, the beauty, history, and adventure of Damariscove lure me back almost every summer.

Watching the weather for a Goldilocks opportunity, I recently identified what appeared to be the perfect Damariscove day: hot, sunny, two- to three-foot seas, and southwest winds between five and ten knots. As soon as I posted a weekday trip with the Penobscot Paddle and Chowder Society, four fellow retirees and a summer vacationer enthusiastically signed on.

We met early in the morning at Ocean Point Boat Landing on the southern end of Linekin Neck. While the weather was fine, southwest winds were clearly stronger than predicted. Considering them manageable, the six of us departed in solo kayaks.

After crossing Fisherman Island Passage, we proceeded along the west side of distinctive Ram Island Lighthouse and barren elongated Fisherman Island. Traversing open water south to the northern extreme of Damariscove, the headwinds increased to about twelve knots, a relief from the humid weather.

Our pivot around the southwestern ear of the island was as anticipated, negotiating menacing ledges in moderately bumpy seas. The Motions were characteristically active. I couldn't help but speculate how many unfortunate vessels had met a catastrophic fate on the same jagged rocks.

A couple of recreational boats cluttered the tiny harbor on our arrival. Probably the thickest seaweed I've ever encountered slowed our landing. Protected from the wind, the heat was oppressive.

The trust maintains a network of trails on the island. As we hiked to cliffs on the east side for lunch, a dubious shark sighting monopolized the conversation. A trek to a tower overlooking the harbor provided an ideal opportunity to discuss a harbor exit strategy. Large swells tend to prevail when attempting to escape southeast. We tentatively decided on that approach and retained the option to retreat west if greeted by treacherous waves.

Moderate swells permitted an uneventful departure when leaving the unique historic island behind. Running north on the east side of Damariscove and Fisherman Islands with a robust tailwind, an expeditious return to the 21st Century was accomplished.

THINGS TO KNOW

Location: Lincoln County, offshore mid-coast Maine

Length: Approximately 10 miles for the described trip. See below for a longer alternative trip.

Difficulty rating: Moderate to difficult

Unique potential hazards: Large waves and rough seas are often encountered entering and exiting Damariscove Harbor on the southern end of the island. Ledges called The Motions are located on the southwest terminus of the island and should be very carefully navigated. There is no best route traveling to and from Damariscove Harbor from Ocean Point, rather wind direction,

Chapter 18 - Damariscove Island

tides, and seas dictate the choice. Water temperatures are cold along the Maine coast year round. Only short exposure in the water can result in hypothermia or drowning. There are many other hazards including larger boats and being swept into rocky shorelines and ledges. It is strongly recommended that paddlers obtain proper instruction from a qualified instructor prior to attempting this trip. That instruction should include suitable dress, self-rescue, assisted rescue, kayak roll, navigation, and what is required for safety equipment and gear. It is further recommended that each paddler carry a GPS, marine chart, and compass, and know how to use them. Never paddle alone, rather a strong team of experienced sea kayakers is always recommended including one participant familiar with the Damariscove trip. Always obtain a reliable weather forecast prior to the trip and if strong winds, particularly offshore winds, bad weather, or rough seas are predicted, don't go.

Directions to Ocean Point: From the junction of Maine Routes 27 and 96 in Boothbay Harbor, follow Route 96 south for about 6 miles to a boat landing and beach at the end. There is some parking available next to the beach and a small parking lot a short distance back on Route 96. As of this writing, no toilet was available at the boat landing or parking lot.

A longer alternative trip: If favorable conditions are present, the trip can be extended by two or three miles traveling to Pumpkin Ledges, Outer Heron Island, and the White Islands. This results in significant exposure to open seas, particularly if the Pumpkin Ledges are included in the itinerary, and should only be attempted when the circumstances are ideal. I generally prefer postponing a decision on the longer trip until after reaching Damariscove Harbor and obtaining first-hand knowledge of the conditions. The traverse between Outer Heron Island and Damariscove Harbor can be hazardous on relatively calm days. This trip should be considered difficult.

Hiking on Damariscove Island: Take hiking shoes or boots, a small pack, and lunch when kayaking to Damariscove. There is a network of scenic trails on the island maintained by the

Boothbay Region Land Trust. Beware of plentiful poison ivy. Visit their website for maps and additional information:
 https://bbrlt.org/trails/

Kayakers paddle along Damariscove Island. (Photo – Ron Chase)

Chapter 19 - Eastern Egg Rock

Eastern Egg Rocks

A seemingly nondescript barren atoll located in outer Muscongus Bay, Eastern Egg Rock does not outwardly appear to be a compelling sea kayak destination. Appearances can be deceiving. For a few weeks each year, migratory Atlantic Puffins breed and nest on the island's gigantic granite boulders.

The colorful seabirds haven't always stopped there. A variety of circumstances drove them from that natural roosting habitat in the late 19th century. A historic restoration effort has resulted in scores of puffins returning each year.

Eastern Egg Rock has a dual attraction for me. Navigating by sea kayak to the remote island is an ambitious undertaking but the reward is a thoroughly entertaining visit with what I consider to be the most extraordinary seabirds to be found on the Maine coast.

Getting there is a challenge. It is situated six miles east of New Harbor, with the exception of tiny Western Egg Rock at about the midpoint, and the journey is completely exposed to the vicissitudes of the open sea. Following an unappealing return crossing to New Harbor in unexpectedly windblown choppy seas several years ago, I concluded that route was too hazardous for a timid senior citizen. Fortunately, departing from the scenic coastal community of Round Pond offers an arguably more benign itinerary.

Benign being a relative term, attentive planning is essential for a safe enjoyable trip. A prerequisite: the puffins must be there. Fortuitously, an inside source recently confirmed their presence. Factors to be considered are winds, seas, tides, and weather. Did I mention winds? Offshore winds are great going out but the destination is Eastern Egg Rock not Spain. Returning into robust headwinds could seem like a journey from the Iberian Peninsula, if you make it back. While onshore winds are preferable when returning, anything over 25 knots gets downright scary for gray panthers posing as kayakers.

Identifying what appeared to be a Goldilocks day, I announced a Penobscot Paddle and Chowder Society trip. Predictably, club interest was significant. A few days later, ten paddlers met early in the morning at the Round Pond Boat Landing on a calm sunny day. Our group consisted of eight solo kayaks, and I paddled a tandem kayak with longtime outdoor friend Suzanne Cole.

Departing with a gentle offshore wind and an outgoing tide, our flotilla traversed through Muscongus Sound into the bay. As we passed between Ross and Haddock Islands, the low profile of Western Egg was visible southeast with a hazy glimpse of distant Eastern Egg beyond. Since landing on Eastern Egg is prohibited, pausing at Western Egg is essential, especially for those of us with elderly needs.

Western Egg was also a critical turnaround point. If offshore winds increased or seas worsened, the trip would be aborted and a visit with the puffins postponed until next year. However, that day the paddling gods smiled on us as on arrival we experienced calm seas and almost nonexistent winds. After a brief respite, we persisted towards Eastern Egg, about three miles east.

Approaching the distinctive boulder pile, my paddling companion observed, "I think those two birds are puffins!" Within minutes, dozens of the delightful seabirds were in our midst. While many floated in the water within yards of our boats, others fluttered rapidly to and from the island in their unmistakable style. While seemingly awkward, they reach flying speeds of 55 miles per hour. A magical time, we lingered for perhaps a half hour bobbing in placid swells just offshore.

Since conditions were exceptional, we decided to paddle around the island. Favorable seas allowed for close exploration of the rugged shoreline. While our puffin playmates were less abundant on the south and east sides, numerous species including terns, guillemots, eiders, and gulls were sighted. The bad boys of

Chapter 19 - Eastern Egg Rock

the seabird world, gulls are a significant threat to the puffin population and "predator management" is necessary for puffin survival on the Egg.

After completing the circumnavigation, our return direction was not obvious as Western Egg blended with islands closer to shore and the mainland. Since several of us had plotted compass bearings in preparation for the trip, that predicament was easily remedied by following a predetermined course.

After a brief interlude on Western Egg, a tailwind and a favorable tide facilitated an expeditious return to Round Pond. A member of the group measured the trip to be 15.8 miles on his GPS. It's difficult to imagine more favorable circumstances for the journey. If I'm still taking air and the puffins come back, we'll try again next year.

THINGS TO KNOW

Location: Lincoln and Knox Counties, offshore mid-coast Maine

Distance: Approximately 16 miles for the described trip. Alternative trips are discussed below.

Difficulty rating: Difficult

Unique potential hazards: Large waves and rough seas are a potential threat once in Muscongus Bay. Landing and departing Western Egg Rock can be treacherous and difficult. The trip from Muscongus Sound to Eastern Egg and back is almost completely exposed and wind direction, tides, and seas determine the conditions. Only short exposure in the water can result in hypothermia or drowning. There are many other hazards including larger boats and being swept into rocky shorelines and ledges. It is strongly recommended that paddlers obtain proper instruction from a qualified instructor prior to attempting the trip. That instruction should include suitable dress, self-rescue, assisted rescue, kayak roll, navigation, and what is required for safety equipment and gear. It is further recommended that each paddler carry a GPS, marine chart, and compass, and know how to use them. Never paddle alone, rather a strong team of experienced sea kayakers is always recommended including one participant familiar with the Eastern Egg Rock trip. Always obtain a reliable weather forecast prior to the trip and if strong winds, particularly offshore winds, bad weather, or rough seas are predicted, don't go.

Directions to Round Pond Boat Landing: From US Route 1 and Maine Route 130 in Damariscotta, drive about 6 miles south on Route 130 to the Upper Round Pond Road on the left in Bristol. Follow Upper Pond Road east for about 2.5 miles to Maine Route 32. Turn left onto Route 32 and continue for about .5 mile to Back Shore Road on the right. Take the Back Shore Road for a short distance, turn right onto Town Landing Road, and go to the boat landing at the end. Get there early as there is limited parking and the trip is a long one. There is a small fee to launch.

Alternative trips:

New Harbor Boat Landing to Eastern Egg: About 12 miles roundtrip, this route is continuously exposed. An afternoon sea breeze can make this rough and hazardous.

Friendship Boat Landing to Eastern Egg: This trip is longer than beginning at Round Pond with no appreciable benefit.

A kayaker enjoys a closeup view of puffins near Eastern Egg Rock. (Photo – Ron Chase)

Chapter 20 - Isle au Haut

Circumnavigating Isle au Haut

We rode the tide south along the eastern shore of the island with nothing between us and the vast expanse of the Atlantic Ocean except a couple of small islands called Little Spoon and Great Spoon. "Spain would be the next stop," Steve observed. As we paddled through the narrows between rockbound Eastern Ear and the extreme southeastern tip of the island, Eastern Head, impressive granite formations became more prominent. After rounding the head and turning west, we saw spectacular, rugged cliffs extending for a couple of miles. These cliffs formed the island's southern boundary.

Steve Ward and I were circumnavigating Isle au Haut in sea kayaks. This view was the highpoint of an exceptional day of paddling. We were traversing Head Harbor and the adjoining bay approximately a mile from shore when a fog bank approached from the west. Almost instantaneously, Western Ear was cloaked in a soupy haze. Using our deck compasses, we quickly took a bearing for the closest point of land and followed with a vigorous paddle towards our new destination. A good decision as thick fog quickly enveloped us and resulted in virtually zero visibility. Carefully following a northerly course, we persevered until reaching the marginal safety of the rocky coastline.

We recognized the sound of lobster boats hauling traps in the area and hugging the shore became necessary to avoid collisions. Staying close together a few feet from the cliffs in gentle swells, we paddled westerly to Western Head then southwesterly to Western Ear. Our maritime charts indicated a navigable channel was located between the ear and head. Attempts to find it in the murky conditions were futile. Warily rounding the ear and heading north, we unexpectedly emerged from the fog. The elongated distinct islands of Vinalhaven and North Haven appeared to our west and the entire western shore of Isle au Haut gloriously opened in front of us.

This was the second day of a three-day sea kayak trip touring Deer Isle Archipelago and the outer reaches of Penobscot Bay. Our journey had begun the previous morning at Old Quarry Campground, located on Buckmaster Neck a couple of miles northeast of the Town of Stonington on Deer Isle.

The Deer Isle archipelago is arguably the premiere sea kayaking experience along the coast of Maine. Dozens of islands of varying sizes provide shelter from the open water and offer paddlers outstanding opportunities for camping and exploration. They also facilitate access to the distant and scenic island of Isle au Haut while minimizing significant exposed crossings.

Numerous potential navigation hazards exist in this area so kayakers should be well-prepared. The clustered islands can cause confusion and fog is a frequent impediment. Paddlers should have strong orienteering skills and be adequately equipped. We each carried deck compasses and nautical maps of the area. Steve also packed a weather radio and GPS. All were needed.

On day one, we launched at the Old Quarry Campground, traveled south out of Webb Cove, and then southwesterly between Russ and Camp islands. Persisting against a modest headwind while negotiating through the complex archipelago, we reached the southern end of Wreck Island. As we left Wreck Island behind, the longest exposed crossing of the day was experienced. Completing the mile-and-a-half traverse, Merchant Island, the northern-most and largest of a collection of islands northwest of Isle au Haut, was passed on the east.

The Maine Island Trail Association (MITA) maintains campsites on several islands in the area. Since the goal was to reconnoiter Isle au Haut, our choice was a site on Wheat Island, a tiny islet just north of Burnt Island and Isle au Haut.

Embarking on the eighteen-mile circumnavigation of Isle au Haut early the next morning with sunny weather, light winds, and a favorable tide, initially we navigated south along the east shore.

Chapter 20 - Isle au Haut

The northern half of the island has a modest amount of development while the southern portion is predominantly Acadia National Park and ruggedly pristine. Angling west at the southeastern terminus, our foggy misadventure commenced.

Diverging from the fog on the southwest periphery of the island and kayaking north for a couple miles brought us to Duck Harbor, the primary access point for Acadia National Park. A regular ferry service operates from Stonington to both the Village of Isle au Haut and Duck Harbor. The park maintains five primitive lean-to shelters at Duck Harbor that can be reserved between May 15th and October 15th. Another park benefit is an extensive network of hiking trails. Our choice was a relatively short hike to the summit of Duck Harbor Mountain. Offering remarkable views of Penobscot Bay and the mountainous mid-coast shoreline, it was an idyllic location for a long, relaxing lunch.

As we exited Duck Harbor, an advantageous tide helped propel us north along the west shore of the island. Passing Trial Point and unique Isle au Haut Lighthouse on Robinson Point, we entered Isle au Haut Thorofare. The attenuated channel between Kimball Island and the Village of Isle au Haut narrowed to a few hundred feet in what was a bustling harbor on arrival. The town is both a working fishing community and home to a relatively small population of seasonal residents. Given an abundance of old homes and the relaxed pace, walking village roads was like stepping back in time. A small general store next to the shore with a convenient boat landing offered an excellent opportunity to resupply. The village is also a popular destination for cyclists who take the ferry and spend the day riding the lightly traveled island roads.

Departing the village, we kayaked north to explore Burnt Island. An almost completely hidden MITA campsite is located on the east shore. From there, a brief paddle returned us to Wheat Island. Approaching our campsite, the seemingly ubiquitous fog again advanced from the west. Within minutes, the whole archipelago was engulfed. Fortuitously, our travels were finished for the day.

We arose to cloudy weather and windy conditions on our final day, and the weather radio indicated a storm was approaching from the southwest. We packed quickly and selected the most direct route to Deer Isle which traversed the outer bay along the southern extreme of the archipelago into Stonington Harbor just east of Crotch Island. From there, a tailwind facilitated a swift two-mile paddle east to Old Quarry Campground ending our expedition just ahead of the storm.

THINGS TO KNOW

Location: Hancock and Knox Counties, offshore mid-coast Maine

Distance: Approximately 41 miles for the described trip

Difficulty rating: Difficult

Unique potential hazards: Large waves and rough seas are a potential threat, particularly on the east side and south end of Isle au Haut. Fog is common throughout the area. Even short exposure in the water can result in hypothermia or drowning. There are many other hazards including larger boats and being swept into rocky shorelines and ledges. It is strongly recommended that paddlers obtain proper instruction from a qualified instructor prior to attempting the trip. The instruction should include suitable dress, self-rescue, assisted rescue, kayak roll, navigation, and what is required for safety equipment and gear. It is further recommended that each paddler carry a GPS, marine chart, and compass, and know how to use them. Never paddle alone, rather a strong contingent of experienced sea kayakers is always recommended including one participant familiar with the Deer Isle and Isle au Haut region. Always obtain a reliable weather forecast prior to the trip and if strong winds, particularly offshore winds, bad weather, or rough seas are predicted, don't go.

Directions to Old Quarry Campground: From the junction of US Route 1 and Maine Route 15 in Orland, travel south on 15 for about 20 miles to Buckmaster Neck Road on the left which is

Chapter 20 - Isle au Haut

about 4 miles south of the Village of Deer Isle. Follow Quarry Campground signs for about 2 miles to the campground, where you can park and launch for a fee. As of this writing, the future of Old Quarry Campground is in doubt.

Alternative trips: There is a multitude of excellent sea kayak trip options in the area. One is to stay at Old Quarry Campground and paddle day trips. Visit their website at: www.oldquarry.com. Exploring the archipelago from one or more of the MITA campsites is another possibility. Visit their website at: www.mita.org. For information on the Duck Harbor campsites, visit the Acadia National Park website: https://www.nps.gov/acad/planyourvisit/duckharbor.htm

Kayakers approach Western Ear on Isle au Haut. (Photo – Ron Chase)

Chapter 21 - Mussell Ridge

Muscle or Mussel Ridge Islands?

The Delorme Maine Atlas calls them the Mussel Ridge Islands. Various other sources including my Maptech Chartbook refer to the archipelago as the Muscle Ridge Islands. I've always assumed some misguided mapmaker from away misspelled the name "mussel" as the islands must be named for the bivalve mollusk endemic to the area. It seems I'm not so clever after all as my research indicates the source of the conflicting moniker is an unsolved mystery. The best explanation I found was provided by Charles and Carol Evarts McLane in their book *Penobscot Bay*. They wrote the Old English spelling for "mussel" was "muscelle" which was "muscle" in Middle English. Wouldn't you know, the McLane's are from away.

Regardless of the name, Mussel Ridge archipelago is one of the finest sea kayak destinations on the Maine coast and perhaps its best kept secret. A large cluster of small and medium-sized islands located east of Spruce Head in western Penobscot Bay, they convincingly compete with more popular areas such as Bold Coast, Muscongus Bay, Deer Isle archipelago, and Mount Desert Island.

Longtime paddling friend Dave Duggan introduced me to the Mussel Ridge Islands more than a decade ago. I've returned almost every year since. Recently, I recruited two retired friends to join me on an excursion. One had just completed his career with the National Oceanic and Atmospheric Administration. As I am a sea kayaking weather worrywart, having an expert along was reassuring for this sometimes apprehensive geriatric boater.

We met at Birch Point State Park near South Thomaston on a beautiful sunny day. The small peaceful beach at the park is another well-kept secret. To reach the islands, one must paddle

Chapter 21 - Mussell Ridge

about two miles across Mussel (or is it Muscle) Ridge Channel to the closest atoll, Otter Island. The channel has a Doctor Jekyll and Mr. Hyde personality. Sometimes a gentle friendly traverse can unexpectedly evolve into a gusty crossing with large swells and choppy waves. Calm conditions existed for our departure. History cautioned wariness as an earlier trip resulted in extremely forceful headwinds during a return that one participant called, "The worst day of my life." I didn't hand out any suggestion cards following that outing.

Once past Otter, the paddling choices are many as an array of islands await scrutiny. Seal sightings are a near certainty as this region has perhaps the largest population of the playful creatures along the Maine coast. While the historic High Island granite quarries to the east were a consideration for exploration, our choice was to travel south to Dix Island, halting for a respite on a gravel beach. A nearby hiking trail is open to the public.

Navigating farther south amongst a multitude of seal inundated ledges and diminutive islets, we stopped for lunch on sandy Bar Island colorfully decorated with a large growth of wild rose bushes overlooking the picturesque beach. Contemplating our remaining itinerary resulted in a decision to paddle around substantial Pleasant Island possibly continuing to distant Two Bush Island and its distinctive lighthouse. Rounding outer Pleasant, a high tide revealed landing on Two Bush would be problematic, so the barren isolated atoll was bypassed. The two bushes are gone, perhaps consumed by sheep that undoubtedly populated the island in the past.

Proceeding north to rugged irregular Hewitt Island, I convinced a skeptic in the group that passage through the narrow gut was possible. Ducking under a low hanging footbridge, the attenuated corridor was successfully negotiated. As we continued north along the west side of Dix Island, scores of frolicking seals entertained.

As we approached Otter Island, the correct direction for our return to Birch Point was indistinct. I had taken a compass bearing from the park to Otter when departing from the beach. I was confident reversing our direction would result in a precise return so that was my choice. Exercising vigilance to avoid heavy motorized boat traffic in the channel, we endured southwest winds approximating ten knots proceeding west. At about the halfway point, Bud Gilbert, who is more familiar with the area, deviated slightly northeast while I stubbornly held to my predetermined course. I missed Birch Point by about a half mile. A strong tidal current was probably the culprit as it couldn't have been operator error. That's my excuse and I'm sticking to it.

The moral of the story: people from away may know their Middle English lexicon but the locals are otherwise more knowledgeable about the Mussel Ridge Islands. Or is it Muscle Ridge Islands?

THINGS TO KNOW

Location: Knox County, offshore mid-coast Maine

Length: Approximately 11 miles for the described trip. Alternative trips discussed below.

Difficulty level: Moderate to difficult

Unique potential hazards: Expect strong currents and heavy boat traffic in Mussel Ridge Channel. Large waves and rough seas are a potential threat in the channel and outside the archipelago. Even short exposure in the water can result in hypothermia or drowning. There are many other hazards including larger boats and being swept into rocky shorelines and ledges. It is strongly recommended that paddlers obtain proper instruction from a qualified instructor prior to attempting this trip. That instruction should include suitable dress, self-rescue, assisted rescue, kayak roll, navigation, and what is required for safety equipment and gear. It is further recommended that each paddler carry a GPS, marine chart, and compass, and know how to use them. Never paddle alone, rather a strong team of experienced sea kayakers is always recommended including one participant familiar with the Mussel Ridge trip. Always obtain a reliable weather

Chapter 21 - Mussell Ridge

forecast prior to the trip, and if strong winds, particularly offshore winds, bad weather, or rough seas are predicted, don't go.

Directions to Birch Point State Park: From the junction of US Route 1 and Maine Route 131 in Thomaston, follow Route 131 south for about 1.5 miles to Westbrook Street on the left. Follow Westbrook Street for about 2 miles to Maine Route 73 in South Thomaston. Turn left onto Route 73 followed by an immediate right turn onto Dublin Road and drive about 1.25 miles to Ballyhac Road on the right. Continue on Ballyhac Road to Birch Point State Park Road on the left. Stop at the entrance and pay a fee. There is a sizeable parking lot with toilets. Boats must be carried to the beach.

Alternative trips: Various trips can be devised exploring the many islands in the Mussel Ridge archipelago using Birch Point State Park as a starting point. Trips on the outside of the islands should be limited to days when the seas are relatively calm. Another alternative is to depart from the boat landing on the causeway to Spruce Head Island. This provides access to the southern Mussel Ridge Islands and a shorter trip to Two Bush Island. At low tide, the Spruce Head Boat Landing is very muddy.

Kayakers paddle along Pleasant Island in Mussel Ridge.
(Photo – Ron Chase)

Chapter 22 - Jewell and Eagle Islands

A Sharking Encounter

Three of us were sea kayaking along the rugged western shore of Upper Flag Island in Casco Bay. Paddling close to my left, Bud Gilbert pointed to a large fin moving in the opposite direction about one hundred feet to our west and yelled, "I think that's a shark!" Play the intimidating Jaws soundtrack, please. My thought, he's just trying to frighten an old man.

Our adventure had begun two days earlier. After studying the weather forecast, I identified what appeared to be a good weather day to kayak to distant Eagle and Jewel Islands in outer Casco Bay. Posting a Penobscot Paddle & Chowder Society trip, my retired friend Bud immediately signed on. The next day another frequent paddling companion, Eggman DeCoster, announced he was able to steal away from his hectic egg delivery schedule to make it a threesome.

Meeting at the Dolphin Marina on Basin Point in South Harpswell early on a calm, partly sunny morning, a last-minute change in the wind forecast had me concerned. The possibility of an offshore afternoon gale had raised its ugly head and the direct route between Eagle and Jewell Islands is completely exposed for about three miles. An examination of our marine charts indicated an option was available for partially protected island hopping from the west on return if gusty northwest winds materialized. An insouciant Eggman promised to tow me if necessary. Elderly misgivings notwithstanding; the trip was a go.

The two-mile paddle past Horse and Upper Flag Islands to prominent Eagle Island was uneventful. The former home of Arctic explorer Admiral Robert Peary and now a state park, the unique distinctive island is a remarkable place to visit. Converted to a museum, daily tours are conducted during the summer.

Arriving before it opened, the Park Ranger, carrying an armload of delicious-looking muffins, was disembarking from a shuttle boat with his staff. Declining to share their tempting pastries while we waited, our intrepid band pushed on towards Jewell, hoping for an afternoon return if winds permitted.

Enduring mildly bumpy conditions resulting from a strong tidal current near sometimes treacherous Cow Ledges during the crossing, our traverse culminated landing on a rocky beach in Cocktail Cove on the northwestern extremity of Jewell. A popular destination for mariners—several sailboats were moored in the cove. Carrying our kayaks to the top of the beach, we hiked about a mile to the southern end of the island to explore two abandoned WWII military towers that had been used for submarine surveillance.

We returned to the beach minutes before an incoming tide engulfed our boats. The ocean gods smiled as a light tailwind and a slack tide were experienced proceeding back to Eagle. The park was open and about an hour was spent touring the museum while enjoying almost continuous banter with the gregarious, hospitable park employees. Free for us senior citizens, Eggman had to pay; there is sometimes justice. The home and island have been preserved much as they were prior to Peary's death in 1920 and they have achieved the intended impression of reverting back to an earlier time.

After we launched from a gravel beach on the north side of Eagle, boat traffic on the traverse to Upper Flag was surprisingly light with gentle seas. Shortly after passing the southern terminus of Upper Flag, we saw the menacing fin.

In the twenty years since I began sea kayaking I've had the good fortune to have sighted many of the more substantial denizens of the deep including a variety of whale and seal species. During paddling excursions in Florida, kayaking with the manatees has been an exceptional aquatic experience. Alas, I've never knowingly seen a shark.

Chapter 22 - Jewell and Eagle Islands

After hearing Bud's dramatic shark announcement, Eggman concurred. I was skeptical, suspecting a dolphin instead while acknowledging I didn't know the difference between a shark and dolphin fin. The arcane sea creature continued out into Broad Sound and our expedition was completed without incident.

The following morning, Channel Six News reported a possible shark sighting at Popham Beach just a few miles from our location during the approximate time of our voyage. According to the broadcast, the beach was temporarily closed and the video they aired showed a fin that looked similar to the one we saw. My research indicates the rear of a shark fin is almost vertical while a dolphin's is curved. The back of the fin observed appeared to be straight.

Reluctant to claim a shark sighting based on this flimsy evidence, I'll let the reader be the judge. However, it seems obtaining a definitive confirmation could have been hazardous.

THINGS TO KNOW

Location: Cumberland County, offshore southern coastal Maine

Length: Approximately 10 miles for the described trip. Alternative trips are discussed below.

Difficulty level: Moderate to difficult

Unique potential hazards: Expect heavy boat traffic throughout Casco Bay but especially in Broad Sound near Eagle and Upper Flag Islands. Ledges and currents west of Eagle Island can be treacherous particularly near Cow Ledges about midway between Eagle and Jewell. Broad Sound often has strong tidal currents. Even short exposure in the water can result in hypothermia or drowning. There are many other hazards including numerous larger boats and the risk of being swept into rocky shorelines and ledges. It is strongly recommended that paddlers obtain proper instruction from a qualified instructor prior to attempting this trip. That instruction should include suitable dress, self-rescue, assisted rescue, kayak roll, navigation, and what is required for safety equipment and gear. It is further recommended that each paddler carry a GPS, marine chart, and compass, and know how to use them. Never paddle alone, rather a strong team of experienced sea kayakers is always recommended including one participant familiar with the Eagle and Jewell Islands trip and Casco Bay. Always obtain a reliable weather forecast prior to the trip and if strong winds, particularly offshore winds, bad weather, or rough seas are predicted, don't go.

Directions to Dolphin Marina: From the junction of Maine Routes 24 and 123 in Brunswick, drive south on Route 123 for about 12 miles to Ash Point Road on the right in South Harpswell. Turn right onto Ash Point Road followed by an immediate right turn onto Basin Point Road. Continue on Basin Point Road to Dolphin Marina at the end. Pay parking and launch fees.

Alternative trips: Boat landings in Portland, Freeport, Brunswick, North Harpswell, and Bailey Island provide for alternative trips to Eagle and Jewell Islands. Dolphin Marina is closest to Eagle Island. These same landings offer opportunities for further exploration of the many islands in Casco Bay.

Information on Peary's Eagle Island State Park: For information on the park and museum visit Friends of Peary's Eagle Island website at: https://www.pearyeagleisland.org/about. If you plan to visit the island, recommend taking dry footwear for touring the museum and hiking on the island.

Information on Jewel Island: For information on Jewell Island trails, visit Maine Trail Finder website at: https://www.mainetrailfinder.com/trails/trail/jewell-island. Camping options are available on the island. Recommend taking hiking shoes or boots to hike the 3 miles of island trails.

Chapter 22 - Jewell and Eagle Islands

A kayaker approaches Eagle Island. (Photo – Ron Chase)

Chapter 23 - Bold Coast

Foggy Exploits on the Bold Coast

Sea Kayaking in the fog is a unique experience. I describe it as the simultaneous sense of serenity yet foreboding. Five of us were on the third day of a five-day expedition from Milbridge to Lubec. We had awoken to dense fog in the morning at our campsite near Jonesport and had been navigating in the thick soup with map, compass, and GPS for the entire day. Our last stop had been on substantial Halifax Island. As it was difficult to locate, consideration had been given to spending the night there. Only mid-afternoon, a collective decision was made to push on to tiny Ram Island, three miles farther east. Limited to just a few feet of visibility while searching for the Scabby Islands which preceded Ram by a half mile, I was having misgivings about our choice. Even though the GPS indicated our course was accurate, an hour had passed since leaving Halifax. Clustered close together to avoid accidental separation, paddling on the outside perimeter of Machias Bay meant missing our destination could be hazardous.

The first positive indicator was the distant muffled sound of crashing waves. While possibly treacherous ledges, they could be our desired objective. Shortly after, the dark shaded silhouette of an island gradually appeared. The GPS confirmed the northern extreme of the largest Scabby Island was nearby. If we followed the same bearing, Ram Island should only be a short distance beyond. Scabby faded from sight but within minutes diminutive craggy Ram Island began to appear.

My sea kayaking mentor, Ken Gordon, had organized the ambitious expedition. Beginning in Milbridge two days before, frequent outdoor adventure companions Brent Elwell, Rich Rockenhauser, and Bruce Weik joined us on a planned eighty-five-mile voyage culminating with a traverse of Maine's fabled Bold

Chapter 23 - Bold Coast

Coast. Departing from Tom Leighton Point, our determined band navigated east in light fog past the northern reaches of Bois Bubert and Pond Islands in outer Narraguagus Bay. Shortly after passing distinctive Shipstern Island, a chilly mist began while traversing Flint Island Narrows south of Dyer Island into Pleasant Bay. The mist increased to steady rain and visibility diminished while advancing below South Addison and entering an attenuated passage between the Drisko Islands. Ken recalled tiny Shabbit Island was located about two miles north and thought it a potential camping option. Cold and weary, Shabbit was our goal.

Approaching Shabbit from the south in rain and fog was a dispiriting experience. The high point only twenty feet above sea level, the scrub-covered islet seemed an unwelcoming place to spend the night. A rocky landing was located below extensive rounded ledges on the north side. An abandoned dilapidated hut was found in bushes just beyond the ledges. Chilled by the rain and in need of warmth and shelter, the wretched cabin was so disgusting everyone elected to erect tents instead.

Sunshine greeted us the following morning, providing an ideal opportunity to dry gear on the ledges prior to departure. As we traveled southeast along Great Wass Island in gentle seas and warm weather, an exploration of an enclosed body of water called The Pond at the southern terminus of Great Wass was our sanguine intention. We rounded Pond Point where calm quickly turned to tumult. Unknown to us, an offshore storm had churned up powerful swells from the southeast. We were entering a cauldron of turbulence. Glancing to the left, I could see surf crashing through a narrow channel into The Pond. Even if entrance could be successfully achieved, exit would be impossible until seas diminished. Yelling to be heard above the din of the crashing waves, the others were emphatically informed that Brent and I were not attempting entry. Ensuring that our tandem kayak remained upright became the primary focus. We found ourselves separated from the group while avoiding hazardous ledges in large swells and the next hour was a continuum of maneuvering northeasterly through Mud Hole Channel in feisty seas before finally reuniting with our companions in the protected waters of Alley Bay. A campsite was located on nearby Kelley Point.

The fog-filled third day began the next morning. Hugging the shore around Kelley Point, an easterly course was plotted for the two-and-a-half-mile traverse of Chandler Bay to Roque Island. Our calculation was on the mark as the initial sighting of Roque was discerned immediately before entering the Thoroughfare leading into Roque Harbor. A welcome respite was savored on Roque Beach at the top of the harbor. Skirting the north shore of the harbor to Bar Island, another bewildering one and a half mile crossing was attempted southeast to Halifax Island. An inexplicable navigation error led us off course to Anquilla Island, slightly southwest of Halifax. While investigating a potential campsite on Halifax, our dubious decision to continue to Ram Island was concocted.

The only acceptable location for tents on Ram Island required securing our kayaks on precipitous ledges above the high tide mark and carrying gear steeply on a boulder-strewn ascent to a grassy knoll. Our arrival upset a territorial denizen of the remote island, an unruly mink who was in a perpetual frenzy. The fog was so murky no one realized a herd of sheep were wandering on the tiny atoll.

A continuation of fog the following day was a significant impediment to the longest exposed crossing of the journey. Almost five miles east to Cross Island, the only plausible interim option to land was rugged Libby Island. Disembarking would be problematic in the fog. The first two miles was uneventful. Shortly after hearing the distant sound of surf crashing on Libby Island, Team Foggy entered the main channel in outer Machias Bay. A strong flooding tide created a continuum of large starboard waves complicating our orienteering efforts and undermining attempts to keep the group together in the dense fog. The eerie blare of a foghorn on a nearby fishing vessel added to our anxiety.

We persevered easterly for about an hour in rough seas. The profile of Northwest Head on Cross Island was barely visible when we came upon powerful currents and breaking waves.

Chapter 23 - Bold Coast

Dismissing any notion of traveling on the outside of Cross, Team Foggy retreated north and found calm in the lee of Northwest Head. As we progressed east through Cross Island Narrows, the sun appeared for the first time in a day and a half. The site of a former Coast Guard lifesaving station on the northeastern shore of the island provided an excellent opportunity to stop for rest and sustenance. Fortuitously, potable drinking water was retrieved from an ancient well.

The return of the sun buoyed our spirits as we proceeded two miles northeast across Little Machias Bay to majestic Great Head south of Cutler. On arrival, a fog bank rolled in with a vengeance. Entering Little River from Western Head, someone suggested visiting Little River Lighthouse. "What's the point?" I inquired. "We can't see it if we can't find it."

Foregoing touristy inclinations, Team Foggy began its quest of the Bold Coast. Consisting of about twenty miles of almost continuous high ocean cliffs and narrow jagged rockbound peninsulas, the Bold Coast is the most spectacular and remote stretch of shoreline on the coast of Maine. Huge tidal ranges, unpredictably strong associated currents, and very few safe havens to land add to the mystique and challenge.

As we persisted northeast through a maze of protruding ledges, an immediate concern was securing a campsite. Following a couple of failed attempts to find a suitable location, Brent remembered observing a cove farther east while hiking the Bold Coast Trail. His recollection was accurate as a secluded gravel beach accessible at any tide was discovered about a mile beyond. The fog appeared to be diminishing as the setting sun raised expectations of a glorious upcoming day on the scenic Bold Coast.

Patchy fog and moderately bumpy seas were immediate challenges on what was expected to be our final day. Modest visibility facilitated safely negotiating around craggy promontories and vertical escarpments as Team Foggy endured northeast. Shortly after crossing Moose Cove, dense murky fog enveloped us. Unable to observe shoreline hazards until the last moment, we were forced farther out to sea. Foghorns from cargo ships cruising through nearby Grand Manan Channel was a reminder that hazards also lurked away from shore.

After we had paddled several hours approximately a half mile offshore in a dismal soupy haze, the high cliffs of West Quoddy Head gradually appeared through the foggy mist. Moving closer to shore, we observed hikers walking the trails high above. Some waved as our kayaks passed.

As we pivoted north after rounding the head, the sky cleared and the sun came out. We appreciated brilliant views of Campobello Island in New Brunswick on the three-mile paddle to Lubec Narrows—the contrast with much of our journey was stunning. Paradoxically, the return shuttle to Milbridge was sunny and clear throughout.

THINGS TO KNOW

Location: Washington County, offshore Down East Maine
Distance: Approximately 85 miles
Difficulty rating: Difficult
Unique potential hazards: Large waves and rough seas are a potential threat on much of the described trip. Fog is common throughout the area. Water temperatures are normally colder along the Bold Coast than the rest of Maine. Even short exposure in the water can result in hypothermia or drowning. Tidal ranges are the most significant in Maine and related currents can be strong and unpredictable. There are many other hazards including larger boats and being swept into rocky shorelines and ledges. This is particularly true along the Bold Coast where there are very few opportunities to safely land. It is strongly recommended that paddlers obtain proper instruction from a qualified instructor prior to attempting the trip. The instruction should include suitable dress, self-rescue, assisted rescue, kayak roll, navigation, and what is required for safety equipment and gear. It is further recommended that each paddler carry a GPS, marine chart, and compass, and know how to use them. Never paddle alone, rather a

Chapter 23 - Bold Coast

strong contingent of experienced sea kayakers is always recommended including one participant familiar with the Down East and Bold Coasts. Always obtain a reliable weather forecast prior to a trip and if strong winds, particularly offshore winds, bad weather, or rough seas are predicted, don't go.

Alternative trips: The Bold Coast trip between Cutler and Lubec can be completed in a long day. Wind and tide forecasts should be obtained so that the most advantageous choice of direction can be determined. A boat landing in South Trescott can be accessed near Boot Cove Road at about the halfway point. It can facilitate completing the Bold Coast in two shorter day trips.

Directions:

Lubec Put-in/Takeout: From the junction of Routes 189 and 191 in West Lubec, drive east on 189 for about 5.5 miles to Water Street in Lubec on the left. Follow Water Street for a short distance to the end where the boat landing is located and some parking is available.

Cutler Put-in/Takeout: From the junction of US Route 1 and Maine Route 191 in East Machias, drive east on 191 for about 14 miles to Cutler. A small landing is located on the right shortly after entering town. Parking is often a problem and it may be necessary to load or unload and park elsewhere.

Kayakers paddle along the foggy Bold Coast. (Photo – Ron Chase)

Chapter 24 - Mount Desert Island: Frenchman Bay and Otter Cliffs

Last Paddle

As I commenced the sport in 2002, sea kayaking is a relatively new activity for me. When you're in your seventies, anything less than twenty years seems like last week. Already eligible for AARP membership when I began, I lacked the risk-taking mentality of younger paddlers. Late fall and winter kayaking on the ocean has never had much appeal. Frigid air, wintry winds, icy water, and frozen hands increase the dangers and decrease enjoyment.

Fifteen years ago, a friend recommended a December trip to Damariscove Island, the far end located five miles off the coast of Linekin Peninsula near Boothbay. It was a cloudy breezy day with temperatures in the thirties when we departed from Ocean Point, navigating past massive distinctive boulders called White Islands to Outer Heron Island in comparatively benign conditions. As we left the protection of Outer Heron for a two-mile open crossing directly into gusty piercing southwest winds to the southern terminus of Damariscove, the character of the excursion changed dramatically. As we approached the southeastern tip, large intimidating swells spewing a frosty spray rocked our tiny crafts. The prospect of accompanying the undulating waves as they crashed into nearby jagged cliffs seemed a disagreeable possibility. Finally achieving relative safety in the sheltered cove; thoroughly chilled, I resolved that cold weather sea kayaking was for younger, tougher paddlers.

Since then, the Penobscot Paddle and Chowder Society fall outdoor weekend on Mount Desert Island has often resulted in my last sea kayak expedition of the year. With the possible exception of the Bold Coast, there is no more spectacular shoreline in Maine than the island explorer Samuel de Champlain called Isles

Chapter 24 - Mount Desert Island: Frenchman Bay and Otter Cliffs

des Monts Desert. Hence, it's an ideal setting to end a season of paddling. Typically, my friend Ken Gordon leads a club sea kayak trip as he did again this year. Several members, mostly elderly boaters, were enthusiastically awaiting his choice. No shrinking violets in our geriatric group, the reality was we were all lobbying for individual preferences.

An offshore storm complicated decision-making. Turbulent seas rendered paddling along the completely exposed rugged eastern shore or touring to outer islands potentially hazardous. Since those were the favored choices, a prolonged discussion ensued. A traverse of picturesque inner Frenchman Bay was the final selection. Infrequently paddled but still exceptionally scenic, the northern sector of the bay offered the benefit of probable sanctuary from predicted prodigious ocean waves. The strategy was a good one as calm conditions were experienced throughout.

Beginning the endeavor at a boat landing on Hadley Point, the island's northern extremity, we launched on the eastern end of Mount Desert Narrows just a short distance from the mainland. Journeying southeast close to shore, locating a landmark called The Ovens was our initial objective. Vertical cliffs with hollowed out caves soon emerged. Paddling into The Ovens is an essential element of the experience; even for seniors posing as youngsters.

As we continued southeast past Salsbury and Hulls Coves, the aptly named Porcupine Islands were directly ahead. Dominating a channel between two of the Porcupines was an immense vessel, the Royal Caribbean cruise ship. Inspecting the ocean liner and reconnoitering the Porcupines became an extended destination.

A sense of insignificance is guaranteed when approaching a cruise ship in a sea kayak. The gargantuan watercraft loomed over us like a small mountain. Surprisingly, no one in our aging group expressed any enthusiasm for embarking on a cruise. A succession of comical observations about the dangers of getting ill while on board followed. While perhaps lacking in good taste, a suggestion that such an outing required a cabin with a "throw up" window was probably the funniest.

Paddling amongst the Porcupine Islands is always a pleasurable diversion. Consisting of several closely connected diminutive atolls extending east towards Schoodic Point, they offer an entertaining escapade while normally ensconced from offshore winds and waves. Completing our exploration, we navigated towards the noted coastal village of Bar Harbor. During the last mile of our voyage, a perpetual view of majestic Champlain, Dorr, and Cadillac Mountains was savored approaching a bustling landing adjacent Bar Island. Fortuitously, our arrival was completed just before an outgoing tide would have culminated in a muddy disembarkation.

On a calm day, prolonging the journey with a ten-mile paddle south along the eastern shore of the island in outer Frenchman Bay to Seal Harbor is a recommended option. The veteran of several such excursions, I believe this section of coastline rivals the Bold Coast as Maine's most spectacular.

Leaving Bar Harbor and traveling south, paddlers parallel Champlain Mountain for about three miles to impressive Schooner Head. A long mile beyond is spectacular Great Head. On one occasion, ominous exploding surf and powerful winds turned back a group of Chowderheads at this location. If the intimidating prominence can be safely negotiated, popular Sand Beach in Newport Cove provides an idyllic location for a respite.

Two of the most iconic locations in Maine are encountered in the next couple of miles: Thunder Hole and Otter Cliffs. When the seas are calm, kayakers can paddle into the entrance of dynamic Thunder Hole. Continuing south, technical climbers can often be observed on the sheer Otter Cliffs and hikers are usually seen rambling on a trail along the edge. After traversing Otter Cove, the remainder of the outing to Seal Harbor passes below the palatial estates of the rich and famous situated on precipitous bluffs high above. The beach in Seal Harbor is an excellent location to exit or launch.

Alas, treacherous seas negated the protracted trip on this day. At my age, I consider myself blessed to have enjoyed another year of exceptional sea kayaking opportunities along the coast of

Chapter 24 - Mount Desert Island: Frenchman Bay and Otter Cliffs

Maine. No cold weather ocean adventures for me. Time is nearing for winter hiking and Nordic skiing instead. My last paddle of the year, fortunes willing, I'll be back in my sea kayak come spring.

THINGS TO KNOW

Location: Hancock County, offshore Down East Maine

Distance: Approximately 9 miles from Hadley Point to Bar Harbor and an additional 10 miles to Seal Harbor

Difficulty: Moderate for the short trip and moderately difficult for the extended version

Unique potential hazards: Large waves and rough seas are a potential threat on the trip, particularly along the eastern shore of Mount Desert Island. Fog is common in the area and safe places to land are limited, particularly between Bar Harbor and Seal Harbor. Even short exposure in the water can result in hypothermia or drowning. There are many other hazards including larger boats. Being swept into rocky shorelines and ledges is a risk and the section between Schooner Head and Seal Harbor can be unusually hazardous. It is strongly recommended that paddlers obtain proper instruction from a qualified instructor prior to attempting this trip. The instruction should include suitable dress, self-rescue, assisted rescue, kayak roll, navigation, and what is required for safety equipment and gear. It is further recommended that each paddler carry a GPS, marine chart, and compass, and know how to use them. Never paddle alone, rather a strong contingent of experienced sea kayakers is always recommended including one participant familiar with Frenchman Bay. Always obtain a reliable weather forecast prior to a trip and if strong winds, particularly offshore winds, bad weather, or rough seas are predicted, don't go.

Directions:

Hadley Point: From the junction of Routes 198 and 3 shortly after crossing onto Mount Desert Island, drive about 3.5 miles south on Route 3 to Hadley Point Road on the left.

Continue on Hadley Point Road to the end where there is a boat landing and parking area.

Boat landing in Bar Harbor: From the Hadley Point Road, continue south on Route 3 for about 7 miles to West Street in Bar Harbor on the left. Turn onto West Street and drive about 1200 feet to Bridge Street on the left. Follow Bridge Street for a short distance to the end where there is a landing. Unload boats and gear and find parking on West Street.

Seal Harbor: From West Street in Bar Harbor, follow Route 3 for about 10 miles to Seal Harbor. There is a small parking area on the right and a beach directly across the highway.

Alternative trip: Depending upon forecasted winds and tides, it may be advantageous to start the trip in Seal Harbor or Bar Harbor paddling north.

A kayaker passes Thunder Hole in Outer Frenchman Bay. (Photo – Ron Chase)

Chapter 25 - Mount Desert Island: Cranberry and Baker Islands

A Waltz on Dancing Rock

Situated about four miles south of Mount Desert Island, historic Baker Island is one of the most unique kayak destinations on the Maine coast. Easternmost of five islands constituting the Cranberry Isles, much of the island is part of Acadia National Park. Baker Island Light Station, a brick lighthouse in the center of the small atoll, marks the southwest entrance to Frenchman Bay. Construction was ordered by President John Quincy Adams in 1828 making it the oldest lighthouse in the area. The island was settled in the eighteenth century; the Gilley family homestead built in 1806 remains. From the lighthouse, a trail leads to the south shore where a mammoth flat slab of granite can be found called "Dancing Rock" or "Dance Floor." In an earlier time, when the Cranberry Isles were inhabited by a substantial year-round population of fishermen, area islanders often held dances at the remarkable location.

The Penobscot Paddle and Chowder Society scheduled four days of outdoor adventures on Mount Desert Island during their Fall Supper Weekend. Mountain hikes, Carriage and Loop Road bike rides, and sea kayak excursions were planned around the island and in Acadia National Park. For fourteen of us a voyage to Baker Island was the goal on day two of the extravaganza.

Since most of the kayakers were camping at Bar Harbor Campground on the northern tip of the island, that was the meeting place on a glorious sunny morning. Chowderheads, and friends of Chowderheads from as far away as Minnesota and Quebec, were in attendance. After formulating a plan for the day's activities, a caravan of vehicles carrying brightly colored sea kayaks traveled south on Route 3 to a public beach in Seal Harbor on the southeastern end of the island. Nearly filling the tiny parking area on the opposite side of the highway and carrying a succession of kayaks and gear across the road slowed busy tourist traffic. The invasion of wetsuit-adorned paddlers mystified early morning sun worshippers claiming sites on the beach.

Consisting of twelve solo kayaks and one tandem team, the entourage departed from the beach in light winds while benefiting from an outgoing tide. We traveled due south past the eastern terminus of Sutton Island towards our first destination, Little Cranberry Island, the two-hundred-acre fishing community and tourist attraction directly ahead. Entering Cranberry Harbor with expansive Great Cranberry Island on the right, our group disembarked on a rocky shore adjacent the ferry landing in the tiny harbor town of Islesford. Several members walked to the Islesford Historical Museum only to find it closed. Others purchased snacks at the local general store.

Paddling south along the southwestern extremity of Little Cranberry, a cone-shaped peninsula named The Maypole, our group navigated east traveling through a narrow channel called The Gut. Emerging from the passageway, distinctive Baker Island entered into view situated about two miles farther east. Approaching low tide, we met with an intimidating continuum of exposed shoals almost connecting Bar Point on Little Cranberry with Baker Island. The sometimes-treacherous ledges were the primary justification for building Baker Island Light Station almost two centuries ago. Weaving through the maze, a circuitous route was detected to a no frills sheltered landing on the northwest prominence of Baker.

A trail led through Gilley homestead to the ancient lighthouse. Trekking southerly, impressive Dancing Rock was located on the rugged southern shoreline. Our large band of kayakers settled in for photo opts and a long lunch while enjoying the scenic coastal views. Seemingly inappropriate to visit the iconic location without a dance, my wife Nancy agreed to a waltz while I simultaneously inflicted my version of the lyrics to Frank Sinatra's "Stranger's in the Night" on her and our bemused companions. Ole Blue Eyes would not have been impressed. From the comfort and security of Dancing Rock, the seas on the outside of the remote isle appeared gentle. A collective decision was made to circumnavigate the island.

As we hiked back to Baker Landing, spectacular views of mountainous Mount Desert Island captured our attention. While proceeding clockwise around the island, we found the perceived calm conditions were actually moderate swells. A flooding tide and numerous exposed ledges necessitated careful maneuvering, especially near Dancing Rock and a perilous offshore ledge named The Thumper.

As we completed the Baker Island tour, a rising tide had engulfed the elongated shoals extending to Little Cranberry. The verdict was to complete the journey with a more direct return to Seal Harbor traveling east of Little Cranberry, a 4.5-mile paddle. The ragged eastern perimeter of Little Cranberry provided an opportunity for some stimulating coastline exploration. Phenomenal vistas of Penobscot, Pemetic, and Cadillac Mountains were continuous during the three-mile crossing to Seal Harbor. While Maine is blessed with many exceptional views, arguably none surpass those experienced on that final traverse.

THINGS TO KNOW

Location: Hancock County, offshore Down East Maine
Distance: Approximately 11 miles
Difficulty: Moderately difficult
Unique potential hazards: Large waves and rough seas are a potential threat on the described trip, particularly on the outside of Baker Island. Fog is common in the area. Only short exposure in the water can result in hypothermia or drowning. There are many other hazards including larger boats and being swept into rocky shorelines and ledges. The shoals between Little Cranberry and Baker Islands can be very dangerous during rough seas. It is strongly recommended that paddlers obtain proper instruction from a qualified instructor prior to attempting this trip. The instruction should include suitable dress, self-rescue, assisted rescue, kayak roll, navigation, and what is required for safety equipment

and gear. It is further recommended that each paddler carry a GPS, marine chart, and compass, and know how to use them. Never paddle alone, rather a strong contingent of experienced sea kayakers is always recommended including one participant familiar with Baker Island and the Cranberries. Always obtain a reliable weather forecast prior to a trip and if strong winds, particularly offshore winds, bad weather, or rough seas are predicted, don't go.

Directions to Seal Harbor: Follow the directions in Chapter 2 to Kebo Street in Bar Harbor. Continue south on Route 3 for about 9 miles to Seal Harbor. There is a small parking area on the right and a beach directly across the highway.

A waltz on Dancing Rock. (Photo – Ken Gordon)

SECTION V. WHITEWATER KAYAKING AND CANOEING

A kayaker is submerged in water on Canada Falls. (Photo – Ron Chase)

Chapter 26 - Dead River

Dead Weekend

A character in Kenneth Roberts's historical novel *Arundel* remarked of the Dead River, "[It's] no more dead than a bobcat after a rabbit." Joining the Kennebec River in The Forks after sixteen miles of almost continuous Class I through IV whitewater, the Dead is in actuality the west branch of the Kennebec and one of the most popular whitewater runs in the northeastern United States.

Beginning in small lakes and ponds in western Maine, the North and South Branches of the Dead converge at Flagstaff Lake in Stratton. What currently constitutes the lake was once a calm section of the Dead River that meandered circuitously for twenty miles, hence the name Dead. In 1950, Long Falls Dam was built, forming the lake and creating a reservoir that regulates flow primarily for hydropower purposes downriver on the Kennebec. An added benefit, scheduled dam releases provide whitewater throughout the dry summer months. As a result, the Dead has become a mecca for enthusiastic boaters in search of paddling thrills and spills.

My first trip on the Dead was in June 1986. Considering ourselves competent canoeists prepared for the challenges of the notorious river, a co-worker and I decided to test our skills in a tandem canoe. The experience was an epiphany. We found a campground on the Dead in The Forks owned by Ed and Marie Webb who also provided a shuttle service on rough logging roads to the preferred put-in where Spencer Stream enters the Dead sixteen miles upriver.

Webb's Campground was an adventure unto itself. Marie ran the campground, organized the shuttle, and collected fees. Ed was shuttle driver extraordinaire and the quintessential Jack-of-all-

Chapter 26 - Dead River

trades who loaded boats onto a trailer and packed paddlers into an open truck bed. There were two coveted seats in the cab with Ed. Everyone else was left out in the elements.

The very personable Marie set up a little table next to the shuttle truck to collect the aforementioned fees. Back then there was what seemed to be a dizzying array of costs. Before loading our boat, Marie required payment for camping, the shuttle, and a special road use charge the Webb's collected for the owner of lands crossed on the drive to Spencer Stream.

My companion and I were quickly in over our heads on the Dead. Even though the dam release was a low one, we struggled mightily from the outset. Every rapid seemed a bewildering assortment of waves surging around and between huge boulders with no obvious route. At about the halfway point, a flip resulted in a short swim. Continuously laboring to stay afloat, the last and reputedly the most difficult rapid, Lower Poplar Falls, weighed heavily on our minds. Entering the intimidating torrent, we were immediately out of control plowing over a couple of ledge drops and filling up in the hydraulics below. Overflowing with water and devoid of stability, a dramatic upset followed. Desperately holding onto our boat and paddles, an enormous effort was required to drag the canoe ashore after swimming much of the falls.

In the over three decades since my first descent, I've navigated the Dead an estimated two hundred times achieving what I call the "Deadhead" distinction. Obsessive compulsive disorder might be the clinical diagnosis. The Dead has been a family affair as both of my sons, my wife, and many other family members have joined me on the river. I've met a host of great friends there and our escapades could easily fill a book.

Recently my outdoor club, the Penobscot Paddle and Chowder Society (PPCS), scheduled a weekend of paddling on the Dead. Sadly, longtime friends Ed and Marie Webb have passed. However, their son Andy and his wife Kim now operate the campground and run the shuttle. Now relaxing in comparative luxury, an enclosed van is provided for the hour-long journey on the Lower Enchanted Road to the put-in. Happily, the road use fees have been discontinued.

On the first day, Gary and Suzanne Cole were trip leaders for a moderately high 3500 cubic feet per second (CFS) release, generally considered a Class III/ IV level. Kayaks were the primary choice of transportation for the high water. After bouncing through choppy rollers at the bottom of Spencer Rips and passing over a huge wave just beyond, some stimulating wave surfing followed on a short pitch called Quattro. Below, protracted Minefield Rapid was negotiated before stopping for lunch at Hayden's Landing, located immediately above complex Hayden's Falls.

Surviving Hayden's by dodging a continuum of potentially troublesome hydraulics, everyone relaxed in a relatively placid stretch called the Doldrums. This was the calm before the storm as the subsequent difficulty level increased appreciably. After passing Enchanted Stream, our intrepid band navigated around a gnarly hole at Elephant Rock and a maze of boulders was negotiated in Horsefly Rapid before entering Mile Long. The longest rapid on the river, Mile Long ends with a baffling assortment of large exploding waves, many concealing boat-flipping holes. Stopping to surf an exceptional wave near Spruce Ledge before successfully maneuvering through formidable Upper Poplar Falls, the excitement ended with a calamity-free exhilarating descent of Lower Poplar Falls. After avoiding numerous intimidating obstacles on "Big Pop," an easy two-mile paddle to The Forks was a time for celebration.

The following day, Chowderheads returned for a 2400 CFS release led by Rick Farnsworth. The lower level attracted more canoes resulting in several minor mishaps particularly on Lower Poplar Falls. Typical of a Dead weekend, more excitement was had than a bobcat after a rabbit.

THINGS TO KNOW

Location: Somerset County, western Maine

Chapter 26 - Dead River

Length: Approximately 16 miles from Spencer Stream to The Forks. The trip can be shortened by about 4 miles by accessing a location called the Gravel Pit which entails driving down an unimproved dirt road to a portage trail. This alternative requires a lengthy carry to the river.

Difficulty ratings and water levels:
    Release 1300 CFS: Class I, II and some III
    Release 1800 CFS: Class I, II and some III. Lower Poplar Falls approaches Class IV.
    Release 2400 CFS: Class II and III, with several sections approaching Class IV
    Release 3500 CFS: Class III/IV
    Release 5500 CFS and above: Class III and IV+

Scouting and required portages: Most rapids are very long. Scouting and portaging are problematic. Spencer Rips is a short walk from Spencer Stream put-in and can be scouted. If paddlers are uncomfortable running Spencer Rips, they should not run the river. A few paddlers scout Lower Poplar Falls from the right or left. A long difficult portage is possible on the right or left. Most paddlers believe running Lower Poplar tight right is easier but requires substantial rock dodging.

Release Information: Brookfield Renewable Energy operates Long Falls Dam and publishes the release schedule each year. The PPCS includes the schedule in its annual Trip Book published each spring. Several paddle clubs and rafting companies post the schedule online.

Shuttle: As of this writing, the only shuttle service to the Spencer Stream put-in is provided by Riverdrivers Camping and Lodging
    http://www.riverdrivers.com/riverdrivers_contact.php,
owned by Andy & Kim Webb. Running your own shuttle is not recommended. It is a long confusing drive on rough roads. The $20 fee for solo canoes and kayaks is well worth the money. Costs vary for other crafts.

Camping and other accommodations:
Riverdrivers Camping and Lodging: Camping and cabins are available at the takeout for the Dead.
Indian Pond Campground: Rustic camping is offered at Indian Pond about 30 minutes north of The Forks:
   https://campmaine.com/directory/kennebec-valley-campgrounds/indian-pond-campground/
Numerous motels and inns are located in The Forks, Jackman, and Bingham
Several rafting companies in the area offer camping options.
Unique potential hazards: The Dead is a very challenging river at all levels. The rapids are often long and extended dangerous swims are possible. It's located in a remote area and largely inaccessible. Paddlers should expect rescue will be extremely difficult and time consuming. Injury, death, and loss of boats are real possibilities. It is strongly recommended that paddlers travel with an experienced group of veteran Dead River paddlers. High water runs are not recommended unless the paddler has a reliable roll.
Directions to take-outs: From US Routes 2 and 201 in Skowhegan follow Route 201 north for 46.3 miles to The Forks. For paddlers shuttling with Riverdrivers, the campground is on the left a short distance after crossing the Kennebec River. The public take-out is the next left turn on the Dead River Road and immediately on the left.

Chapter 26 - Dead River

A kayaker paddles Hayden Rapid on the Dead River. (Photo – Ron Chase)

Chapter 27 - Kennebec Gorge

Big Mama is Waiting

We had exceptional weather and an excellent turnout for a paddle on the Kennebec Gorge. A western Maine whitewater treasure located in Moxie Gore, "the gorge" is four miles of continuous big volume whitewater that flows from Harris Dam to Carry Brook. After Carry Brook, the rapids gradually calm until joining the Dead River in The Forks, nine miles farther south.

The second day of the Penobscot Paddle and Chowder Society (PPCS) Summer Picnic extravaganza, I was Trip Coordinator. In the spirit of club balladeer Kyle Duckworth's great tune about the search for peace and harmony between sometimes discordant canoeists and kayakers, both were well represented with only minimal conflict. Ryan Galway and Jason McAllister paddled a tandem canoe while John Brower and Evan Eichorn were in solo open boats. Allen Gaskell, Brent Elwell, Dylan Brown, and I navigated kayaks. Dylan was supposed to be in an open boat but showed up wearing a kayak to bewilderment of the easily confused Trip Coordinator.

Since several paddlers were relative newcomers to the big water run, describing the rapids was the dominant topic of conversation throughout. Consequential Big Mama Rapid was the recipient of a preponderance of the discussion. While most of the rapids have fairly distinct routes, Big Mama is very difficult to predict. Near the end of two hundred yards of large, breaking rollers, Big Mama Wave is the biggest and baddest of all. Mercurial is the best way to describe the mammoth swell. Sometimes a huge wall of foam rises up and crashes down on much smaller kayaks and canoes. Most of the time, it unpredictably surges and undulates, leaving approaching paddlers wondering about their fate. The breaker may elevate them several feet into the air and violently regurgitate the near helpless victims into the churning waves

Chapter 27 - Kennebec Gorge

below or miraculously mellow to a smooth tongue allowing boaters to slide serenely through. If paddlers come out of their boats in the gorge, Big Mama is likely the culprit. There is little time for an assisted rescue. Swimmers must quickly gather themselves, their boats, and paddles into an eddy at the bottom. Otherwise, they'll endure a very long unpleasant swim through the huge waves of Upper and Lower Alleyway to Cathedral Eddy.

Tandem canoeing is relatively rare in the gorge, so Ryan and Jason were our primary concern. They were on their game from the outset. Everyone had clean runs at Taster and Rock Garden Rapids with some intriguing surfing on Disappearing Wave in between. The entire group cautiously entered Big Mama Rapid and caught a squirrely eddy part way down on river right to discuss strategies for confronting Big Mama Wave. I suggested they follow my line. My intent was to approach the monster roller in the middle and then angle left when breaking over the top. That would set me up to drive hard through the irregular waves below and catch a large eddy on river left. Big Mama was uncooperative, pitching me unceremoniously into the air and perfunctorily propelling my kayak towards cliffs on the right. After precariously bracing through the tumultuous diagonal waves below, I found myself on the wrong side of the river in a micro eddy, but present and accounted for. "A thoroughly uninspiring performance," someone later observed.

Following close behind, my companions attempted to duplicate the misguided route. The volatile billow responded by elevating some, surfing others, and pampering a few. When the tandem team blasted over the top of the infamous boat thrasher, their eyes were the size of tennis balls. Despite Big Mama's best efforts, everyone remained upright. Inexplicably, some ended by unintentionally joining me on river right while others finished left.

With renewed confidence, we paddled around Good-bye Hole, rode the waves of Upper Alley Way past Whitewasher Hole, and most attained quality air time on Big Kahuna Wave. After catching our breath in an eddy on the left, Lower Alley Way was navigated to Cathedral Eddy without incident. A tranquil, majestic location with sheer cliffs on both sides, the calm water of Cathedral Eddy provides a stark contrast to the turbulence above. As has been my habit over the years, I announced to no one in particular, "We're not swimming the Alley Way today." It's much easier to be cocky once you're safely ensconced in Cathedral Eddy.

After some excellent surfing in Z-Turn Rapid, Magic Falls was next on our dance card. There is a huge hole on top left that can swallow large rafts. Hence the name, Magic Falls. It was decision-making time for our group. Would we take the sporting route punching Magic Hole or run the more benevolent Highway? The hole sometimes flips rafts so the probability of getting some rolling practice in a kayak or canoe was high. A few hundred yards of big waves and holes waited menacingly below. A hiking trail leads to Magic Falls from Carry Brook, so there was a sizeable audience of onlookers, known as vultures, anticipating the carnage. Most of our group chose a less intimidating drive down the Highway. A great surfing wave just above the hole seductively lures imprudent kayakers. Brent and I couldn't avoid the temptation. Alas, we disappointed the expectant viewers remaining in our boats.

Easier rapids brought us to Carry Brook. More Chowderheads joined us for the "float" out. A laid back group if there ever was one, they were guilty of felonious lallygagging, which is worse than criminal milling. I exchanged my kayak for a tandem canoe and a beautiful girl, my wife Nancy. The first couple of miles of the lower section contain several entertaining rapids and big waves followed by a placid float to The Forks. It was a glorious day on a marvelous river. Big Mama will be waiting with some daunting contrivances for our next visit.

THINGS TO KNOW

Location: Somerset County, western Maine
Length: Approximately four miles from Harris Dam to Carry Brook. It is an additional nine miles from Carry Brook to The Forks.

Chapter 27 - Kennebec Gorge

Difficulty ratings and water levels: From May 1st through mid-October, the minimum daily dam release between 10 AM and 1 PM is 4800 CFS which is considered Class IV in the gorge and Class I, II, and III below Carry Brook. Four 8000 CFS releases are scheduled sometime during that timeframe, Class IV+ in the gorge. There are also scheduled 2400 CFS afternoon releases on most Saturdays and some Sundays that are Class III/IV. The releases can change without notice as a result of power demands or high water levels on the lakes above.

Scouting and required portages: The gorge is a deep canyon with steep cliffs on both sides. With the exception of Magic Falls, scouting and portaging are not possible.

Release Information: Brookfield Renewable Energy operates Harris Dam and publishes the release schedule each year. The PPCS includes the schedule in its annual Trip Book published each spring. Several rafting companies post the schedule online.

Shuttle: There is no regular shuttle service for the Kennebec. It may be possible to arrange one by contacting Riverdrivers Camping and Lodging

(http://www.riverdrivers.com/riverdrivers_contact.php), owned by Andy & Kim Webb.

Camping and other accommodations:

Riverdrivers Camping and Lodging: Camping and cabins are available at the takeout for the Dead in The Forks, just a short distance from the lower Kennebec take out.

Indian Pond Campground: Rustic camping is offered at Indian Pond about 30 minutes north of The Forks near the gorge put-in at Harris Dam: https://campmaine.com/directory/kennebec-valley-campgrounds/indian-pond-campground/

Numerous motels and inns are located in The Forks, Jackman, and Bingham. Several rafting companies in the area offer camping options.

Unique potential hazards: The Kennebec Gorge is very challenging at all levels. The rapids are long with large waves and extended dangerous swims are possible. It's located in a remote area and largely inaccessible. Paddlers should expect rescue will be extremely difficult and time consuming. Injury, death, and loss of boats are real possibilities. It is strongly recommended that paddlers travel with an experienced group of veteran Kennebec Gorge paddlers. High water runs in the gorge are not recommended unless paddlers have reliable rolls. The section from Carry Brook to The Forks is easier but the same potential hazards exist.

Directions to access points and take outs: From US Routes 2 and 201 in Skowhegan follow Route 201 north for 46.3 miles to The Forks. Called the Ballfield, the take out for the lower Kennebec is just across the bridge over the Kennebec River and immediately on the right. To reach the take out at Carry Brook for the Kennebec Gorge, turn right before the bridge over the Kennebec onto Lake Moxie Road and drive 5.3 miles to Indian Pond Road. Turn left onto Indian Pond Road and continue 3.9 miles to Carry Take Out Road on the left. Follow the rough Carry Take Out Road for about two miles to the end where there is a large parking area on the left. Boats must be carried steeply up or down the long stairs. To reach Harris Dam, return to Indian Pond Road, turn left, and drive about 3 miles to a gatehouse where paddlers must sign in. Follow gatehouse directions on where to park and how to gain access to the river. A steep carry down a long stairs to the put-in below the dam is always necessary. On some occasions, it is possible to drive to the top of the stairs and on others a longer carry from the parking area is required.

Tandem canoeists challenge the Alley Way on the Kennebec Gorge. (Photo – Rapid Shooters)

Chapter 28 - West Branch of The Penobscot

The Finest Surf and Turf in Maine

Flowing beneath the shadows of Maine's tallest mountain, Mount Katahdin, the West Branch of the Penobscot River is arguably the most challenging whitewater regularly paddled in New England. Below McKay Power Station, the West Branch churns up several sections of Class III through V rapids in the next eleven miles. A short distance away, Knife Edge and the three major peaks of Mount Katahdin provide the most extensive alpine mountaineering environment in Maine. Katahdin and the Penobscot would furnish three of us with the state's finest surf and turf weekend adventure.

Five kayakers from the Penobscot Paddle and Chowder Society (PPCS) met at McKay Station on a warm summer day. As we peered into Ripogenus Gorge from the cliffs above, we could see the water level was obviously high: 3400 cubic feet per second (CFS) to be precise. A good medium range is 2000 to 2400 CFS. Above 2600 is high and over 3000 is too high for an old man. As the water rises in the gorge, the additional volume funnels with increasing intensity and velocity into a massive hole called Exterminator. As far as I know, it's never exterminated anyone, but I've witnessed a couple of dislocated shoulders. The key to a successful run is skirting Exterminator on the left, catching the eddy below, and then navigating through a slightly easier lower part of the gorge called Staircase. At 3400 CFS, it would be a Class V undertaking.

I'm always amazed at how quickly things happen in the gorge at high water. In seconds, paddlers are in the turbulence where effective paddling techniques are essential. Almost immediately, a powerful diagonal wave that feeds unsuspecting boaters directly into the bowels of Exterminator was reaching out to grab me. Having been there and done that, I angled my boat left with all the momentum I could generate, broke over the menacing wave, and crossed an eddy line that seemed a foot high. My companions were close behind, some catching a micro eddy with me, others simply kissing the edge of Exterminator and tumbling into Football Eddy below. A few moments later, we were all gathered there.

The downriver view from Football Eddy was a horizon line of exploding waves. "Go as far right as you can get," my longtime paddling friend Jonathan Wheaton advised. Lacking a better plan, I went far right. Apparently, it wasn't far enough right, as I was instantly upside down in what seemed like a giant washing machine. Rolling up, something knocked me over again. Popping up once more, I grabbed an eddy in time to watch three of my buddies enduring the same unsolicited rolling practice. Rolling frightens me. There are rocks down there; a person could get hurt!

So it went running The Heaters, Trouble Maker, and a long, twisting rapid culminating with an inhospitable hole called Telos. Just ahead was the most difficult rapid on the river, Cribworks. "Do you want to scout it?" Jonathan asked as we sat in a tiny eddy above. "Hell no, it scares me to look at it," I responded. He departed the eddy disappearing into the cauldron below. I followed about twenty yards behind. Spectators sardonically known as vultures hovered on a large rock above, but I never gave them a glance. Big waves, big holes, and big rocks constituted my singular view of the world. At the bottom of a steep, narrow channel called Turkey Shoot, I submerged in a cloud of violent foam and completed my third roll of the day just above a section of the rapid called Boulder Pile. If the name sounds intimidating, it should. Threading my way through the jagged rocks of Boulder Pile without incident, I joined Jonathan in calm water at the end. There we waited for our three counterparts who had the good judgment to scout the rapid resulting in calamity-free descents.

Below Cribworks, we continued through Class II/III Bonecrusher and Big Eddy Rapids followed by some play spots with excellent surfing opportunities to Big Ambejackwockamus Falls, a solid Class IV. Called Big A, the three-stage falls includes a near-river-wide keeper hole that has claimed lives. Passing just to the right of the invidious hydraulic, and boofing over a vertical

Chapter 28 - West Branch of the Penobscot

ledge landed us into a welcome eddy. Below Big A, entertaining Class II Horse Race Rapid flowed for 1.3 miles to Nesowadnehunk Deadwater.

After lunch at Nesowadnehunk Deadwater Campground, consequential Nesowadnehunk Falls was next on the agenda. A ten-foot drop into a violent hole followed by huge breaking waves that usually flip paddlers, the insouciant younger members of our group enjoyed multiple sorties down the dramatic falls.

Traveling farther downriver, the day culminated with some exhilarating Class IV paddling on Abol and Big Pockwockamus Falls. Both difficult, they are uniquely different. Steep and shallow Abol Falls requires deliberate navigation around a pair of unpleasant holes in the middle. Whereas, Big Pock is a long rapid mandating multiple maneuvers to avoid holes, pour overs, and breaking waves. Everyone had successful runs and no more rolling for me, always a good thing.

While tenting at a beautiful campsite on Nesowadnehunk Deadwater, dessert wars provided the evening entertainment. I brought a six-pack of cream horns, a banned substance where I live. Greg Winston challenged my claim to dessert supremacy with a huge, chocolate chip Whoopie Pie. However, the *piece de resistance* was Randy Berube's almost homemade, single crust blueberry pie. Randy had baked and baked, but had an assist using frozen blueberries and store-bought crust. He also knew how to intimidate the competition by showing up with a container the size of a shoe box that unfolds into a double-tiered table with a stove burner.

Fortified with the 10,000-calorie dessert, three of us decided to test our mountaineering skills on Mount Katahdin the following morning. Our intrepid trio represented the three primary stages of life: Dylan Brown – youth, Randy – middle age, and me – senility. Leaving before sunrise for Baxter State Park, we arrived at Roaring Brook Trailhead early in the morning. Hiking up Chimney Pond Trail, an old acquaintance was encountered who asked if Dylan was my grandson. Unarmed, I ignored the question.

Self-preservation dictated I assume control of the pace. After a couple of miles, we turned right onto the North Basin Cut-Off

Trail and traveled through a thick spruce forest to Hamlin Ridge Trail. Rising between the Chimney Pond cirque and North Basin, Hamlin Ridge is a spectacular, majestic ascent. Breathtaking alpine views continued for much of the remainder of the day. Crossing over Hamlin Peak, our journey persisted descending to the Saddle and then climbing steeply to Baxter Peak, the high point in Maine.

A final decision on traversing Knife Edge had been postponed until the wind conditions could be assessed at the summit. They were benign which facilitated a glorious crossing. After scrambling precipitously to the top of Pamola Peak, a much-needed respite ensued. Here, senility trumped my dubious leadership skills. I missed the Helon Taylor Trail, erroneously guiding us down Dudley Trail instead. There is a silver lining in every cloud. Descending the Dudley Trail provided Dylan with an opportunity to climb to the very tip of Pinnacle Rock for an obligatory photo op. I stopped shimmying up that daunting, attenuated boulder about forty years ago. After a refreshing water break at Chimney Pond, our truly remarkable surf and turf weekend concluded with an easy hike down Chimney Pond Trail to Roaring Brook. I noticed Dylan was limping on the way out. Yes!

THINGS TO KNOW

Location: Piscataquis County, north-central Maine

Length: Approximately eleven miles for the described paddle. The Golden Road parallels this section of the Penobscot River and there are multiple opportunities to set up shuttles in order to drive around flatwater sections or shorten trips. A frequent PPCS day trip begins at McKay Station in the morning ending at Nesowadnehunk Deadwater for lunch, about six miles. In the afternoon, we often drive to Abol Bridge and complete the approximately 2.5-mile Abol and Pockwockamus Falls section. Reversing the sequence is also a common stratagem.

Chapter 28 - West Branch of the Penobscot

Difficulty ratings and water levels:
    Release 2000 to 2400 CFS: Rip Gorge and Cribworks – Class IV/V and below Class II, III & IV
    Release 2400 to 3000 CFS: Rip Gorge and Cribworks – Class IV/V and below Class II, III & IV
    Release above 3000 CFS: Rip Gorge and Cribworks – Class V and below Class II, III & IV+

Scouting:
    Scout Rip Gorge from the cliffs above at McKay Station on river right
    Scout Cribworks from Vulture Rock on river left
    Scout Big A on river right. Have a definite plan for avoiding the keeper hole.
    Scout Nesowadnehunk Falls on river left
    Scout Abol Falls on river right
    Scout Big Pockwockamus Falls on river right

If paddlers have any doubts after scouting, the following portages are strongly recommended:
    It is possible to lower boats down a slide below Exterminator and Staircase in Rip Gorge.
    Portage Cribworks on river left
    Portage Big A on river right
    Portage Nesowadnehunk Falls on river left
    Portage Abol Falls on river right or left
    Portage Big Pock on river right

Release Information: Flow information is available from April 1 through October 15. Call Waterline hotline at 1-800-452-1737. At the prompt, dial in the six digit site code: 234114. Beware that water levels change without notice.

Shuttle: There is no shuttle service on the West Branch of the Penobscot. The Golden Road parallels the river and setting up private shuttles at various locations is quite easy.

Camping and other accommodations:
Chewonki Big Eddy Cabins & Campground: https://bigeddy.chewonki.org/
    Abol Bridge Campground: http://abolcampground.com/

Abol Pines State Campsite: On river left below Abol Bridge
Nesowadnehunk Deadwater State Campsite: On river right below Horse Race Rapid
Numerous motels and inns are located in the Millinocket area.

Unique potential hazards: The West Branch is very challenging at all levels. The rapids are often long and extended dangerous swims are possible. It's located in a remote area. Paddlers should expect rescue will be difficult and time consuming. Injury, death, and loss of boats are real possibilities. It is strongly recommended paddlers travel with an experienced group of West Branch veterans. Runs on Rip Gorge, Cribworks, Big A, Abol Falls, and Big Pockwockamus Falls are not recommended unless paddlers have a reliable roll.

Baxter State Park Information: See an alternative to winter in Baxter State Park at the end of Chapter 1.

Directions: To reach the take out for the lower section (Abol and Big Pockwockamus Falls), from the junction of Routes 11 and 157 in Millinocket, turn right onto Katahdin Avenue, keep straight at .2 mile on Bates Street, at .8 mile the road changes to Millinocket Lake Road, at 6.4 miles road changes to Millinocket Road, at 1.2 miles road changes to Millinocket Lake Road, at 5.7 miles turn left on Golden Road, at .7 mile turn right on Golden Road, at 4.5 miles arrive at Abol Bridge. Return on the Golden Road for a short distance to Nevers Corner Road on the right. Follow the rough dirt road for 1.5 miles to a short path on the right that leads to the water. That is the take out. To launch for the lower section, return and cross Abol Bridge, turn left, and immediately carry boats to the river. To reach Nesowadnehunk Deadwater, continue west on the Golden Road for about 4 miles to the parking area and campground on the right. McKay Station is about 6 miles further west on the Golden Road on the right. A sign marks the entrance to the parking area. Unless the gate is open, paddlers will have to carry boats down to the put-in.

Chapter 28 - West Branch of the Penobscot

A kayaker runs the cribworks on the West Branch of the Penobscot.
(Photo – Phyllis Wheaton)

Chapter 29 - Canada Falls on South Branch of the Penobscot

Mercurial Canada Falls

Contrary to its name, Canada Falls is not located in Canada. However, it's not far away as it is situated northeast of Jackman in a remote area just a few miles east of the Canadian border. Actually a 3.5-mile section of the South Branch of the Penobscot River, it is referred to as Canada Falls by virtually everyone in the paddling community. The reason is simple: an abundance of exciting whitewater compressed into that short segment of river.

Generally considered the authority on all things whitewater, the American Whitewater Association rates Canada Falls Class III/V; Class V is deemed the most difficult level navigable. I call it one of the most challenging whitewater descents this old man is still attempting.

Canada Falls Dam at the outlet of Canada Falls Lake controls the flow of water. As a result of licensing negotiations with paddling representatives, the dam operator Brookfield Renewable Energy is required to provide releases most Saturdays during the summer, pool levels on the lake permitting. Specified flows vary from 500 to 750 cubic feet per second (CFS), higher levels being more difficult.

My Canada Falls escapades began nearly 30 years ago, and the thrills and spills continue to the present. A few years ago, I organized a Penobscot Paddle & Chowder Society (PPCS) trip on Canada Falls subsequently christened "A Day at the Beach." What does one do at the beach? Swim! A large group had joined me, eighteen to be precise, and the water level was unexpectedly high resulting in a considerable amount of what paddlers call "river carnage." Multiple swims occurred at each of the most hazardous rapids: Slide Falls, Cabin Rapid, Upper Split Decision, and Lower

Chapter 29 - Canada Falls on South Branch of the Penobscot

Split Decision. An almost river wide keeper hole at the bottom of Cabin Rapid recirculated two paddlers for what seemed an eternity before they were thankfully regurgitated still breathing but exhausted.

Recently, two paddling friends announced a Canada Falls trip. Recalling "A Day at the Beach," I verified the discharge would be 600 CFS, a medium level. Eight kayakers and a canoeist constituted our group.

Getting to Canada Falls is an ambitious undertaking. A four-hour drive from central Maine, the last portion is on rough logging roads to the takeout near Pittston Farm, a historic logging community. From there, one must travel on North Maine Woods controlled lands to a launch site below Canada Falls Dam. Gaining access through the gated entrance is a tediously slow process requiring completion of paperwork and payment of fees. Good news: old people get in free!

The first few rapids were routinely stimulating but pushier than anticipated. I suspected the water level was higher than 600 CFS. As we arrived at imposing Slide Falls, an explosive wave and undulating boil menacingly awaited at the bottom. The falls usually randomly select a couple of victims for a bumpy upside-down shallow water experience in the run out. Some misadventures were encountered but no carnage.

Cabin Rapid was the next difficult falls on the agenda. The complex descent requires maneuvering to a wearisome micro eddy on river right followed by an awkward ferry above the intimidating keeper hole to river left. I botched the ferry. Only an infrequent geriatric adrenaline rush avoided calamity.

The ensuing sector was a continuum of steep, technical falls with few opportunities to regroup. Everyone had successful plummets down Upper Split Decision. Rarely does an excursion on Canada Falls end without someone involuntarily leaving their boat. Our good fortune ended on Lower Split Decision. Guardedly approaching a horizon line adjacent to a boulder pile, one kayaker accidentally tumbled into an unforgiving hole next to an immutable rock wall. After several herculean but abortive attempts to roll, he departed his boat bounding over shallow ledges downstream. Numerous members of the group were required to affect a difficult rescue of kayaker, paddle, and craft. Fortuitously, nothing was damaged but his pride.

After completing the exciting voyage, the actual flow was confirmed to be almost 750 CFS instead of the 600 scheduled. While this may not seem significant to the uninitiated, safety is an important reason for the precisely negotiated levels. I have driven to Canada Falls for a scheduled 500 release and found none despite plentiful water. On "A Day at the Beach," 600 CFS was promised but a formidable 1200 delivered. No advance notice was provided regarding any of those changes even though a communication mechanism is readily available. Their inexplicable behavior begs the question, who is making the decisions at Brookfield Renewable Energy and why?

Will I paddle Canada Falls again? Probably! "Never gonna grow up."

THINGS TO KNOW

Location: Somerset County, northwestern Maine
Length: Approximately 3.5 miles
Difficulty ratings and water levels:
  Release levels 500 to 750 CFS: Class III/ IV+
  Release levels over 750 CFS: Class III/V
Scouting: Setting up safety with throw bags recommended at all scouting locations

Scout Slide Falls from river right. The falls are located just below a small island.

Scout Cabin Rapid from river left. Have a definite plan to avoid the keeper hole at bottom.

Scout Upper Split Decision from river left.

Scout Lower Split Decision from river left.

If paddlers have any doubts after scouting, the following portages are strongly recommended:

Portage Slide Falls on river right.

Chapter 29 - Canada Falls on South Branch of the Penobscot

Portage Cabin Rapid on river left.
Portage Upper Split Decision on river left.
Portage Lower Split Decision on river left.

Fees: See North Maine Woods website for fees: https://www.northmainewoods.org/information/fees.html

Release information: Brookfield Renewable Energy operates Canada Falls Dam and publishes the release schedule each year. The PPCS includes the schedule in its annual Trip Book published each spring. Flow information is also available by calling Waterline hotline at 1-800-452-1737. At the prompt, dial in the six digit site code: 235119. Inexplicably, the published release information has not been reliable in recent years.

Shuttle: There is no shuttle service for Canada Falls. Private shuttles are required on the rough roads .

Camping and other accommodations:
Pittston Farm: http://www.pittstonfarm.com/
Seboomook Wilderness Campground: https://seboomookwildernesscampground.com/
Wilderness campsites at Canada Falls Dam
Numerous motels and inns are located in the Jackman and Rockwood areas

Unique potential hazards: Canada Falls is very challenging at all levels. Many of the rapids are difficult and dangerous swims are possible. It's located in a remote area and largely inaccessible. Paddlers should expect rescue will be extremely difficult and time consuming. Injury, death, and loss of boats are real possibilities. It is strongly recommended that paddlers travel with an experienced group of Canada Falls veterans. A reliable roll should be considered a prerequisite.

Directions: From the junction of US Route 201 and Maine Routes 15 and 6 in Jackman, drive east on 15/6 for 13.5 miles to Demo Road on the left. Follow the rough dirt Demo Road for 14.6 miles to Northern Road. Turn left onto Northern Road and drive 11.5 miles to a bridge over the South Branch of the Penobscot River. After crossing the bridge, the take out and a parking area are on the immediate left. To reach the put-in, turn left out of the parking area and continue to the nearby North Maine Woods gate. After signing in and paying the fee, travel a short distance and take the first left turn onto a very rough dirt road. Drive about 3 miles to the put-in and parking area on the left.

A canoeist enters the Slide on Canada Falls. (Photo – Ron Chase)

Chapter 30 - Orbeton Stream

Misadventures on Orbeton Stream

Arguably the best whitewater run in Maine, Orbeton Stream flows from Redington Pond beneath the slopes of Saddleback Mountain tumbling southeasterly into the Sandy River near Phillips. From the normal put-in on rugged Potato Hill Road, it's a short five miles of continuous Class II, III, IV & V whitewater to Reed's Mill Bridge and another three miles of easier rapids to Toothaker Pond Road Bridge shortly before joining Sandy River.

The exciting voyage begins with about two miles of tight, technical non-stop Class II/III rapids with a moderate to steep gradient before reaching Grisham Falls. Since it is a precipitous, twisting, boulder-strewn cataract pockmarked with holes, I rate Grisham Falls Class V. At the end, the current flows directly into a large, jagged rock which obstructs most of the channel. I've watched many good boaters flip, roll, or swim after meeting up with Grisham's unforgiving rock, and have had my share of collisions and underwater misadventures there. Grisham becomes more difficult and a lot less appealing at lower levels when most boaters practice their portage slalom skills, hiking through a troublesome boulder pile on river right. A short distance below, Perham Stream enters on the left.

Acquiring additional volume and encountering a steeper gradient after Perham, the character of the stream changes becoming almost uninterrupted Class IV whitewater until Reed's Mill Bridge - making it Class IV/V at most water levels. A mile below Perham, the main current flows to the right of an island and First Island Rapid begins. A succession of steep attenuated drops, First Island is as close to Maryland's renowned Upper Yough in difficulty and character as anything I've experienced in Maine. Bouncing from eddy to eddy, paddlers must boat scout their way through the maze. Peering over the edge of horizon lines, punching through holes, and boofing over rocks, catching the next eddy for a moment's respite—all are essential before plummeting further downward. Eddies are small and turbulent, mandating invocation of the one boat per eddy rule allowing little opportunity to commiserate with fellow paddlers. Shortly after, Second Island Rapid begins on the left. The longest, steepest, and narrowest falls on the river, I rate it Class IV/V. A five-stage drop filled with holes and inconveniently located rocks, there is little room for error. Although I've witnessed such attempts, backwards is not the recommended technique. The next major obstacle is Bridge Rapid, not as intimidating as Second Island—the labyrinth of massive boulders makes it very difficult to find unimpeded routes.

Passing under Reed's Mill Bridge, I've generally exhausted my daily ration of adrenaline. Fortunately for us elderly folks, calmer waters await. Following some Class II rapids, the river turns abruptly left and the paddler confronts a long, moderately steep boulder garden with no obvious route. Normally the best option is to negotiate through the rocks to far river left where a very narrow channel avoids the worst of the congestion. Easier rapids and a fast current carry one to a significant ledge drop with some nasty holes that can be avoided by aggressively paddling down a tongue left center. From there, quick water flows to the lower takeout.

Short of standing on the bridge staring down at the painted gauge on the lower left abutment in Reed's Mill, determining the Orbeton Stream water level is an imprecise exercise in gauge extrapolation. Most regular Orbsters use the online USGS Sandy River gauge at Madrid (pronounced *MAD-Drid*) as an indicator of the probable water level. If the online gauge is between 100 and 400 cubic feet per second (CFS), Orbeton is probably runnable. However, depending on whether or not the water is rising, falling, or the Orb is feeling contrary, it could be as low as 1.0 or high as 4.5 on the gauge when actually arriving at Reed's Mill Bridge. Not a service available to everyone, I use the "Ask Randy" method. If my friend Randy Berube says it's runnable, it usually is. In my opinion, the optimum level is between 1.25 and 2.5. Lower levels

Chapter 30 - Orbeton Stream

become increasingly scratchy and the steep drops can be very tight, bumpy, boat (or body) beaters, particularly Grisham Falls. Because much of the Orb has a creek-like character; higher levels get pushy and, at some personally subjective point, the fun ends and survival begins.

Almost every day on the Orb there is a story to tell and I've had many memorable experiences. Perhaps the most remarkable run of Grisham Falls I've witnessed was when teenage Amanda Shorette vanquished the intimidator. Possessing modest skills, I fully expected Mandy would take the hike on river right. Instead, she pushed aggressively between approach boulders, punched a couple of holes in the narrow entrance slot, and ran up onto Grisham Rock. The unforgiving obstacle catapulted her backwards violently slamming her kayak against the rock wall on river left. Abruptly flipping onto a downstream rock, she attempted several rolls before coming up with a smile. Impressive would be a serious understatement.

Several years ago, First Island Rapid was the scene of an extended river misadventure and rescue. Morrill Nason, the legendary Waterman, was shredding with my wife Nancy. Missing a must catch eddy about halfway through the falls and crashing into an immoveable rock, they flipped. Shredders don't move rocks or roll. Not surprisingly, a concerted effort to rescue Nancy immediately ensued, leaving The Waterman floating downriver largely ignored. Randy and I caught up with her clinging to a rock precariously located above a steep ledge descent with a very unpleasant-looking hydraulic directly beneath. From a boulder about 40 feet upstream on river left, a throw bag was tossed to her with very basic instructions, "Once we start pulling, don't let go, no matter what." Pulling with all of the power we could muster, she was completely submerged until safely reaching our grasp. After salvaging the shredder, somebody remembered The Waterman who was impatiently waiting wrapped on his own rock farther downstream. A second rescue was belatedly affected.

Easily my most memorable day on Orbeton began on a warm sunny morning in April 1994. We were a group of five canoeists:

Brent Elwell, Doug Field, Colby Libby, the late Ted Lombard, and me. A different paddling era, back then, real men and real women paddled real canoes, not the mamby-pamby, microscopic present-day canyaks. Our smallest boat was a 12-foot beast, considered tiny at the time. Just back from a successful whitewater trip in the southeastern United States, I was feeling cocky. That would soon come to an abrupt halt.

The Reed's Mill gauge was running high and rising. In assessing upstream conditions, I observed substantial snowpack and some remaining ice shelves along the shore. Using a convoluted form of misguided group think, our injudicious band decided to attempt what we believed then (and I've never heard it contradicted) a first descent of Perham Stream.

Beginning in East Madrid about a mile before converging with Orbeton, a multitude of strainers and a large logjam were immediately confronted necessitating a portage along the steep, narrow creek. Progressing downstream, the intensity increased as the turbulent mountain freshet was extremely tight and precipitous. Probing a long, narrow decline, Brent jumped from his boat and frantically signaled me to move hard left. Only making it part way, I was upside down tumbling downstream on submerged rocks. A fistful of bloody knuckles was the price for rolling up. The experience foreshadowed the remainder of the day.

Above us, the weather was not cooperating. Temperatures rose dramatically, a violent thunderstorm developed with a continuous downpour, and the water level started rising dramatically. Scouting the last rapid at the confluence with Orbeton, we concluded there was no safe route. All of us walked except Ted, who had a phenomenal run in his 13-foot Mohawk Canoe. A perfectionist, Ted had the most precise paddling skills I've ever observed. I swear he could run Magic Falls on Maine's Kennebec River punching the hole with three paddle strokes. Typically, he'd flip and roll if there was a large, fawning audience.

Orbeton Stream was no longer a stream, rather a raging torrent. Besides lightning, thunder, and pouring rain, the fog was so thick only a few feet of visibility remained. Doug rammed into a

Chapter 30 - Orbeton Stream

rock and dragged his boat off the river. Somehow, Colby got ashore after swimming. Brent came out of his canoe and swam at First Island Rapid. Remarkably he managed to self-rescue hauling his boat up onto a steep snowbank. Although the others could be heard yelling, Ted and I lost sight of everyone continuing our perilous descent. Somewhere in First Island Rapid, my boat swamped. Grabbing a tree branch with one hand, I bailed with the other. Shortly after leaving the unstable eddy, a large hole again filled my canoe. This time there was no branch to grab. Plowing awkwardly downstream in a 400-pound unmanageable barge, I flipped in Second Island Rapid. Missing a roll, I jumped ship fearing a long upside-down journey that might not end until Reed's Mill Bridge or beyond. My boat continued without me. As I staggered in a couple of feet of wet snow, Ted could be heard yelling that he was stuck in a hole and needed help. Responding that I couldn't see him and didn't have a throw bag, a harsh invective was his retort – then silence.

Toiling in the deep snow, I stumbled into Doug and Brent. A little later, Colby was encountered singlehandedly towing his canoe and mine. Converging on Reed's Mill Bridge, the fate of our remaining companion was paramount in our minds. Much to our surprise, the perfectionist was still in his boat coolly relaxed in an eddy below the bridge searching for the gauge. A futile endeavor, the gauge was completely underwater. Our best guestimate is that it was at least six feet and climbing!

Exhausted as darkness approached, this was a day in which wisdom and common sense were scarce commodities. For inexplicable reasons that escape me now—perhaps it was a case of dueling bad judgment—Brent, Ted, and I decided to continue to the Toothaker Pond Road takeout. Doug and Colby would pick us up. Persisting downstream with minimal daylight, we skirted big waves in what is usually a boulder-strewn rapid. Soon after, it was dark. Huddling close together as the flooded stream propelled us rapidly along, our game plan was simple: when the roar of falls could be heard we'd pull out and drag around. Finally, something went right.

I've returned to Orbeton many times since, never once failing to pause and recall the exploits and mishaps of that day—not just our misadventures but Ted's truly remarkable open-boat success in the fog during a storm with the level over 6 feet. It was probably his finest paddle. Sadly, he died a young man in his early thirties later that year. Nowadays, when I get to Reed's Mill Bridge, if the water level is over 3 feet, I walk away.

THINGS TO KNOW

Location: Franklin County, western Maine

Length: Upper section from Potato Hill Road to Reed's Mill Bridge approximately 5 miles. About 3 more miles to Toothaker Pond Road Bridge

Difficulty ratings and water levels:
  Gauge reading up to 3.0: Class IV+
  Gauge reading over 3.0: Class IV/V

Scouting: Setting up safety with throw bags recommended at both scouting locations
  Scout Grisham Falls on river right.
  Scout Second Island Falls from river left.
  Boat Scout First Island Falls from eddies. The rapid is too long for land scouting.

If paddlers have any doubts after scouting, the following portages are strongly recommended:
Scout Bridge Rapid from the take out before beginning the paddle. If it causes heartburn, paddle somewhere else.
  Portage Grisham Falls on river right.
  Portage Second Island on river left.

Determining water levels: Visit USGS Maine Streamflow online: https://waterdata.usgs.gov/me/nwis/current/?type=flow. If the Sandy River Madrid gauge is 100 to 400 CFS, Orbeton may be at a runnable level. Drive to Reed's Mill Bridge and view the painted gauge on the lower left bridge abutment for the actual level.

Chapter 30 - Orbeton Stream

Unique potential hazards: Orbeton Stream is very challenging at all levels. Almost continuous, many of the rapids are difficult and dangerous swims are possible. It's located in a remote area and largely inaccessible. Paddlers should expect rescue will be extremely difficult and time consuming. Injury, death, and loss of boats are real possibilities. It is strongly recommended that paddlers travel with an experienced group of Orbeton Stream veterans. A reliable roll should be considered a prerequisite.

Directions: From the junction of US Route 2 and Maine Routes 4 and 27 in Farmington, drive north for 2.5 miles on 4 and 27. Bear left onto Route 4 and continue for about 23 miles to Reeds Mill Road in Madrid. Turn right onto Reeds Mill Road and drive about 5 miles to Reeds Mill Bridge over Orbeton Stream. This is the takeout for the upper section. To reach the Toothaker Pond Road takeout, continue south on Reeds Mill Road for a short distance, turn right on Fish Hatchery Road, and drive about 1.5 miles to Toothaker Pond Road. Turn right onto Toothaker Pond Road and continue for about a mile to the bridge over Orbeton Stream. This is the lower takeout. To reach the put-in for the upper section from Reeds Mill Bridge, continue south on Reeds Mill Road for about 2 miles to Bray Hill Road. Turn left onto Bray Hill and drive about 1 mile to East Madrid Road. Turn left onto East Madrid Road and follow for about 2.5 miles to East Madrid. Cross the bridge over Perham Stream and continue for about .5 mile to Potato Hill Road on the left. Follow Potato Hill Road for about 1.5 miles to a bridge over Orbeton Stream. The put-in is just before the bridge on the left. Beware, sections of the Reed's Mill Road are often in poor condition and the Potato Hill Road is an unplowed snowmobile trail in the winter, often impassable until late spring. For the truly determined, pulling boats down the Potato Hill Road on the snow is an option.

Kayakers navigate Bridge Rapid on Orbeton Stream. (Photo – Ken Gordon)

Chapter 31 - Webb River

Weaving the Webb

Hidden away in the rural community of Carthage, except for locals Webb River is relatively unknown. Three exceptions are whitewater boaters, avid fishermen, and Russ.

Each spring, scores of enthusiastic paddlers converge on the Webb as soon as ice is out for some excellent Class II/III whitewater. A free-flowing river, it's unique in that a comparatively large watershed keeps water levels elevated long after other mountain freshets are impassably low.

I first "discovered" the Webb in the spring of 1989. The late Terry Tzovarras and I were returning from paddling exploits on Sandy River. Traveling south from Weld on Route 142, we crossed a bridge over an engaging stretch of whitewater. Shortly after, two more appealing rapids appeared beside the road. Promptly halting our journey, a shuttle was arranged and our first descent accomplished. I've been hooked ever since, completing at least one hundred outings.

This spring has been an exceptional one even for the Webb. Regular rainstorms and heavy snowpack have kept it at a runnable level for virtually the entire season. As usual, my outdoor club, the Penobscot Paddle and Chowder Society, scheduled a couple of trips. Wallowing in my unrestrained semi-retirement status, that was insufficient for me.

I have a wild card, my old friend Russ Moody. If I qualify for Webb Head status, Russ is the Webb River god. On a recent trip, I asked how many times he'd paddled it. He paused for a moment and responded, "So many times, I don't know…hundreds for sure."

Not only does the prolific Mr. Moody paddle the Webb but he's the unofficial caretaker. He and Greg Hamilton painted a gauge on a bridge abutment at the bottom of Schoolhouse Rapid in the tiny hamlet of Berry Mills. Regularly used by paddlers and fishermen, the gauge is the primary indicator of conditions on the remainder of the river. When new obstructions and hazards materialize, they often miraculously disappear shortly after Russ detects them.

The U.S. Geological Survey (USGS) maintains gauges on many rivers and streams throughout the country and readings are available online. Apparently unaware of the Webb's significance, they've omitted that important waterway. However, I have a system. If the online gauges for nearby Sandy and Swift Rivers are high, history tells me the Webb will soon follow.

When indications are positive, my next step is to text Russ. This may be a shocking revelation for some as my reputation as a technology resistant Luddite is notorious. In fact, I only recently learned what a text was. That people actually send and receive them while driving is both amazing and frightening. If something is important enough, I adapt. Russ told me the quickest most efficient way to reach him is by text, so that's what I do, hoping of course he's not driving when responding. Not much of a typist with my thumbs, I write something like, "Webb today at 11?" A man of many words, his response is normally, "OK."

Russ and I have completed that ritual five times this spring. We're not wearing the river out and both agree our durable plastic kayaks will outlive us. We may be wearing ourselves out. Not youngsters, he's one of the few people I boat with older than I am. I sometimes worry that when we're observed paddling, witnesses may suspect we're escapees from a local nursing home and report us to the geriatric police. When the river is at flood, dementia might be their concern which could prompt a Silver Alert.

Our most recent outing on the Webb was typical. A beautiful sunny day, we met at the traditional takeout next to the last rapid, the very same spot where Terry and I left a vehicle over 30 years ago. Commenting that the actual water level was higher than anticipated, we detected a few obnoxious blackflies but they weren't biting. "It won't be long," Russ commented. Leaving his car, we

Chapter 31 - Webb River

drove a short four miles north and carried our kayaks through the woods for about 200 yards to a steep narrow rapid.

That's where the entertainment began. The Webb is a continuum of fun rapids. Both of us commenced the paddle by surfing a wave on the first falls. Dodging rocks and surfing more waves two old men tumbled through a series of narrow Class II/III rapids to the Route 142 Bridge. Easier whitewater followed to a location where a large fallen tree blocked most of the channel, forcing a difficult maneuver through alders on the far right to avoid it.

From there quick water meandered circuitously through a pasture. Just below a small bridge, a steep rapid angled right followed by another precipitous drop where the current flushed through a strainer and pillowed up against a large boulder midstream mandating a determined move left. Below, an ancient motorboat that high water had flushed downriver from Webb Lake was nestled in a stand of bushes on the right. Shortly after, where the river flows under a canopy of hardwoods, the most entertaining wave surfing of the day ensued.

Traversing through a long falls and more play spots brought us to four consecutive rapids that collectively constitute the most difficult whitewater on the river, normally Class III+ but more demanding in high water. The second drop necessitated maneuvering through a maze of boulders before executing an extreme right turn at the bottom to avoid a large hole. The fourth falls, Schoolhouse Rapid, required negotiating around several holes before passing under the bridge at Berry Mills. The gauge read .5, a medium low level.

Beyond Berry Mills, the river separates into three narrow twisting channels that often accumulate debris. Carefully navigating through the right passage, we passed underneath a low hanging snowmobile bridge farther downstream. More quick water and some easy Class II paddling culminated with the final rapid, a technical Class III requiring several challenging maneuvers.

When finished, Russ retrieved his rod and began fishing. He doesn't keep the fish, taking nothing but satisfaction from the Webb.

As noted, my first Webb descent was with longtime friend Terry Tzovarras. He and I shared many outdoor adventures together canoeing and winter hiking. Unfortunately, he passed away in 2011. His always cheerful demeanor and colorful personality are very much missed.

THINGS TO KNOW

Location: Franklin County, western Maine
Length: Approximately 4.5 miles
Difficulty ratings and water levels:
    Gauge level -1.5 to 3.0: Class II/III
    Gauge level over 3.0: Class II/ III/IV
Gauge location: Driving north on Maine Route 142 in Berry Mills, take a right turn and cross a bridge over Webb River. Immediately turn right. The gauge is visible from the street on the lower river right bridge abutment.

Scouting and portages: Rapids on the Webb are not normally land scouted or portaged. Boat scouting is recommended to ensure that whitewater is free of hazards. The rapids at the takeout and above the bridge in Berry Mills are indicative of the difficulty level. When in doubt, paddlers should get out of their boats and scout or portage.

Determining water levels: Visit USGS Maine Streamflow online:
    https://waterdata.usgs.gov/me/nwis/current/?type=flow.
If the Sandy River Madrid gauge is over 200 CFS and the Swift River gauge is over 700 CFS, Webb River will probably be a medium low level in the 0 to .5 range on the painted gauge. This extrapolation is more accurate in the spring.

Shuttle: There is no shuttle service for Webb River. Easy private shuttles on paved roads are required.

Chapter 31 - Webb River

Unique potential hazards: Webb River is challenging at all levels. Many rapids are moderately difficult and dangerous swims are possible. The Webb is notorious for collecting strainers and other hazards. Their locations and frequency cannot be predicted. Injury, death, and loss of boats are real possibilities. It is strongly recommended that new paddlers travel with an experienced Webb River veteran.

Directions: From the junction of US Route 2 and Maine Route 142 in Dixfield, drive north on Route 142 for about 7 miles to a bridge crossing over Webb River. Continue for a short distance to wide dirt shoulder on the right next to a rapid. That is the normal takeout. To reach the put-in, follow Route 142 north for 3.5 miles through Berry Mills to the remnants of an old road on the left that leads to the river. There is space to park vehicles next to the road.

A kayaker paddles a rapid on Webb River. (Photo – Ron Chase)

Chapter 32 - Ducktrap River

Stalking the Duck

How do you know you're paddling Ducktrap River? The weather is lousy. Inclement weather seems to be an inherent part of the Ducktrap experience and it's not a coincidence. Water levels rise and fall rapidly on the tiny Lincolnville body of water mystifyingly called a "river." Hence, the opportunity for a quality whitewater adventure is generally near the end of a significant rain event.

When heavy rains occur, a small subculture of "river rats" start watching gauges to determine when their favorite whitewater river or stream has increased to an advantageous volume. My primary sources for gauge information are American Whitewater and USGS websites. As water measurements climb and choices increase, a whirlwind of emails and phone calls follow; as rats debate the options and lobby for their preference.

In the weather according to Ron, early November is often a time of heavy rains. That was true again this fall. Several storms dumped copious amounts of precipitation on our area. Because the Duck has a minuscule watershed, it peaks earlier than most rivers and drops just as dramatically. In short, the window of opportunity is very narrow.

Recently, during the morning of a substantial deluge, an online inspection of the Ducktrap USGS gauge indicated it was a respectable 150 cubic feet per second (CFS) and surging upward. A Duck devotee for several decades, I began advocating for an afternoon voyage on the elusive whitewater gem. Four friends with the Penobscot Paddle and Chowder Society responded to the call. A trip was on!

Several factors make the Duck a compelling paddling encounter. Tumbling down a bucolic valley that approaches gorge status

Chapter 32 - Ducktrap River

shortly before reaching the sea, it is one of the few Maine whitewater streams flowing directly into the ocean. The escapade includes a significant Class IV waterfall and about three miles of excellent whitewater.

Our intrepid band met in stormy weather at the seawall takeout in Lincolnville where the Duck joins Penobscot Bay. There are two primary launches – a seven-mile descent from Route 52 or a shorter version beginning at Tanglewood Camps about three miles downstream. Since most of the whitewater is below Tanglewood and conditions were typically atrocious, the abbreviated alternative was chosen. Epitomizing whitewater diversity, we were a variety of crafts – two kayaks, a canoe, and a two-person inflatable vessel called a shredder. An elderly cold water sissy, I wore a dry suit to protect aging bones from the elements. My younger tougher companions survived quite nicely sporting damp colder wetsuits. The mere fact they're called wetsuits explains my dry suit preference.

Tanglewood Camps is a boater friendly place. A 4H Camp and Learning Center, Tanglewood is operated by the University of Maine Cooperative Extension. For decades, they've graciously allowed access to the Duck whenever road conditions permitted.

We departed from a cove adjacent to the camp; the weather was typically Duck-like, rain, wind, and fog. Beginning in calm water, we passed under a snowmobile bridge and immediately portaged around debris and trees blocking passage. Called strainers in the vernacular of the whitewater world, blow downs are always a potential hazard on the attenuated twisting waterway. Shortly after, Kendall Stream entered on the left. During our excursion, the USGS gauge averaged 200 CFS. Since the gauge is located upriver on a Route 52 bridge abutment, side streams below raised the actual flow experienced to an estimated 350 CFS.

Around the bend, the excitement began. The first rapids are the most challenging; a series of ledge drops progressing in difficulty to Class III just before plunging over Twitchell Pitch. American Whitewater rates Twitchell Class V. It's not that demanding but certainly Class IV. Since the approach is a horizon line, I always pull off to scout and take safety precautions. Stopping isn't easy as paddlers must catch a tiny eddy on river left in turbulent water immediately above the falls. Our group successfully executed the precarious maneuver. After scouting and discussing the best route for negotiating the perilous pitch, two participants were posted with throw bags at the bottom and a cameraman midway. Excellent runs were executed by all, followed by the usual triumphant exaltations.

Below the pitch over two miles of continuous Class II whitewater provided an excellent opportunity to experiment with various paddling techniques, particularly wave surfing. Unwanted rescue practice interfered with our agenda when one member of the group flipped and was unable to roll in the shallow fast-moving current. Following a substantial effort, boat and paddler were reunited, but his paddle was lost. Fortunately, the shredder carried a spare.

Finishing the rapids, we passed under the unique two-tiered Ducktrap Bridge in heavy fog and navigated across a pool that may be the source of the moniker "ducktrap" to the seawall takeout. If there aren't cold gusty winds blowing at the takeout, you haven't been paddling the Duck.

THINGS TO KNOW

Location: Waldo County, mid-coast Maine
Length: Approximately 3.5 miles from Tanglewood Camps and 7 miles from Route 52
Difficulty ratings and water levels:
Gauge level 125 CFS to 400 CFS: Class II/IV
Gauge level over 400 CFS: Class III/IV+
Gauge location: From the junction of Maine Routes 52 and 173 in Lincolnville Center travel about 4 miles east on 52 to a bridge over Ducktrap River. The gauge is on the lower left bridge abutment. There is a small turnoff for those who want to launch there.

Chapter 32 - Ducktrap River

Scouting and portages: Twitchell Pitch should be scouted or portaged on river left. After passing Kendall Brook on river left, navigate through a series of Class II/III rapids. As the intensity and difficulty increases, move hard left and catch a small eddy. This is a difficult maneuver that needs to be anticipated. Scout or portage the pitch before deciding to run the falls. Boat scouting other rapids to ensure they are free of hazards is recommended.

Determining water levels: Visit USGS Maine Streamflow online: https://waterdate.usgs.gov/me/nwls/current/?type+flow. If the CFS is between 125 and 400, it should be a fun run. The river becomes progressively more difficult as the volume increases.

Shuttle: There is no shuttle service for the Duck. A relatively easy private shuttle is possible.

Unique potential hazards: Ducktrap River is challenging at all levels. Many rapids are moderately difficult and Twitchell Pitch is a Class IV (rated Class V by American Whitewater). Dangerous swims are possible. The Duck is notorious for collecting strainers and other hazards. Their locations and frequency cannot be predicted. Injury, death, and loss of boats are real possibilities. It is strongly recommended that new paddlers travel with an experienced Ducktrap River veteran and follow his or her lead to the eddy above Twitchell Pitch.

Directions:

Takeout: From the junction of US Route 1 and Maine Route 173 in Lincolnville, drive north on Route 1 for about 1.5 miles. Just before crossing the bridge over Ducktrap River, turn right onto Howe's Point Road and drive a short distance to the seawall parking area at the end.

Tanglewood Put-in: From the takeout, return to Route 1, turn left and then take the next right onto Ducktrap Road. Continue for about 1 mile to a right turn onto Tanglewood Road. Drive about 2 miles to the end. Park on the left near some camp buildings and carry boats on a path to the river. If the Tanglewood gate is closed, return and go to the Route 52 put-in.

Route 52 Put-in: Return to Ducktrap Road and turn right. Drive about .5 mile and turn right onto Slab City Road. Continue for about 4 miles to Route 52. Turn right and follow Route 52 for about 1.5 miles to Ducktrap River. There is a small parking area on the right after crossing over the river.

A kayaker descends Twitchell Pitch on Ducktrap River. (Photo – Ron Chase)

Chapter 33 - Gulf Hagas on West Branch of the Pleasant River

Falling for Gulf Hagas

Plunging into the foamy abyss, I immediately recognized trouble. Sinking deeper, I could feel my kayak being sucked into the backwash beneath the falls. My first thought, "I'm too old for this stuff."

Having just plummeted over twenty-foot Billings Falls, my plate was full. Counseling myself to roll, I tried and failed. A second attempt failed. The power of the hydraulic was so intense it was impossible to set up for a third, my paddle sinking straight down instead. Assuming more unsuccessful attempts would simply waste energy, bailing was my reluctant decision.

Yanking off my spray skirt, I forced myself out of the kayak. Swimming towards bottom, my goal was to reach the downstream current optimistically hoping it would propel me away from the hydraulic. The technique worked. Rising from darkness, rays of sunshine penetrated the water. My son Adam had jumped the falls just ahead of me. I hoped he'd be there when I surfaced. He was. A couple of strong swim strokes later, I was holding onto his kayak. Moments after, my boat and paddle flushed out from under the falls and the three of us were reunited on a ledge deep in Gulf Hagas Gorge.

There were five of us, four kids and myself. I say kids because one was my son and the other three were about his age. Catching my breath, I was reminded of the whitewater axiom, "There are old kayakers and bold kayakers, but no old bold kayakers." Disproving that adage became my goal.

Rick Hartley was next over the falls. Younger and stronger, he seemed to have a perfect line. Instant replay! Swallowed into the backwash, Rick thrashed wildly attempting multiple rolls. Another rescue was needed. Fortunately, Daryn Slover and Greg Winston had clean descents. Our third waterfall in less than a half mile, two more remained. Reportedly, the waterfalls were the easy part.

Located in south central Piscataquis County, Gulf Hagas is arguably the premier creek run in New England. The American Whitewater Association rates it Class V in difficulty. Gulf Hagas is actually the name of the gorge the West Branch of the Pleasant River flows through. Remarkably spectacular, it's often called the Grand Canyon of the East. We were too busy to enjoy the views.

The trail along the cliffs is an outstanding Maine wilderness trek. Ironically, the Gulf Hagas Rim Trail was one of the first family hikes Adam participated in when he was five. Trudging high above decades ago, kayaking waterfalls was beyond our wildest dreams. A lot has changed. On that trip, he was so tired I had to carry him out. Now, Adam had rescued me in the turbulent whitewater below.

Most kayakers use high volume creek boats to paddle Gulf Hagas. The four youngsters in our group had them, I didn't. Constantly compensating for the low volume stern on my Dagger RPM, I regretted the decision throughout the trip. As Adam says, "It's an old man's boat."

Gulf Hagas begins with a whimper, winding through a swampy section of flat water for about a mile and a half. Turning right around a small island, the character of the river transforms dramatically. Entering the first rapid called Stairs Falls, the water tumbles through a narrow ravine, over a vertical waterfall, and ends with a couple of complicated ledge drops. The lower end of Stairs Falls can be seen from the western terminus of Gulf Hagas Rim Trail. Soon after, a fourteen-foot waterfall charmingly called Faceplant Falls is encountered. Uneventful descents were completed by our crew as calm water above allowed maximizing boat speed, facilitating launches extending well over the rim. A safe landing at the foot of Faceplant is essential as Billings Falls is just below.

Normally, the strategy for successfully running a waterfall in a kayak is to generate enough velocity above the falls to clear any

Chapter 33 - Gulf Hagas on West Branch of the Pleasant River

backwash at the bottom. That is particularly difficult at Billings Falls as a complex maneuver is required just above the lip slowing the approach. Hence, the unplanned swims.

Below Billings, and out of view from the hiking trail, is the most dangerous rapid on the river called Amuck. Most paddlers portage the lower section laughingly proclaiming, "Don't run amuck." Our cautious choice was to carry right. The reason is simple. The steep, boulder-strewn descent constricts to just a few feet in width at the end, creating serious pinning potential. The fourth waterfall, Buttermilk Falls, is just below. Buttermilk is easier than it looks as kayakers are able to drive aggressively from right to left jumping most of the rocks and backwash directly below the nearly vertical decline.

After Buttermilk, a fairly long continuous section of steep narrow Class IV/V whitewater is engaged. The canyon in this sector is extremely constricted with vertical cliffs on both sides, making it difficult to scout from shore or for a boat-deprived kayaker to hike out. Consequently, careful boat scouting was our choice. Three rapids in particular warranted attention: Jaws, Turnstile, and Hammond Pitch. Jaws had been the scene of numerous misadventures and close calls, including a bow pin that nearly ended in tragedy. Recognizing the hazard, the menacing final pitch was carried. Turnstile is a multi-stage, narrow falls that looks like Jaws, but less constrained. Hammond Pitch, the last and easiest of the waterfalls, is a gentler version of Buttermilk. Shortly after, the difficulty level moderated until reaching the takeout.

Fortunately, after Billings Falls, our group did not suffer any further mishaps. Everyone acknowledged that it had been a very challenging day. Close calls had been numerous and several emergency rolls were necessary to avoid serious consequences.

Gulf Hagas had been a great adventure. Am I going back? Nope. I'm too old.

THINGS TO KNOW

Location: Piscataquis County, north central Maine

Length: Approximately 5 miles

Difficulty Rating: Class V
Gauge: The bridge abutment at the put-in is the gauge. Level with the abutment is medium, minus 5 inches minimum, and plus 8 inches probably maximum. It was medium for our trip.
Scouting and portages: Scouting Gulf Hagas is quite difficult but essential. On our trip, Stairs Falls was reconnoitered river left, Faceplant Falls river right, Billings Falls river right, portaged lower Amuck river right, scouted Buttermilk Falls river right, portaged lower Jaws river right, and boat scouted everything else. A case could be made for portaging everything but then why bother to paddle the river? When in doubt, paddlers should get out of their boats and scout or portage.
Shuttle: Private shuttles are necessary on old logging roads.
Unique potential hazards: Gulf Hagas is the most difficult and dangerous whitewater in this book. Almost continuous, many of the rapids and waterfalls are extremely hazardous. It's located in a remote area and largely inaccessible. Paddlers should expect rescue will be extremely difficult and time consuming. Injury, death, and loss of boats are real possibilities. Prior to deciding to paddle, hiking the Gulf Hagas Rim Trail is recommended. If you're not comfortable with the prospect of kayaking what you can see from the cliffs, don't go. What you can't see is more difficult. It is strongly recommended that paddlers go with an experienced group of Gulf Hagas veterans.
Directions: From Brownville Junction, drive 5 miles north on Maine Route 11 to Katahdin Iron Works Road on the left. Follow Katahdin Iron Works Road for 7 miles to the Katahdin Iron Works Gate and pay the fee. Continue on Katahdin Iron Works Road for about 7 miles to the Appalachian Trail and a large parking area. This is the takeout for the whitewater trip and the beginning of the Gulf Hagas Rim Trail. Follow Katahdin Iron Works Road for approximately 5 miles to a bridge over West Branch of the Pleasant River. This is the put-in.

Chapter 33 - Gulf Hagas on West Branch of the Pleasant River

A kayaker leaps Billings Falls on Gulf Hagas. (Photo – Daryn Slover)

Chapter 34 - Cathance River

Eggman Delivers on Cathance River

"*...Man, you should have seen them kicking Edgar Allen Poe, I am the Eggman...*" —The Beatles

The Cathance River is *my* river. Well, not really, but I like to think so. Unlike some places, in Maine you can't own a river or stream. If it's navigable, the public has right of passage and landowner boundaries are limited to the low water mark. Where is the low water mark, you ask? Good question. Safe to say if you're on a Maine river or stream in a kayak or canoe, you're legal – probably.

Located in my hometown of Topsham, the Cathance travels through a picturesque wilderness area, most of which cannot be accessed without hiking or paddling. Judging from the placid waters at the put-in and takeout, one would never guess that a whitewater gem blesses the unseen portion of this tumultuous four-mile stretch of water. Consisting of one long, technical rapid and five cataracts, the American Whitewater Association describes it as a Class III/IV creek with two Class V waterfalls.

Because it has a relatively large watershed for a small river, the Cat can often be paddled when others are too low. Spring is primetime. I regularly check the river level and my paddling buddies, particularly the younger ones, generally start calling about levels and anticipated ice-out in late February or early March.

A couple of years ago, my son and another young paddling friend, Ryan Galway, coaxed me into a late winter run, insisting ice was out – not exactly. Seal launching kayaks and canoes on a snowbank at the put-in, we broke through several stretches of ice with our paddles. Menacing, overhanging ice shelves on the rapids

Chapter 34 - Cathance River

added an extra level of intimidation. Despite the chilly conditions, a good time was had by all.

A painted gauge adorns the Interstate 295 bridge abutment at the put-in. Boating companions and I have paddled the river between 1.5 and 4.5 on the gauge. The low end is too bony and the escapade gets pushy and more dangerous over four feet.

Finding the Cat gauge a little over 2 feet earlier this spring, I called my paddling buddy, the Eggman. Why the Eggman? Sorry, you have to have a "need to know." He had been itching to run the Cat for a couple of years, but wanted a safe relatively easy level for his first descent. "This is your day," I announced to a skeptical Eggmeister. "It's the perfect *first-time* level with warm, sunny weather to scout the rapids."

Since the Eggman is exclusively an open-boater, I sweetened the proposal by promising to paddle my much maligned, battered, and bruised Mohawk Viper canoe. In order to keep it afloat, each spring I add another layer of Plumber's Goop to the many cracks and gouges. It's old and ugly, but serviceable – sort of like me.

The Eggman nailed a complex, circuitous line on the first rapid called Z Turn, catching a small eddy next to a nasty hole at the bottom of the descent. Styling, he negotiated the slot, avoided the undercut, and navigated through the boulder pile on the following three cataracts. No paddling on eggshells for the Eggster this day—he was on a roll.

The biggest, meanest falls on the excursion was next. Called Little Gorilla, or more euphemistically, Magic Carpet Ride, I rate it Class V. Careening through a narrow gorge, it begins with some precise obstacle dodging followed by a 90-degree left turn down a steep, shallow slide into a churning foam pile with boulders waiting just below the surface. Partway down the slide, an intimidating rock formation extends out from river left at head level, encouraging paddlers to stay right to avoid decapitation. While not technically difficult, the drop deserves respect. I watched my son flip upstream on the slide in a kayak, separating his shoulder. And, I've witnessed several near catastrophic collisions. The portage is dangerous, too. A friend cracked a rib slipping on icy rocks while carrying his kayak around the falls. I've never observed a canoe attempt Little Gorilla. Eggman and I carefully studied potential routes and decided not to tempt offending the river gods. Instead, we gambled on the portage. It's not hard to find, I've worn a fairly distinct path on river right.

The final falls is a somewhat easier version of Little Gorilla, but a more straight-forward, two-stage ledge drop that tumbles into a sticky hydraulic at the bottom. At most water levels, the line is right to left to right, blasting through some breaking waves, powering down the final slide, and punching the hole as far right as possible. Speed and angle are paramount. Several very good boaters have been turned sideways in the hydraulic, all swam. No problem for the Eggman, who delivered a perfect route and exited the hydraulic sunny-side up.

The debutante was now a certified Cathead. "…Goo goo g'joob…"

THINGS TO KNOW

Location: Sagadahoc County, mid-coast Maine
Length: Approximately 4 miles
Difficulty ratings and water levels:
    Gauge reading 1.5 to 4.0: Class III, IV, and V
    Gauge reading over 4.0: Class IV/V
Scouting: Scout Z Turn river right or left, First Drop river right, Second Drop river right, Boulder Pile river right or left, Little Gorilla river right, and final drop river right. Look for debris or strainers in each of the rapids.
Portages: Portages should be considered on all of the rapids scouted and can be accomplished on the same side. Recommend portaging Little Gorilla.
Gauge: Located at the put-in and boat landing on dead end Old Augusta Road, the painted gauge is on the I-295 bridge abutment directly across from the landing.
Unique potential hazards: Cathance River is very challenging at all levels. Rapids are difficult and dangerous swims are

Chapter 34 - Cathance River

possible. It's located in a remote area where access is problematic. Paddlers should expect rescue will be very difficult and time consuming. Injury, death, and loss of boats are real possibilities. The Cathance is notorious for collecting strainers and other hazards. Their locations and frequency cannot be predicted. It is strongly recommended that new paddlers travel with an experienced Cathance veteran and all horizon line descents be scouted for debris. There is a dangerous waterfall just below the takeout. Don't run it. The landing is too shallow.

Directions: From the junction of Maine Route 196 and US Route 201 in Topsham, drive north on 201 for about .75 mile to a right turn on the Old Augusta Road. Follow the dead end Old Augusta Road for about .5 mile to the end. The boat landing and put-in is located there. To reach the takeout, travel east on Route 196 from the junction of Routes 201 and 196 in Topsham for about 1.5 miles to a short connector road to Maine Route 24 (Middlesex Road) on the left. Follow Route 24 east for about 1.5 miles to the Cathance Road on the left. Take the Cathance Road for about 1 mile to the Cathance River. There are parking areas on the left and right at Head of Tide Park. Take out on the left before the bridge or on the right after the bridge. Be extremely careful paddling below the bridge as there is a dangerous waterfall on the immediate left.

A kayaker plunges down Little Gorilla on the Cathance River.
(Photo – Ron Chase)

SECTION VI. NORDIC SKIING

A skier negotiates a steep descent in Mount Blue State Park. (Photo – Ron Chase)

Chapter 35 - Mount Blue State Park

Skiing the Winter Blues Away

Much of the snow had melted and it appeared an early spring was imminent. Two blockbuster storms later, excellent conditions for late winter cross-country skiing had returned throughout most of Maine.

Mount Blue State Park offers one of the finest Nordic skiing opportunities in western Maine. Located in the mountainous region of Weld, the park has about fifteen miles of trails groomed for classic skiing. Consisting of five loop trails of varying length and difficulty, there is something for virtually every cross-country ski enthusiast.

Since the trail system does not get the same continuous attention provided at most commercial ski areas, snow conditions can vary from superb to downright scary. Having experienced scary several times during the twenty-five years I've been skiing at Mount Blue, I watch for the right combination of snow, its consistency, and weather. Prior to the almost two-hour drive from Topsham, I check the park website for a status report on their grooming efforts.

My preferred park ski is the ten-mile Maple Trail Loop. Other choices are two-mile Birch Trail and shorter circuits on Fox, Moose, and Pine Trails. All the loops except Pine Trail depart from various points on Central Trail which begins at park headquarters. Pine Trail starts on the western end of Moose Trail.

The extensive Maple Trail offers a wide variety of wilderness settings and several different skiing challenges. Passing through fields, densely wooded areas, and old farmlands, it seems the skier is always climbing or descending. About midway through the trek, a scenic overlook offers an excellent chance to pause for a respite while enjoying phenomenal views.

Chapter 35 - Mount Blue State Park

The trailhead for Central Trail is located next to park headquarters on Center Hill Road in Weld where there is a large parking area. Several winter activities are available, including a skating rink with a heated yurt. Snowshoe, snowmobile, and ski trails all leave from the parking lot next to a kiosk where trail maps are available. Sliding is an option on nearby Center Hill and arrangements can be made with park staff for winter camping. The day use fee is $5 for adults. Old people like me who are Maine residents 65 or over get in free. I'd rather be young and pay the fee!

After the heavy snowfall, I announced a Penobscot Paddle and Chowder Society (PPCS) ski trip in the park. Two club outdoor regulars, Ken Gordon and Eggman DeCoster, enthusiastically agreed to join me.

The three of us met at the parking area, intent on skiing Maple Trail Loop. Trails had recently been groomed with set tracks. A fresh layer of powder from the previous night provided an exceptional ski-friendly surface. Leaving on Central Trail, Center Hill Road was soon crossed and shortly after the Moose and Fox Trail junctions were passed. Climbing steadily, the first serious downhill test was encountered. The steepest drop in the trail network, I've had more than my share of mishaps on the irregular, attenuated pitch. The new snow facilitated effective snowplow turns and all descents were accident free.

Just beyond is the junction for Birch and Maple Trails. Bearing left, Maple Trail Loop began. Climbing a long gradual hill, an aging vacant farmhouse was observed on the left. Just beyond, an open field was traversed with excellent views northwest. As we entered a dense hardwood forest, an invigorating circuitous descent was savored before again crossing Center Hill Road. After a short uphill, we engaged a steep twisting downward slope. Adhering to the "caution" sign is strongly recommended. Complicated by a narrow road intersecting in the middle, a snowbank often provides unwanted airtime. The tricky attention-getting plunge was successfully negotiated without incident.

Following a gradual serpentine downhill section that angles south, the longest ascent of the day began. Turning right in a conifer forest, we arrived at a lean-to located at the junction of a spur trail leading to Hedgehog Hill Overlook. A precipitous knoll, it was a split decision on whether to herringbone to the top or leave skis behind. Retaining his skis, Ken made the right choice. Eggman and I experienced an exhausting climb wading in thigh deep snow. Regardless of the choice, everyone enjoyed the exceptional panoramic vista of Tumbledown and Jackson Mountains from the scenic ridge.

After lingering on the impressive escarpment for a relaxing lunch, our outing continued with another long, gentle downward gradient. Pivoting abruptly west, an exhilarating protracted decline ensued before spanning a bridge over Fran Brook at the bottom. The price for the downhill was a lengthy climb that took us through part of Birch Trail loop and back to Center Hill Road. Soon after, we rejoined Central Trail ending the Maple Trail tour.

We completed our trek with a steep ascent followed by a gradual decline and one final road crossing. About three hours was spent on the excursion, including lunch at the overlook. Park literature says Maple Trail loop is ten miles long and Central Trail an additional half mile. Irrespective of the distance, it's a rigorous workout on a remarkable trail system.

THINGS TO KNOW

Location: Franklin County, western Maine
Trail distances and difficulty ratings:
Maple Trail Loop and Central Trail: 11 miles – moderate to difficult
Birch Trail Loop and Central Trail: 3 miles – moderate
Fox Trail Loop and a portion of Central Trail: 1.5 miles - easy
Moose Trail Loop and a portion of Central Trail: 2 miles - easy
Moose Trail and Pine Trail Loops and a portion of Central Trail: 3 miles - easy to moderate

Chapter 35 - Mount Blue State Park

Views: Exceptional from Hedgehog Hill

Fees: Fees are posted on the kiosk. The cost for an adult to ski is $5. Maine residents 65 and older are not required to pay entrance fees.

Unique potential hazards: Conditions can vary substantially on all trails. A fast icy surface can be hazardous. Recommend contacting the park regarding snow conditions in advance of a planned ski. Remote sections of Maple Trail Loop may make rescue problematic. Pick up a trail map at the kiosk.

Trail characteristics: The trails are narrow and groomed for classic skiing only.

Other Activities:

Two snowshoe trails depart from the parking area:

-Center Hill Trail is a 3-mile out and back to Center Hill.

-The Rock Trail is a 3-mile out and back to a rock overlook.

Access to snowmobile trails is provided from the parking area. A skating rink is adjacent to the parking area and the heated yurt is next to it on the right.

Skates and snowshoes can be rented at the yurt.

Winter camping can be arranged with park officials.

Sliding options are available at Center Hill.

Directions: From the junction of Main St. and Maine Route 156 in Wilton, travel north on 156 for 13.2 miles to Weld and turn right onto Center Hill Road. Drive .4 mile and bear left continuing on Center Hill Road. After an additional 1.2 miles, turn right at Mount Blue State Park Headquarters and enter the large parking area. Trailheads are at the far end of the parking area and the yurt is to the right.

Skiers on Mount Blue State Park Center Trail. (Photo – Ron Chase)

Chapter 36 - Harris Farm

A Sure Cure for Cabin Fever

A friend once said, "If you live in Maine, you need to embrace winter." She was right. After too many years of misspent youthful winters, I found the antidote for cabin fever. Identify the things you love to do and discipline yourself to get out and do them. Eventually, you'll be a winter devotee addicted to short days and long cold winter nights. All right, that's goofy talk. However, you may find yourself looking forward to your favorite winter activities in the fall, enjoying an abundant winter agenda, and feeling a sense of loss when spring arrives.

There are lots of excuses to stay huddled on the couch addictively binge-watching whitewater videos and reruns of old Patriot's Super Bowl victories. Limited daylight, frigid weather, ice storms, lousy traveling, the flu, snow removal—the list seems endless. If you think things are tough now, they were worse when I was a kid. I know, you've heard that before. But really, back then there were no Patriot's Super Bowl victories to watch over and over and whitewater videos didn't exist. I can remember when my grandparents had the only television in the neighborhood and viewing hours on the three stations were from four to ten. Life was tough.

Some winter activities require a substantial commitment of time, money, and travel such as snowmobiling, downhill skiing, or one of my favorites, winter mountaineering. Not so with cross country skiing. A pair of skis and poles, boots that fit, the usual winter garments, and you're ready to ski the winter blues away. And, the sport is old people friendly.

One of my favorite cabin fever treatment clinics is Harris Farm X-Country Ski Center in Dayton. There is much to like at Harris Farm. A fourth-generation family business, it reminds me of several farms that flourished in Randolph when I was growing up. Howdy Doody and the Mouseketeers were hit TV shows then. When I arrive at the farm, it's like stepping back in time… without Howdy.

If you don't have ski equipment or lack skills, you're in luck at Harris Farm. They rent skis, boots, and poles. Lessons are available by appointment. Snowshoeing, sliding, and fat tire biking are also options. A family friendly place, it's common to see parents guiding their miniature progeny on the easy trails or pulling babies in sleds. Cabin fever is a virtual impossibility when playing at the farm.

A confessional is in order. Something I don't like about many commercial Nordic ski areas is short trails crisscrossing one another, often going in circles. I feel like a rat in a maze experiment. If you like that sort of thing, it's an option at Harris Farm. However, a big attraction for me is that I can ski the perimeter trails on both sides of the road for about two and a half hours without once repeating a section of trail. It's easy, even for us doddering geriatrics, just keep making right turns. The satisfying result is the impression of a wilderness skiing expedition.

A frequent outdoor companion, Eggman DeCoster, and I met at the farm for an afternoon ski. Both old people, the Eggster is still fully engaged in employment as a carpenter but not opposed to stealing a mental health day for cabin fever rehab.

It was a beautiful, breezy winter day, the trails were expertly groomed and in superb condition. Fortuitously, Eggie was game for my favorite perimeter ski.

Beginning across the road from the lodge, we turned right, of course, dropped into a dense forested area, and glided the rolling hills of the intermediate Cold Water Brook Trail. Following about a mile of exhilarating skiing, Cold Water connected with the easy Joe Buzzell Trail network in a large open field. Joe Buzzell and Joe Buzzell Extension continued for a prolonged period on the northwestern and southwestern boundary of the trail system. Persisting to the more difficult Farm Forest Trails, the sector ended with a challenging descent on Express Way. The Eggmeister lost his colorful stocking cap but stayed upright.

After climbing steeply on Deer Run Trail, we crossed Buzzell Road and joined the Out-to-Pasture Trails. Cruising down Maternity Loop in an open field and negotiating demanding Lucky Logger, the Bobcat Loop was next. Traveling to the far eastern terminus of the trail network, consequential Buck Bramble was successfully navigated before returning to the lodge on Sokokis Woods and Pole Barn Run Trails.

In frequent need of cabin fever therapy, this was one of my many regular visits to the Harris Farm clinic. I'll keep returning until the snow is gone and the streams open for whitewater paddling. When that happens, I'll miss winter skiing.

THINGS TO KNOW

Location: York County, southern Maine
Trail Distances:
   Joe Buzzell Lane: 5 miles
   Bobcat: 3 miles
   Estimated distance of described perimeter trip: approximately 10 miles
   Cold Water Brook: approximately 1 mile
   Farm Forest: approximately 1 mile
   Out-to-Pasture: approximately 1 mile

Difficulty levels:
   Cold Water Brook: Intermediate
   Out-to-Pasture Trails: Easy except difficult Lucky Logger
   Bobcat Loop: Intermediate and difficult
   Joe Buzzell Trails: Easy and intermediate
   Farm Forest Trails: Intermediate and difficult

Views: Very nice in the open fields of Joe Buzzell and Bobcat Loop Trails

Fees: Rates vary depending upon activity, age, student, weekday, and weekend. See the ski center website for specifics: http://www.harrisfarm.com/x-c-skiing.html

Unique potential hazards: Conditions can vary substantially on all trails. A fast icy surface can be hazardous. Recommend contacting the center regarding snow conditions in advance of a planned ski. Pick up a trail map at the lodge.

Trail characteristics: Most trails are groomed for classic and skate skiing. Check with the center on the status of grooming.

Other activities:
  Snowshoeing, fat-tire biking, and sliding
  Equipment rentals are available for skiing, snowshoeing, fat-tire biking, and pulk sleds

Directions: From the junction of Interstate 95 and Maine Route 111 in Biddeford, drive 5.5 miles west on 111 to Maine Route 35 in Lyman. Turn right onto 35 and go 3.9 miles to Gould Road on the right. Follow Gould Road for .3 mile to Buzzell Road. Turn right onto Buzzell Road and go .3 mile to Harris Farm on the left.

A skier descends Express Way at Harris Farm. (Photo – Ron Chase)

Chapter 37 - Rangeley Lakes Trails Center

In Search of Bobcats and Snow

It had been a difficult winter for cross-country skiing in the Maine foothills and coastal plain. A succession of mixed precipitation storms had resulted in minimal snowpack and often icy surfaces.

Two of my favorite commercial ski areas, Harris Farm in Dayton and Pineland Farms in Pownal, had been open only sporadically. Despite aggressive grooming when operating, snow conditions had often been mediocre. Crusty hard-packed trails can be a boon for skilled skate skiers but ancient classic skiers like me fear for our lives when careening downhill in icy tracks or desperately trying to hold a snowplow on frozen precipitous turns. While climbing is a more benign activity, ascending on slick surfaces can be extremely arduous and a lack of traction unforgiving on aging joints and muscles.

Still, cross country skiing is a beneficial sport for us old folks and easier on the anatomy than winter mountaineering. A preference for many of us is to combine both activities into our winter outdoor agenda. In search of quality snow, my friends and I had made several trips to Jackson Ski Touring Center located in New Hampshire's Mount Washington Valley. Although it had also endured some rainstorms, Jackson had accumulated a deep snow base and regularly groomed its trails to a satisfactory level.

Excellent skiing is not the only attraction at Jackson. With 150 kilometers of ski trails spanning 60 square miles of highlands, it offers several extended trips many find appealing. However, Jackson has a significant disadvantage as it entails a long drive from many points in Maine. A few of us elderly pseudo-weather geeks carefully analyze forecasts, strategically planning visits to preferred Maine ski areas when conditions appear optimum. Trips to Harris Farm and Mount Blue State Park immediately after snowstorms had proved successful. Unfortunately, both trail systems worsened significantly soon after.

In search of snow, a group of seniors took advantage of their semi-retired status for an impromptu two-day ski trip to Rangeley Lakes Trails Center in Dallas Plantation following a snowstorm. Situated at the foot of majestic Saddleback Mountain, the center provides 55 kilometers of trails for Nordic skiing, snowshoeing, and fat tire biking.

When five of us arrived in Rangeley, our first observation was that there was no shortage of snow in the area. Snowbanks were piled high resulting in narrow streets and many road signs were buried. Snowmobiles filled the motel parking lot and gas stations were cluttered with them – all positive indicators for our ski plans.

The ski center is operated by Rangeley Lakes Cross Country Ski Club. The hub for activities is a sizeable yurt that functions as the ski lodge where passes are purchased and equipment rented. Light lunches and snacks are sold, and a changing room is available in the hospitable refuge. A medium-sized parking lot is adjacent to the yurt and a larger area located across the street.

Most of the trails had already been groomed when departing from the yurt on Tote Road Trail. Snow conditions were exquisite. My longtime outdoor amigo Ken Gordon and I teamed up to explore an extensive array of trails, much of it on the network perimeter. Gliding along on a beautiful breezy sunny day, we were also in pursuit of a bobcat known to frequent the area.

Passing through a major trail intersection at Tote Road's end, a gradual climb on Bridge Trail led to distinctive Junction Rock. Turning left on Lower Pump House Road, recent bobcat tracks were encountered. Alas, the elusive critter was nowhere to be seen. Continuing on, Outer Limits Trail was joined where I hoped to spot an asteroid. Ken's skepticism prevailed. After traversing Lower Pipeline back to the Tote Road junction, an exacting one mile climb on Upper Pipeline was experienced followed by a rollicking descent to the yurt on challenging Larry Hall Trail.

Day two offered another almost cloudless sky with near perfect snow. Ken and I added Sisu, View, and Nat's Alley Trails to our itinerary. Rated most difficult, Sisu was very manageable due to exceptional snow conditions that facilitated effective snowplow turns. View lived up to its moniker with a phenomenal vista of the Saddleback Range. More bobcat tracks and fresh scat were identified high on scenic Nat's Alley Trail but the furtive feline remained concealed. My guess, it was secluded in nearby bushes enjoying a silent sarcastic guffaw at our expense. Another invigorating cruise down Larry Hall Trail followed, completing our two-day excursion on the thoroughly entertaining Rangeley Lakes Trails.

The Rangeley area is a mecca for wildlife sightings. On another visit, my wife Nancy and I spotted a lynx twice on the same day near the ski center. Not quite believing our eyes, the yurt manager confirmed that several had been seen in the area.

THINGS TO KNOW

Location: Franklin County, western Maine
Trail distances and difficulty ratings:
    Geneva Loop: 3.27 kilometers - easier
    Tote Road: 1.8 kilometers - easier
    Zapolsky Trail: 1.54 kilometers - easier
    Lower Pipeline: 1.42 kilometers – easier
    Lower Pumphouse Road: 2.4 kilometers – intermediate
    Outer Limits: 2.76 kilometers – easier
    Sisu: 1.76 kilometers – most difficult
    View Trail: 1.83 kilometers – intermediate
    Hoffman's Run: .71 kilometer – intermediate
    Bridge Trail: 3.5 kilometers – intermediate
    Upper Pumphouse Road: 1.6 kilometers – intermediate
    Nat's Alley: .88 kilometer – intermediate
    Upper Pipleline: 1.5 kilometers – intermediate
    Larry Hall Trail: 3.12 kilometers – intermediate and most difficult
    Pulp Run: 1 kilometer – most difficult
    Moose Alley: .89 kilometer – intermediate

Jeff's Trail: .67 kilometer – intermediate

Views: Exceptional from View Trail and Nat's Alley

Fees: Rates vary depending upon activity, age, and full or half day passes. See the ski center website for specifics:
https://rangeleylakestrailscenter.org/

Unique potential hazards: Conditions can vary substantially on all trails. A fast icy surface can be hazardous. Recommend contacting the center regarding snow conditions in advance of a planned ski. Remote sections of Outer Limits, Lower and Upper Pumphouse, Nat's Alley, and Larry Hall Trail may make rescue problematic. Pick up a trail map at the yurt.

Trail Characteristics: Most trails are groomed for classic and skate skiing. Check with the center on the status of grooming.

Other activities:

Snowshoeing, fat-tire biking, and back country skiing

Equipment rentals are available for skiing, snowshoeing, and fat-tire biking.

Non-winter activities include running, walking, and biking.

Directions: From the junction of US Route 2 and Maine Routes 4 and 27 in Farmington, drive north for 2.5 miles on 4 and 27. Bear left on Route 4 and continue for 28.8 miles to Dallas Hill Road on the right in Rangeley. Turn right onto Dallas Hill Road and travel 2.4 miles to Saddleback Mountain Road on the right. Follow Saddleback Mountain Road for 2.5 miles to the ski center, yurt, and parking area on the left.

Chapter 37 - Rangeley Lakes Trails Center

A skier at the Rangeley Lakes Trail Center. (Photo – Ron Chase)

SECTION VII. LAKE PADDLING

A kayaker paddles along the cliffs of Mount Kineo on Moosehead Lake. (Photo – Ron Chase)

Chapter 38 - Moosehead Lake

Moosehead Lake Surf & Turf

Call me quixotic but I like surf and turf outdoor adventures. What's a surf and turf? One definition is a sea kayak or canoe trip combined with a mountain hike. There are other variations. While this may seem bizarre to the uninitiated, it's an excellent way to combine three popular outdoor activities, paddling, hiking, and camping.

Fortuitously, Maine has a number of excellent surf and turf options. In recent years, I've led Penobscot Paddle and Chowder Society (PPCS) trips on Donnell Pond and Schoodic Mountain, Tunk Lake and Black Mountain, and Attean Lake and Mountain. Fall is my season of choice for these outings because there is less competition for campsites and no bugs. With the exception of dragon flies, I've never met a bug I liked. The wonderful dragon flies consume copious amounts of blackflies.

This year, my focus was on what I consider to be Maine's quintessential lake surf and turf, Moosehead Lake and Mount Kineo. What better choice than Maine's largest lake and arguably the state's most distinctive summit? The missing link was finding willing victims to join me.

When in need of outdoor companions, I fall back on my most reliable source, Chowderheads with the PPCS. Within hours of announcing my proposed escapade, three of the usual suspects, Brent Elwell, Suzanne and Gary Cole, had enthusiastically signed on. I could write a book about the adventures the four of us have shared over the past thirty years. Now that I think of it, that's what I'm presently doing.

All of us retired from our respective careers; I'm the oldest. How did this oldest thing happen? Not that long ago, I was the youngest in everything: baby of my high school class, the youngest

IRS Revenue Officer, and more. When I'm shipped to the home, perhaps I'll temporarily regain the youngest status before passing on to my eternal reward.

Surf and turf trips entail logistical complexities. Foremost, you need more stuff. Essential is a vessel large enough to carry all paddling needs, camping equipment, and hiking gear. Canoes provide greater space but are slower and more exposed to often gusty lake winds. We chose sea kayaks.

While an out and back expedition is simpler to arrange, traversing large lakes is more interesting and theoretically easier when planning for winds. Having twice experienced the ubiquitous Moosehead winds, I knew they could be very challenging and unpredictable. Since the forecast called for light breezes out of the northwest, I plotted a traverse from Rockwood to Mount Kineo, then southeast to Lily Bay State Park.

Camping at the state park the night before, we left a vehicle for the return shuttle. One of the few benefits of being old in Maine is that a resident 65 or older is exempt from state park day use fees. The two youngsters in our group had to keep shelling out money while receiving little sympathy from Gary and me.

As we departed from the boat landing in Rockwood, gentle winds and bright sunny skies were on the menu for our mile-long paddle north to Mount Kineo State Park. With a perpetual view of that magnificent rock-faced peak, the crossing was nothing short of spectacular.

From the Kineo boat landing, we hiked the Carriage Trail along the shore and then ascended Indian Trail to the summit where a fire tower provides 360-degree views. Indian Trail skirts along vertical cliffs affording splendid vistas of the southern half of the lake.

Returning from the three-mile hike, our southeasterly kayak journey began with idyllic conditions: a light tailwind, sunny skies, and wonderful views of the surrounding mountains. Paddling for about five miles past Harris and Cowan Coves and rounding Big Dry Point into Spencer Bay offered phenomenal profiles of Big and Little Spencer Mountains. After discovering a southeast-

Chapter 38 - Moosehead Lake

facing campsite about two miles east of the point, a truly exceptional fall evening ensued.

After awakening just in time to catch a glimpse of a brilliant sunrise, we consumed a leisurely breakfast while plotting our strategy for the day. From the sheltered campsite, powerful northwest winds appeared to be gusting down the lake.

Attempting to avoid the blustery gales for as long as possible, we paddled east to Spencer Narrows and crossed the bay. When we turned southwest into Lilly Bay, steady, forceful starboard winds and three-foot breaking waves were encountered. Brent accurately observed, "These are serious ocean-like conditions." Yelling above the din, a collective agreement was made to cross the top of Lily Bay with the hope of finding shelter next to Sugar Island.

After a rollicking 1.5-mile passage, protection from the powerful winds was attained in Galusha Cove. Skirting the east side of Sugar Island, the remainder of our paddle to Lily Bay State Park was uneventful. Alas, more park fees were assessed against the youngsters.

This had been my third kayak trip on Moosehead. The first was an attempted journey north to south from Northwest Cove to Greenville Junction. After being forced to stop at Toe of the Boot due to formidable winds, the trip was cancelled the next morning over fears that one member of the expedition was suffering a heart attack.

The second was a traverse south to north from Greenville Junction to Northwest Cove. The change in direction was based on a forecast for winds from the south. After completing the arduous, time-consuming shuttle, strong headwinds from the north were endured the entire first day. On the following day, gusty winds from the east resulted in three to five-foot swells for much of the remainder of the expedition.

If you plan a paddle trip on Moosehead, expect strong winds, probably from the least desirable direction.

THINGS TO KNOW

Location: Piscataquis County, north central Maine

Length: Approximately 16 miles for the described trip. A traverse south to north is approximately 40 miles.

Difficulty level: Moderate to difficult

Views: Some of the most spectacular in Maine, particularly approaching Mount Kineo and on the mountain

Unique potential hazards: Expect large waves and strong winds anywhere on Moosehead Lake. Substantial recreational boat activity often presents a hazard on the lake. It is strongly recommended that paddlers obtain proper instruction from a qualified instructor prior to attempting this trip. That instruction should include suitable dress, self-rescue, assisted rescue, kayak roll, navigation, and what is required for safety equipment and gear. It is further recommended that each paddler carry a GPS, map, and compass, and know how to use them. Never paddle alone, rather a strong team of experienced kayakers is always recommended including one participant familiar with Moosehead Lake. Always obtain a reliable weather forecast but don't depend on it. Be prepared for changing conditions. Sections of Indian Trail on Mount Kineo require boulder and rock scrambling increasing the risk of serious falls.

Directions:

To Lily Bay State Park: From the junction of Maine Routes 15/6 and Lily Bay Road in Greenville, drive north on Lily Bay Road for about 8.5 miles to Lily Bay Park Road on the left. Enter and pay fees.

To Rockwood Boat Landing: From the junction of Maine Routes 15/6 and Lily Bay Road in Greenville, drive north on Routes 15/6 for about 18 miles to Village Road on the right in Rockwood. Follow Village Road for a short distance to Kineo Dock Road on the right. Continue on Kineo Dock Road to the end where there is a large parking area and boat landing.

Chapter 38 - Moosehead Lake

Information on Lily Bay State Park: Visit the state park website at:
http://www.stateparks.com/lily_bay_state_park_in_maine.html

Information on hiking Mount Kineo: Visit Maine Trail Finder website at:
https://www.mainetrailfinder.com/trails/trail/mount-kineo-state-park

Information on Moosehead Lake campsites and trails: Visit Moosehead Lake Shoreline Public Lands website at: https://www.maine.gov/dacf/parksearch/PropertyGuides/PDF_GUIDE/moosehead-lake-shoreline-guide.pdf

Kayakers paddle towards Mount Kineo at Moosehead Lake. (Photo – Ron Chase)

Chapter 39 - Mooselookmeguntic, Cupsuptic, and Richardson Lakes

Traversing the Big Lakes

I had two good reasons to organize a trip on the big lakes of western Maine. First, a traverse of Cupsuptic, Mooselookmeguntic, Upper Richardson, and Lower Richardson Lakes is one of the most exceptional paddling experiences in Maine. Second, I thoroughly enjoy blending large Maine lake trips into my sea kayaking schedule.

Because it is a physically demanding, logistically challenging expedition, enlisting at least one willing victim was a necessity to efficiently complete the required shuttle. I began marketing the scheme to my regular outdoor companions. About a dozen paddlers expressed an interest as a result of my lobbying efforts.

Several factors make planning the journey exacting. The shuttle over backcountry roads is about sixty miles in distance, weather and wind direction can be significant factors, and availability of campsites in this managed wilderness area is sometimes problematic.

The choice of vessel is another issue. On my first traverse with my son Adam about thirty-five years ago, we used a tripping canoe. On a second outing, everyone paddled sea kayaks. Canoes carry more gear but kayaks are faster and easier to navigate in strong winds. When winds increase and waves get rough, kneeling is often necessary in a canoe. Kneeling with my aging arthritic joints and replacement knee is simply too uncomfortable. A kayak has become my lake craft of choice.

I estimated the paddling distance to be about thirty miles with a portage in the middle and a long shuttle on both ends, so three days seemed the requisite timeframe to complete the endeavor. Since identifying a perfect three-day weather forecast with only two days advance notice, my recruitment efforts were minimally successful. Frequent outdoor accomplice Brent Elwell signed on and we'd both be piloting sea kayaks. Since the forecast called for

Chapter 39 - Mooselookmeguntic, Cupsuptic, and Richardson Lakes

winds from the northwest on the first two days, our selection was a north to south traverse beginning at the top of Cupsuptic Lake. The excursion would entail traveling south through much of Mooselookmeguntic, portaging around Upper Dam, and continuing south through Upper and Lower Richardson Lakes ending the journey in the tiny community of South Arm.

Stephen Phillips Memorial Preserve manages campsites on Mooselookmeguntic Lake. I was able to reserve one on Brandy Point ideally situated two miles east of Upper Dam for the first night. The Richardson Lakes have a multitude of campsites. Trusting an aging elderly memory, my recollection was they were available without reservations.

We met at a large parking area near the boat landing in South Arm where Brent's kayak and gear were loaded onto my vehicle and his car left for the return shuttle. Wearing masks to protect against spreading Covid-19, ominous unwelcome rain clouds threatened on the one-and-a-half-hour drive to Cupsuptic. Approaching the Town of Oquossuc, Height of Land Overlook on Route 17 provided a stunning panoramic view of much of our upcoming voyage.

We benefited from a gentle tailwind as the sun was shining and skies partly cloudy when departing from Cupsuptic Boat Landing. The Saddleback Mountain Range dominated views in the east. Traveling southeasterly through a narrows near Oquossoc, we noted that Bald Mountain on our left and highlands to the right created the impression of an inland fjord.

Passing Stony Batter Point, we navigated south and experienced continuous views of substantial Toothaker Island in the distance with Height of Land and Bemis Mountain towering above. We enjoyed plentiful bird sightings throughout the excursion—a family of Canada Geese led the way to our campsite on scenic Brandy Point opposite Student Island. The forecast called for a slight chance of showers. We thought we would use reverse psychology on the weather gods, so a tarp was erected to ensure a dry overnight.

After an idyllic stay at Brandy Point, a brief paddle west brought us to Upper Dam. An excellent trail facilitated the portage around the dam and a modest release was sufficient to maneuver through the rock-strewn outflow into Upper Richardson. A tailwind propelled us rapidly south to Black Point Campsite.

My senior moments seem to be increasing exponentially. A sign announced South Arm Campground now manages all camping on the Richardson Lakes. A cell phone call confirmed every location was reserved. Instead of a delightful evening blithely ensconced on one of the many sandy beaches, the disappointing revelation resulted in a long day paddling to South Arm.

Since the weather was superb and the wind continued to cooperate, our tiring odyssey was completed in good spirits despite the setback. We had thoroughly enjoyed one of Maine's finest outdoor adventures.

THINGS TO KNOW

Location: Franklin and Oxford Counties, western Maine
Length: Approximately 30 miles
Difficulty: Easy to moderate
Unique potential hazards: Paddlers should be wary of potential gusty winds, particularly from the northwest. Kayakers and canoeists should have strong paddling skills and be familiar with self-rescue and assisted rescue techniques. It is further recommended that each paddler carry a map and compass and know how to use them. Never paddle alone. Always obtain a reliable weather forecast prior to the trip.
Directions:
South Arm Boat Landing: From the junction of U.S. Route 2 and Maine Route 5 in Rumford Point, drive north on Route 5 for about 12 miles to Andover. Shortly after crossing a bridge over the Ellis River, turn left onto South Arm Road at a junction with Route 120. Travel north on South Arm Road for about 11 miles to the boat landing on the left. A large parking area is located across the road and up a short hill.

Chapter 39 - Mooselookmeguntic, Cupsuptic, and Richardson Lakes

Cupsuptic Boat Landing: From the South Arm Boat Landing return on the South Arm Road to Route 120. Drive southeasterly on 120 for about 11 miles to a short connector road near Hale that crosses over the Swift River to Route 17. Follow Route 17 north for about 22 miles to the Height of Land Overlook, a great spot to stop for a break and to enjoy a panoramic view of your upcoming adventure. Continue north on Route 17 for about 12 miles to Route 16 in Oquossuc. Turn left onto Route 16 and drive about 6 miles to the Cupsuptic Boat Landing on the right where there is a small parking lot.

Obtaining Campsites:
Mooselookmeguntic Lake: Stephen Philips Memorial Preserve
https://www.stephenphillipswildernesscamping.com/
Upper and Lower Richardson Lakes: South Arm Campground (https://campmaine.com/directory/western-lakes-mountains-campgrounds/south-arm-campground/)

A kayaker navigates south on Mooselookmeguntic Lake. (Photo – Ron Chase)

Chapter 40 - Donnell Pond

Donnell Pond Surf & Turf

We were luxuriating with one of the most impressive views in the State of Maine. As we sat atop Hancock County's Schoodic Mountain on a clear, calm morning, Frenchman Bay and the majestic peaks of Mount Desert Island provided an enthralling panorama. First on the mountain, John and I had departed our campsite on Schoodic Beach immediately after breakfast. An invigorating 1.5-mile hike had culminated at the spectacular barren mountaintop.

Donnell Pond Public Lands consist of over 14,000 heavily forested acres that include several rugged mountains enveloping remote ponds and lakes. An extensive trail system meanders over and around the summits that dominate the conservation area. Numerous scenic campsites have been established along the shores of lakes and ponds. Yet the recreational wonderland is a relatively well-kept secret.

While possible to connect with several trailheads by road, the campsites can be reached only by hiking or watercraft. The substantial effort required to access them probably explains their limited use. The unique setting lends itself to one of my favorite fall exploits, a surf and turf. Surf and turf is loosely defined as combining a canoe or kayak trip with a mountain hike, preferably including at least one night of camping. The allure of crisp cool evenings and bug-free campsites makes autumn the ideal time for the multifaceted undertakings.

An excellent two-day forecast inspired me to post a Penobscot Paddle and Chowder Society Donnell Pond Surf & Turf Trip. My longtime friend John Brower signed on. At age 79, he is one of a handful of outdoor playmates older than I am. Our combined ages constituted a depressing Team Sesquicentennial.

Chapter 40 - Donnell Pond

We met at a boat landing on the western terminus of Donnell Pond in Franklin on a serene, sunny fall day. John was paddling a lightweight solo Kevlar canoe and I my new expedition kayak. Ever since a knee replacement I've struggled with kneeling in a canoe when winds and whitewater necessitated it. After two painful canoe trips this spring, I relented and purchased an expedition kayak that would in theory transport sufficient gear for multiday trips while capable of effective whitewater navigation. A flat-water expedition, this was a test of its carrying capacity. My verdict, it was a success as there was room to spare.

Paddling due east for a couple of miles towards distinctive Caribou Mountain, we turned south into a narrow channel opposite Redmans Beach Campsites. A trailhead for Caribou Mountain begins at the beach. Our goal was the more dramatic peaks farther south.

Continuing a southerly course, Caribou, Black, and Schoodic Mountains surround the lower arm of the pond suggestive of an inland fjord. As we approached spacious sandy Schoodic Beach, colorful tents materialized at both ends. Fortuitously, ample space remained in the center for two elderly paddlers and their camping gear. The site came equipped with an ancient picnic table that didn't appear to have much life left. The hope was the three of us would survive a few more meals.

After setting up camp, the turf portion of our excursion began. Black Mountain Cliffs Loop Trail originates and ends at the beach. Hiking counterclockwise for a half mile brought us to a parking area with additional trailheads to Black and Schoodic Mountains. Parking there provides alternative access to the campsites on Schoodic Beach for those unwilling or unable to travel by water. From the parking area, Black Mountain path climbed steadily in a densely wooded environment for 1.2 miles to a junction above the cliffs. Leaving the loop trail, a hilly route continued north for a short mile to spectacular East Peak on Black Mountain. Expansive views from the summit revealed breathtaking vistas of Tunk Lake and Mountain, Frenchman Bay, and Mount Desert Island. Tranquil and sublime, we lingered at the top captivated by the moment. The only other hikers encountered that day were approaching from the south as Team Sesquicentennial departed. Returning towards Black Cliffs, a junction leading to Caribou Mountain was cause for contemplation. Sorely tempted to add another peak to our collection, the math didn't work. A return in the dark seemed a certainty. Persisting to the loop trail, our endeavor ended with a steep descent along the cliffs to the beach.

Our night camping on the shore was idyllic. Mild temperatures and a light breeze facilitated a leisurely dinner while experiencing a brilliant sunset. The dazzling red sky portended a sailor's delight. The following morning found us contentedly situated on the summit of Schoodic Mountain. After hundreds of shared adventures spanning decades, we both agreed, it didn't get any better.

THINGS TO KNOW

Location: Hancock County, Down East Maine

Length: For the described trip: 6 miles paddling roundtrip, 6 miles hiking Black Mountain, and 3 miles hiking Schoodic Mountain

Difficulty: Easy to moderate

Views: Donnell Pond is very picturesque, while views from the summits of East Peak on Black Mountain and Schoodic Mountain are some of the finest in Maine.

Unique potential hazards: Paddlers should be wary of the potential for gusty winds, particularly from the north and northwest. Kayakers and canoeists should have strong paddling skills and be familiar with self-rescue and assisted rescue techniques. It is further recommended that each paddler carry a map and compass and know how to use them. Never paddle alone. Always obtain a reliable weather forecast prior to the trip. Some areas on Black and Schoodic Mountains require boulder and rock scrambling increasing the risk of serious falls.

Directions to the Franklin Boat Landing: From the junction of Maine Routes 182 and 200 in Franklin, drive north on

Chapter 40 - Donnell Pond

Route 182 for about 1.5 miles to Donnell Pond Road on the right. Follow Donnell Pond Road for about 1.25 miles to the boat landing. There is a large parking area with a toilet before the landing on the right.

Map of Donnell Pond Public Lands, trails, campsites: Visit: https://www.maine.gov/dacf/parksearch/PropertyGuides/Maps/FullSize/donnellpondmap.pdf

A canoeist traverses Donnell Pond. (Photo – Ron Chase)

SECTION VIII. CANOE TRIPS

A tandem canoe team runs a rapid on the Machias River. (Photo – Ron Chase)

Chapter 41 - Machias River

Tumultuous Times on the Machias River

Forget the St. John, Allagash or Moose Rivers. As far as I'm concerned, the Machias River is the best canoe trip in Maine, maybe all of northeastern United States. A free-flowing river with a large watershed, it begins in the lakes region of northern Washington County then meanders and tumbles for eighty miles to the sea in the coastal community of Machias.

Meaning "bad run of water" or "bad little falls" in Passamaquoddy, the Machias has virtually everything for the adventurous paddler. Narrow, scenic whitewater streams connect five small to medium lakes in the upper reaches of the river. A few miles after leaving the last downriver lake, First Machias, it joins the West Branch and becomes a much more substantial body of water. Beginning with Long Falls between Third and Second Machias Lakes, there are at least eight Class III rapids, some more difficult in high water. Depending on water levels and paddling skills, a few may need to be portaged. Most consider spectacular Class V Holmes Falls to be a mandatory portage, especially in a tripping canoe.

Numerous access points on the Machias offer a very unique feature for a canoe camping river, allowing for a multitude of tripping options from single day adventures to weeklong expeditions. While paddling the entire river is always my first preference, a favorite shorter version is a thirty-mile stretch from Third Machias Lake to the top of Holmes Falls.

My tumultuous affair with the Machias began in the late 1970s when my wife Nancy and I completed an overnight trip from Third Machias Lake to Airline Rapids at Route 9. Lacking wetsuits, we wore cotton jeans instead. The wet frigid garments were desperately discarded for dry replacements the moment we were off the river. Indicative of how much we (well, maybe I) loved the sport and river, I thought we were having fun despite being near hypothermic for the better part of both days. In the ensuing forty years, I've completed about thirty trips on the Machias, having recruited an abundance of victims. Some have remained friends.

Perhaps my most unforgettable trip began at the outlet of Third Machias Lake on Friday the 13th, April 1984. Undeterred by triskaidekaphobia, three friends and I launched in two tandem canoes at near flood conditions with about two feet of snow on the banks. To say we lacked adequate paddling skills would be a serious understatement. At the time, I thought eddies were two or more people named Ed and ferrying was something accomplished when traveling to the island of Vinalhaven. Instead of being a narrow technical rapid, at very high water Long Falls consisted of large standing waves pockmarked with nasty holes. Never crossing our minds to portage, somehow my Mad River Explorer and its inept occupants miraculously survived although filled to the gunnels. Team Two wasn't so fortunate, swimming much of the rapid in icy water while clinging to their heavy, overloaded canoe.

Reuniting paddlers, gear, and boat, we proceeded downstream in a series of rapids that are usually Class II. Attempting to negotiate more standing waves, Team Two was again quickly in the water only this time separated from their boat. An epic chase in deep snow ensued. The canoe with some gear was recovered but mercifully it was too badly damaged for them to continue. Dragging boats and gear up a steep hill affectionately named "Chase Mountain" by my companions, tenting on the snow in damp sleeping bags was our plight that night.

The following morning, the four of us hauled the damaged canoe and most of our gear about a half mile through dense woods in deep snow to the Little River Road. While Team Two walked back to their vehicle, my apprehensive partner and I continued downriver, across the south end of Second Machias Lake, and navigated a flat water stretch to the Stud Mill Road on the north end of First Machias Lake. Arriving at a bridge on the Stud Mill Road, Team Two was waiting in their truck informing us of

Chapter 41 - Machias River

a minor logistical problem: First Machias Lake was completely covered with ice. In our rush to launch, no one had considered stopping to check for ice on the lake.

Fortuitously, a shuttle vehicle with two shuttle bunnies was now available; bad rabbits might be a more accurate description. After chauffeuring us around the lake, another night was spent tenting on the snow at what is now called Wonderland Campsite at the outlet of First Machias Lake. While the bad rabbits continued to shuttle, my tandem partner and I paddled in snow showers to Airline Rapids the next day, an exploit that included a frigid boat filling misadventure at Carrick Rips. On the following day, a rollicking ride in a cold rainstorm through Little Falls and Wigwam Rapids to Holmes Falls was endured. Our inexperienced technique on difficult rapids was to choose a line, point the boat downriver, and plow straight ahead, usually filling up but somehow remarkably staying afloat. Adding insult to injury, a sinister landlubber had deflated all the tires on my vehicle at the take out. Thankfully, the bad rabbits were available for assistance.

While no subsequent trip has been quite as noteworthy or traumatic as the April 1984 fiasco, the Machias is always an adventure. The following spring, my brother-in-law Mike Moody and I became seriously hypothermic after swimming Third Wigwam Rapid during a significant snowstorm. In order to avoid the 1986 trip, he broke his ankle. In April 1989, the late Terry Tzovarrus and I began an excursion at the outlet of Fifth Machias Lake in heavy rain. With the exception of one sunny morning, it rained for the entire outing. We were thoroughly waterlogged when finally finishing in the village of Machias several days later.

Occasionally, the weather cooperates on the Machias resulting in some of my finest outdoor experiences. A few years ago, Doug Field, Helen Hess, Eggman DeCoster, Kim Perkins, and I duplicated the 1989 expedition with great weather and near perfect water levels.

Another trip began with a bad omen, a vehicle mired in mud on a seldom used access road to Fifth Machias Lake. Following an extended vehicle rescue, our large group encountered low but passable water levels on the streams above Second Machias Lake. After dozens of successful runs on Long Falls, the river gods frowned on me. My accomplice and I wrapped my ancient Dagger Dimension Canoe in the bony run out. Forty-five years of paddling canoes and kayaks on a multitude of rivers notwithstanding, I lost my first boat on a rapid etched in my mind. The Machias has a way of humbling paddlers. Surprising my fellow travelers, I was comfortable with the bush whack out to the Little River Road, having danced that rumba in the snow more than thirty years before.

My two most recent trips were memorable for substantially different reasons. A year ago, a group of four encountered flood levels on an excursion from First Lake to Whitneyville. Paddling solo canoes, we filled up at Carrick Rips and Airline Rapids. Recognizing the raging water presented potentially perilous consequences, six rapids were portaged the following day. Two of us who had paddled the Grand Canyon agreed Great Falls was comparable in difficulty. In short, it was no place for tripping canoes. Everyone took out above the usually easy Class II falls in Whitneyville on the final day of the expedition.

This year, the pandemic added a new dimension to the always challenging river experience. Achieving appropriate social distancing was the most significant obstacle. Using masks, careful separation, sanitizing, and various other techniques, I joined Rick Farnsworth and his hardy group of three enjoying good weather, perfect water levels, and no black flies on an outing from Third Machias Lake to Holmes Falls. After years of struggling while kneeling in a canoe as a result of a knee replacement, I completed my first descent in an expedition kayak. Success was the verdict.

What are my plans for next spring? I expect to be back on the Machias in my expedition kayak. Hopefully, the trip will begin at Fifth Machias Lake and end at the bridge above Bad Little Falls in Machias. If the water comes up in the fall, I may spend a few days on the best tripping river in Maine.

Chapter 41 - Machias River

THINGS TO KNOW

Location: Washington County, Down East Maine

Length: Approximately 80 miles from Fifth Machias Lake to the finish. The outing from Third Machias Lake to Holmes Falls is about 30 miles. Several other trips of various lengths are possible. See access points below.

Difficulty rating: Class I, II, and III. Several rapids increase to Class IV in difficulty when the water level is high.

Determining water level: Inexplicably, the USGS stopped operating the Whitneyville gauge on the Machias River several years ago. In defiance of any apparent logic, they continue to maintain a gauge on Old Stream, a relatively minor tributary of the Machias. In my opinion, the Machias watershed is too important. They should close the Old Stream gauge and reopen the Machias. Since the closing, I have extrapolated USGS gauge readings on Old Stream and the Narraguagus River to determine the approximate Machias level. If the Old Stream gauge is between 60 and 180 cubic feet per second (CFS) and the Narraguagus gauge is between 500 and 1600 CFS, everything on the Machias should be runnable. The small streams on the upper section will be very scratchy below those levels and the Class III rapids will become more difficult and dangerous above. Visit the USGS website to determine gauge levels:
 https://waterdata.usgs.gov/me/nwis/current/?type=flow.

A summary of the river, scouting, and portages: Narrow 5th Machias Stream flows for 10 miles from 5th to 4th Lake. About midway through, there are 3 ledge drops that should be scouted and possibly portaged. 4th Lake is approximately 4 miles long before emptying into 4th Lake Stream which has a couple of easy Class II rapids before joining 3rd Lake after about 2.5 miles. The paddle to the outlet of 3rd Lake is 6 miles. From the outlet, there are a couple of Class I/II rapids followed by a short section of dead water and then another Class II rapid. After a mile of flat water, Long Falls is encountered, the longest technical rapid on the river. It can be scouted or portaged on either side. A mile of continuous Class II rapids follow to 2nd Lake. The paddle across 2nd Lake and the stream connecting to 1st Lake is about 2.5 miles and another mile arrives at the outlet of 1st Lake. After 4 miles of flat water a couple of easy rapids indicate Class III Carrick Rips is just ahead, scout or portage on the right. Below Carrick, the West Branch enters on the right. Several easy rapids are found in the 5 miles to the Airline (Route 9). Class III Airline Rapids begin at the bridge and should be scouted or portaged on the right. With the exception of a couple of easy rapids, flatwater continues for about 5 miles to Little Falls, a Class III (Class IV at high water as a steep pitch in the middle forms a river wide hole). A portage trail is on the left. Five miles of calm water continues to Mopang Stream on the right. Around the bend, the Wigwams begin. Consisting for four significant rapids or pitches in two miles, the first is the longest and should be scouted or portaged on the right. The second is a long Class II followed by a pool and then the Third Wigwam which is similar in character to Little Falls and should be scouted or portaged on the left. Immediately below is the Fourth Wigwam, a short Class II. Three miles of calm water brings the paddler to Holmes Falls which should be portaged on the left. A dangerous 15-foot waterfall, it should not be run. After about a half mile of quick water, Deadman's Island is reached. There is a stone memorial to an early settler named Obadiah Hill on the island. The downstream end is a good place to plot a strategy for approaching Little Holmes Falls which is just below. At most levels, Little Holmes is a challenging technical Class III to the right of a lower island and Class IV to the left. Both are difficult to scout but take the time to scout or portage on the right. Eleven miles of flat water continues past Old Stream and Smith Landing on the left to Great Falls, the longest most difficult high volume rapid on the trip. Class III at low to medium levels, it rises to Class IV in high water. Scout or portage on the right. Six miles of flat water follows to a falls in Whitneyville. The far-right channel is a steep Class II and the left channel Class IV. Two miles of calm water ensues to Munson Pitch, a Class II normally run left. A short section of easy rapids are encountered after another two miles. Just beyond is a

Chapter 41 - Machias River

gorge that is Class II at low and medium levels and Class III in high water. Class I/II rapids continue to the takeout in Machias on the left just above the bridge. Bad Little Falls, a very dangerous waterfall begins under the bridge.

Access Points:
  Outlet of 5th Machias Lake: Road 42-00-0
  4th Machias Lake: Grand Lake Stream Road
  Outlet of 3rd Machias Lake: Little River Road
  2nd Machias Lake: Little River Road
  Entrance 1st Machias Lake: Stud Mill Road
  Wonderland Campsite, Outlet 1st Machias Lake: Machias River Road
  Log Landing Campsite, Outlet of West Branch: Machias River Road
  Machias Rips Campsite: Airline (Maine Route 9)
  Holmes Falls: Holmes Falls Road
  Smith Landing: Smith Landing Road
  Whitneyville: U S Route 1A
  Machias: Takeout, U S Route 1

River Campsites:
  Outlet of 5th Machias Lake
  4th Machias Lake
  Outlet of 4th Machias Lake
  Prune Island, 3rd Machias Lake
  Outlet of 3rd Machias Lake
  2nd Machias Lake
  Outlet of 2nd Machias Lake
  Wonderland Campsite, Outlet of 1st Machias Lake
  Log Landing Campsite, Outlet of West Branch
  Machias Rips Campsite, Airline Rapids
  Little Falls Campsite, Little Falls
  1st Wigwam Campsite
  3rd Wigwam Campsite
  Holmes Falls

Little Holmes Falls
Smith Landing
Great Falls

Shuttle Services: Dan Pelletier, Maine Guiding Wilderness Adventures: http://maineguiding.com/ and Sunrise Canoe and Kayak: http://www.sunrisecanoeandkayak.com/maine-canoe-trips/machias-river.htm

Unique potential hazards: There are many challenging rapids including those on 5th Machias Stream, Long Falls, Carrick Rips, Airline Rapids, Little Falls, the Wigwams, Little Holmes Falls, and Great Falls, some that rise to Class IV in high water. Paddlers should have Class III paddling skills. Dangerous swims are a risk and injury or death a real possibility. Extreme caution should be used when approaching Holmes Falls and the takeout in Machias. Inexperienced canoe trippers should consider hiring a guide.

Directions:

Access Points above the Airline: Start at Machias River Road about 1 mile west of where Maine Route 9 crosses over the Machias River and follow the State of Maine Machias River Guide: https://www.maine.gov/dacf/parksearch/PropertyGuides/PDF_GUIDE/machiasriverguide.pdf

Access Points below Airline: Obtain and follow The Maine Atlas: https://www.amazon.com/Maine-Atlas-Gazetteer-Delorme/dp/089933282X

Takeout in Machias: Traveling north on U S Route 1 in Machias, turn left onto Water Street immediately after crossing the bridge over the Machias River. The takeout is next to a sizeable parking lot on the immediate left.

Chapter 41 - Machias River

A canoeist descends First Wigwam Rapid on the Machias River. (Photo – Ron Chase)

Chapter 42 - Allagash River and Tributaries

What's a Musquacook?

A tributary of the Allagash River, Musquacook Stream is located in a remote area east of that iconic waterway. Flowing northwesterly, it joins the Allagash about midway through the river section of the traditional canoe trip.

Musquacook had been on my bucket list ever since two friends paddled it eight years ago. At my age, time was running out. The problem is that the window of opportunity to navigate the arcane stream is very limited. Ice has to be out, the old logging roads accessible, and adequate water for an enjoyable, exciting paddle is necessary. For me, there is an additional prerequisite, no black flies. That narrows the chances to a handful of days each spring.

I called premiere Allagash shuttle aficionado and owner of Pelletier Camps, Norm L'Italien, on a Wednesday evening. He reported roads were rough but passable and ice was out. Adding in his distinctly French Canadian accent that there was plenty of water and no black flies, he cautioned, "If you're going, do it soon. Remember, you'll be on your own with unknown conditions. No one has been there since last May."

Early the following Tuesday morning, Norm's crew was shuttling us to Musquacook. We were a team of four, including three retirees. Ken Gordon paddled an expedition kayak while Eggman DeCoster, Brent Elwell, and I solo canoes. The confusing labyrinth of roads was muddy with numerous partial washouts, but the van driver safely delivered us to a bridge over a fast-moving stream everyone hoped was the correct one. According to online gauge readings, the Allagash watershed was running in excess of 5000 cubic feet per second, more than five times the normal flow for the canoe trip. The actual level for Musquacook was unknown but presumed high. The weather forecast was unsettled and stormy throughout our planned excursion with periodic rain,

Chapter 42 - Allagash River and Tributaries

possibly snow, and strong headwinds. Our choice was to tolerate the unpleasant weather or wait another year. We knowingly selected the former.

Initially a fast-moving current, the intensity quickened to steady whitewater. There were two primary concerns: the possibility of dangerous strainers blocking the stream and a ledge drop reputed to be a difficult Class III. Rounding a bend early on, we encountered a large fallen tree that obstructed navigation. Since water was high, negotiating to the right and pushing through alders on what would normally be the shore, successfully avoided the impediment. Shortly after, another downed tree was confronted in the midst of a rapid. Halting our heavy vessels just above, we decided that dragging our boats around the hazard was the only option. Progressing in search of the elusive falls and evading a continuum of blow downs were constant challenges.

The river gods smiled on us as no additional significant obstacles were encountered. The presumed formidable rapid was traversed without realizing it. In fact, the sustained entertaining whitewater never exceeded Class II in difficulty. Following a couple of miles of flat water, we arrived at Allagash River. The substantial efforts expended to paddle Musquacook had been justified as it was a thoroughly stimulating endeavor.

Powerful headwinds greeted us on the Allagash. With a forecast for heavy rain, snow, and temperatures in the low thirties, stopping early at Five Fingers Brook campsite was the consensus decision. After setting up tents, a large tarp was erected over the picnic table and firewood gathered before hunkering down. A cold weather sissy, I pitched a small tarp over my tent for added protection. Shortly after, the rain began.

Lingering in our warm sleeping bags, we arose late the following morning. If it snowed in the night, early morning rain had washed it away. After we enjoyed a brief clearing, rain vindictively recommenced shortly after launching. While the high water pushed us along, an unrelenting headwind was an unwelcome adversary. Following a stop at closed Michaud Farm Ranger Station, we traversed through a succession of small islands that brought us to spectacular Allagash Falls, a mandatory portage.

While any portage is a chore, Allagash Falls Trail is in excellent condition. Completing the arduous task ahead of schedule, we progressed north into a persistent gale to Big Brook Campsite where wind and rain continued throughout the night. As we embarked early on our final day, the remaining ten miles were accomplished despite, you guessed it, enduring an uncompromising headwind with steady showers. No black fly problems for us; too cold, wet, and windy.

My bucket list reduced by one, I have an eye on another obscure tributary that flows into the Allagash, Chemquasabamticook Stream. Can't pronounce it, don't know anyone who has been there, but I want to paddle it.

My previous trips on the Allagash have been family affairs. In 1983, my wife Nancy, our youngest son Adam, and I completed the entire 92-mile Allagash Wilderness Waterway from Chamberlain Bridge at the southern terminus of Chamberlain Lake to Allagash Village. Adam was five at the time and the outing was a great adventure for all three of us. Many exciting challenges were experienced including enduring strong winds and large waves on the big lakes, a visit to ancient abandoned locomotive engines near Eagle Lake that once transported logs south, navigating the Class II whitewater on Chase Rapids, and portaging impressive Allagash Falls. Adam rode in the middle of an 18-foot Old Town Voyageur Canoe. In order to keep him entertained, we took our time, stopped to swim regularly, and one day was spent hiking and exploring the Round Pond area.

A few years later, Adam and I completed the trip beginning at Churchill Dam, avoiding the big lakes. On that occasion, he paddled a whitewater kayak and I a solo canoe loaded with gear. More recently, he and I were joined by a large group of friends, again beginning at Churchill Dam.

The Allagash Waterway is a tale of two paddling experiences. The first forty miles is primarily big lakes. The remainder is essentially a river trip with whitewater, quick water, and narrow lakes.

Regardless, an excursion on the Allagash River is one of Maine's finest outdoor adventures.

THINGS TO KNOW

Location: Piscataquis and Aroostook Counties, northern Maine

Length: Approximately 40 miles for the described Musquacook and Allagash trip. The entire Allagash Waterway is 92 miles and the approximate distance from Churchill Dam to Allagash Village is 55 miles.

Difficulty rating: Class I/II

Determining the water level: Visit USGS website at: https://waterdata.usgs.gov/me/nwis/current/?type=flow and click on Allagash.

Scouting and portages: Allagash Falls is a mandatory portage. Inexperienced whitewater paddlers may want to stop and scout sections of Chase Rapids below Churchill Dam. When the waterway is open, arrangements can normally be made with the ranger at Churchill Dam to portage gear or boats and paddlers around Chase Rapids.

Shuttle Services: Pelletier Camps: https://pelletiers.mainerec.com/ and Allagash Guide Service: https://www.allagashguideservice.com/maine-canoe-trips/canoe-trip-shuttle-transportation/ . From my viewpoint, the easiest shuttle method is to drive to Allagash and have a shuttle service transport paddlers, boats, and gear to the put-in. Another option is to drive to the put-in in your vehicle and have a shuttle service drive it out. Some boaters arrange to be flown in by float plane.

Unique potential hazards: There are several challenging Class II rapids, including the long sector of Chase Rapids just below Churchill Dam. Paddlers should have solid Class II whitewater paddling skills. Consider having the ranger at Churchill Dam portage gear or boats and paddlers. Dangerous swims are a risk and injury or death is a real possibility. Officials on the waterway do a good job of keeping it free of strainers and hazardous debris; however there is always a possibility of their presence. Paddlers should be extremely cautious approaching Allagash Falls. There are signs in advance and the takeout is on the right. A missed eddy could result in being swept over the falls. Paddlers attempting Musquacook Stream should expect to encounter dangerous strainers. Inexperienced canoe trippers should consider hiring a guide.

Directions:

Chamberlain Bridge: Follow the directions in Chapter 1 and Chapter 4 to reach the junction of the Golden Road and Telos Road from Millinocket. From that junction drive north for about 25 miles on Telos Road to Chamberlain Bridge where there is a Ranger Station, landing, parking area, and toilets.

Churchill Dam: From Chamberlain Bridge, travel over a series of logging roads for about 35 miles to Churchill Dam where there is a Ranger Station, landing, parking area, and toilets. This drive is very confusing and road problems are common. It should not be attempted without a GPS and map.

Allagash Village: From the junctions of US Route 1 and Maine Routes 11 and 161 in Fort Kent, drive north on paved Route 161 for about 30 miles to Allagash Village. There are several options to takeout most involve paying a parking fee. Recommend consulting with the local shuttle services, see above.

Chapter 42 - Allagash River and Tributaries

A canoeist navigates Long Lake Dam on the Allagash. (Photo – Ron Chase)

Chapter 43 - West Branch of Penobscot and Chesuncook Lake

Skunked on the West Branch

I love fall canoe trips and my brother-in-law, Mike Moody, is an avid bird hunter. As a result of some friendly negotiations, we agreed to combine our interests into a canoe trip on the legendary West Branch of the Penobscot River. The late October journey would begin not far from where the venerable 19th century journalist and nature lover Henry David Thoreau and his Penobscot Indian Nation guide Joseph Attean entered the West Branch after portaging from Moosehead Lake on one of their famous Maine wilderness explorations. Unlike Thoreau, our excursion would end on Steamboat Landing at the southern terminus of substantial Chesuncook Lake.

The plan was for me to have primary responsibility for paddling from the stern, while Mike assisted from the bow pausing to hunt when the opportunity arose. Ducks and partridges would be his primary quarry, but bagging an elusive Canada goose a secondary goal. Since he was in need of ammunition, the last stop on our drive to the river was Indian Hill Trading Post in Greenville. While there, I purchased a cot to elevate my aging bones above the ground during the cold nights that were forecasted for the expedition. Carefully guarding his nickels, Mike elected to forego the extravagance.

Launching on the West Branch just below a popular whitewater run at Roll Dam, we navigated flat water for about eight miles to Lobster Stream. Leaving the river and following the shallow tributary into picturesque Lobster Lake, we selected a campsite on scenic Ogden Point. No migratory birds had been observed during the day, but geese could be heard honking at night. Once the sun went down, the temperature dropped

Chapter 43 - West Branch of Penobscot and Chesuncook Lake

dramatically. Toasty warm in my sleeping bag on the cot, I observed it was unfortunate Mike had to sleep on the cold ground. Expletive deleted.

We arose early, but a search for the noisy geese proved futile. Wherever we explored, the wily birds seemed to be squawking on a distant side of the lake. As we departed from Lobster Lake, a strong current helped propel us downriver. After we stopped for lunch at Lone Pine Campsite, additional sites were observed on Big Island beyond. While they were empty and otherwise met our needs, our decision was to journey farther along to an expansive site called Little Ragmuff on river left. No game birds were spotted during our time on the river. A cold night, I inquired as to Mike's comfort. Seemingly out of sorts, he said something under his breath.

Up early, Mike had no luck hunting partridge before breakfast. Shortly after we departed on a raw chilly gray day, a twisting, shallow Class II rapid was negotiated. Arriving at a large pool of dead water, Boomhouse campsite was on the right. After filling our water containers from an ancient hand pump, we hiked south into the old logging community of Chesuncook. On return, Mike spotted a Spruce Partridge, a protected bird.

Turning Graveyard Point into Chesuncook Lake, we encountered unusual calm paddling south past the Village of Chesuncook and along the west shore of the upper lake region. The often-tempestuous body of water was remarkably serene as we continued south to scenic Sandy Point Campsite where exceptional views of the Katahdin massif were the reward for our efforts. During our trip down the lake, several geese were observed on the opposite shore. They seemed to be taunting us with their loud honking. Sandy Point was a partridge-free zone so delicious grouse breast sautéed in white wine and butter failed to make the evening menu.

Powerful winds developed during the night and a fierce gust blew our canoe dangerously close to the lake. Forced to leave the violently trembling tent to retrieve the fugitive boat in cold howling conditions, we were able to secure it to a large log in a sheltered location. Returning to our tent and the warmth of my elevated cot, I expressed an avuncular concern for Mike's well-being. Uncharacteristically intense, he threatened to throw the cot into the lake with me in it.

Winds dissipated around dawn, so we broke camp before breakfast in hopes of avoiding more blustery weather in the open water that would prevail during much of the remainder of our voyage. Hunting had to be postponed until protection from potential squalls could be ensured. After a breezy crossing above Caribou Lake to Caribou Point, a potent tailwind catapulted us rapidly south in three- and four-foot swells.

The thrilling escapade in turbulent waves required constant attention to our paddling duties, allowing no time for hunting. A formation of Canada geese flew directly overhead while we were preoccupied maneuvering through the tumultuous waters. "No hunting" signs welcomed us on arrival at Steamboat Landing. Mike never needed the ammunition he purchased in Greenville. In my opinion, he would have been better served buying a new cot, a thought I kept to myself.

THINGS TO KNOW

Location: Piscataquis County, northwestern Maine
Length: Approximately 50 miles
Difficulty rating: Easy to moderate with one Class II rapid
Water levels: The release from Seboomook Dam above Roll Dam can be determined by calling 1-800-452-1737 and entering the six-digit code 235120. While a minimum release is sufficient to complete the river trip, levels are often increased during the summer to facilitate whitewater boating at Roll Dam. Primarily a flat-water trip, it can be completed from ice out in the spring to late fall.
Unique potential hazards: Paddlers should have Class I/II skills. Dangerous swims are a risk and injury or death is a real possibility. A popular trip in summer months, vacant campsites may

Chapter 43 - West Branch of Penobscot and Chesuncook Lake

be scarce. Dangerous gusty winds on Chesuncook are always a potential risk.

Directions:
Take out at Steamboat Landing: From the junction of Route 15/6 and Lily Bay Road in Greenville, drive north on Lily Bay, Sias Hill, and Greenville Roads for about 38 miles to the Golden Road. Turn right on Golden Road and go about 5 miles to a left turn leading to Steamboat Landing. Expect the roads to be rough.

Put-in at Roll Dam: From Steamboat Landing, drive north on Golden Road past the junction with Greenville Road for about 21 miles to a left turn leading to Northeast Carry about two miles before a bridge over the Penobscot River called Hannibal's Crossing. Prior to the turn, stop to pay road and camping fees at the North Maine Woods Caribou Gatehouse. Follow the road past Northeast Carry for about 11 miles to Roll Dam on the right. Again, expect the roads to be rough.

Alternative Trips: It's possible to continue following Thoreau's odyssey by traversing the top of Chesuncook Lake, navigating northeast on Umbazooksus Stream and Lake to the strenuous two-mile Mud Pond Carry. After hardy adventurers complete the portage, a short paddle across Mud Pond and down a steep narrow outlet stream leads to Chamberlain Lake. From that point, there are options to end the excursion at Chamberlain Bridge, continue north on the Allagash trip (See Chapter 42), or complete the Webster Stream and East Branch trip (See Chapter 46).

The view from Sandy Point Campsite on Chesuncook Lake. (Photo – Tom Meredith)

Chapter 44 - St. John River

Realizing a Dream on the Elusive St. John

I began canoe tripping in 1974. From the outset, a goal was to paddle the legendary St. John River in northern Maine. In the subsequent decades, plans were made several times to complete the iconic canoe trip. On each occasion, low water or impassable roads prevented realization of my objective.

Finally, veteran St. John trippers Carolyn Welch and Dave Lanman invited my wife Nancy and me to join them on their planned trip. Although skeptical it would actually become a reality, we sanguinely signed on. A few days before the anticipated departure, Carolyn announced the roads were open, water levels moderately high, and a shuttle operator, Sean Lizotte, owner of Allagash Guide Service, had been engaged. A deluge of telephone calls and email messages quickly followed. A final roster of participants was determined, meals assigned, and the meeting time and place established. This time, it seemed the St. John was really going to happen.

On a cool mid-May afternoon, five tandem canoe teams met at a large cabin owned by Sean in Allagash Village. Giant chunks of ice had been observed scattered along the St. John River bank during our drive from Fort Kent. Sean reassured us ice was out on Baker Lake, the preferred starting point. While everyone knew Carolyn and Dave, the evening was spent with the others getting acquainted as canoe packing strategies were refined.

The outside temperature was a balmy 27 degrees when the group arose early the following morning. After breakfast, Sean and his assistant, Roger Kelly, transported the entire assemblage on a four-hour drive to the outlet of Baker Lake. A team of six departed just ahead of us and another group of six decided to spend the night at Baker Lake to avoid congestion on the river.

Obviously, others had recognized this was the ideal window of opportunity for a St. John trip.

Embarking early afternoon, a steady current propelled our exuberant team of canoeists nine miles to Flaws Bogan Campsite. A covered picnic table was a welcome accoutrement and the first of many delicious communal meals was served. Doubting our culinary skills, Nancy and I were intimidated.

Slightly warmer than the previous morning, we were on the river at nine. One overly enthusiastic team was so excited they forgot to untie their canoe before attempting to depart. On a glorious day with partly sunny skies and comfortable paddling conditions, twenty-three miles were attained before reaching the intended campsite at Ledge Rapids. Nancy and I set up a sun shower, providing a pleasant late afternoon indulgence. Our salmon and pasta meal appeared to pass muster so everything was copacetic.

Up early the following morning with overcast sky, Team St. John broke camp and departed. After paddling a short distance, we replenished our water supply in a spring near Moody Bridge. While stopping at historic Nine Mile Bridge for lunch, an ancient railroad steam shovel provided entertainment for the history buffs. In earlier times during an era of the great logging drives, this area was a whirlwind of activity. Some of the remnants remain. Completing twenty-one miles, extensive ice shelves along the shore and huge blocks of ice seemingly tossed onto the river bank underscored our arrival at Seven Islands Campsite. After another great meal, Nancy and I drew dishwashing duty. A weather radio report wasn't so encouraging; rain and snow were forecast during the coming days.

We awoke to gray skies and cool temperatures the next day. Excitement was in the air as demanding whitewater rapids were on the agenda. Following a break at Simmons Farm, the Class II Basford Rips were successfully traversed. Just below, Class III Big Black Rapids were scouted on river left. The exciting waves were negotiated without incident. Shortly after, a campsite was selected

Chapter 44 - St. John River

near the outlet of Big Black River, culminating a twenty-one-mile paddle. Ominously, the sky and air looked and felt like snow.

Rain and snow fell during the night. Heavy wet snowflakes persisted through breakfast, prompting a conversation about the wisdom of breaking camp, given the inclement weather. The snow subsided and a decision was made to proceed. Shortly after turning the first bend, we were confronted with heavy snow driven horizontally by a powerful headwind. While there was some momentary second-guessing, our intrepid band persevered downriver. The snow dissipated but a bitter headwind persisted. Arriving at Ouellette Farm Campsite for lunch after sixteen miles of frigid paddling, hypothermia was a concern for some. Instead of continuing, establishing camp was deemed the wiser choice. The temperature dropped below freezing during the night.

Frost coated our tents the following morning. Another overcast day with the threat of rain, the most challenging rapids on the journey lay ahead. A few miles of quick water brought us to Big Rapids. After exhaustively scouting the two-mile rapid from river left, the big waves and intimidating ledge drops were triumphantly navigated. The successful paddlers stopped to bail their canoes at the bottom while emphatically celebrating the exhilarating escapade. The expedition ended about four miles downriver at Dickey Bridge in Allagash Plantation.

Another night at Sean Lizotte's cabin in Allagash provided an idyllic setting to reminisce about the many exploits our group had shared. Happy hour was a rousing affair. For Nancy and me, it was the culmination of a longtime dream fulfilled.

THINGS TO KNOW

Location: Piscataquis and Aroostook Counties, northern Maine
Length: Approximately 105 miles for the described trip
Difficulty rating: Class I/II with two Class III rapids

Determining water level: Visit USGS website at: https://waterdata.usgs.gov/me/nwis/current/?type=flow and click on St. John at Dickey and Nine Mile Bridge. Paddlers navigate the St. John at very low to exceptionally high levels. During our six-day trip, the Nine Mile Bridge gauge varied from 9500 cubic feet per second at the beginning to 3500 approaching the end, moderate levels.

Scouting and portages: Scouting Big Black and Big Rapids recommended. Inexperienced whitewater boaters may want to portage both.

Shuttle Services: Pelletier Camps: https://pelletiers.mainerec.com/ and Allagash Guide Service: https://www.allagashguideservice.com/ . From my viewpoint, the easiest shuttle method is to drive to Allagash and have a shuttle service transport paddlers, boats, and gear to the put-in. Another option is to drive to the put-in in your vehicle and have a shuttle service drive it out. Some boaters arrange to be flown in by float plane.

Unique potential hazards: There are two challenging Class III rapids and several easier ones. Paddlers should have solid Class II whitewater paddling skills. Dangerous swims are a risk and injury or death a possibility. Inexperienced canoe trippers should consider hiring a guide.

Directions to Allagash Village: See Chapter 41. Driving to Baker Lake is not recommended. The roads are confusing and even when passable often in marginal to poor condition. The drive should not be attempted without a GPS and map.

Chapter 44 - St. John River

Canoeists persevere in a snowstorm on the St. John River. (Photo – Ken Gordon)

Chapter 45 - Moose River Bow Trip

You Always Forget Something on a Canoe Trip

The trip had been planned for weeks. Four of us intended to paddle the famous Moose River Bow Trip in two tandem canoes. I would supply my Old Town Voyageur and Mike Breau was bringing his Old Town Tripper from Portsmouth, New Hampshire.

When Bob Smith and I met Mike and my co-worker, Bill Laidley, at the Greyhound Bus Station in Augusta, they both were departing from the bus. Mike didn't have his vehicle or canoe. He had forgotten his canoe. You always forget something on a canoe trip.

The actual story was more arcane but just as enigmatic. Mike's car had broken down the day before so he decided to load a duffle with his gear, catch the bus, and make the best of it. So there we were in the Greyhound bus station parking lot on a cold, late October day: Four wannabe canoe trippers, gear for a three-day canoe trip, one tandem canoe, and one tiny 1978 LUV truck with a bench seat that fit three maximum. What ensued was the most bizarre and serendipitous canoe trip I've experienced.

With three of us in the cab and Mike relegated to the truck bed in his sleeping bag surrounded with gear and sheltered by the canoe, we embarked on the 110-mile drive to Attean Pond near Jackman. While Mike deservedly shivered in the back, a strategy was devised by those of us benefiting from the warmth inside. Bill and I would load most of the gear in the canoe and paddle. Mike and Bob would hike carrying light packs and meet us at strategic points on the journey. In the relative comfort of the truck cab, it seemed a remarkably simple efficacious plan.

After dispatching the hikers onto the Canadian Pacific Railroad tracks on the north side of Attean Pond to begin a five-mile

Chapter 45 - Moose River Bow Trip

slog along the tracks to the western terminus of the pond, Bill and I launched from Attean Pond Boat Landing. The hike and paddle were relatively uneventful, culminating in all of us meeting at the 1.2-mile portage trail to Holeb Pond. This was one of the rare moments when one canoe was advantageous. Completing the arduous portage, the determined hikers continued west along the tracks on the south shore of Holeb Pond while Bill and I traversed the pond to a campsite on the western end. After unloading gear, I paddled a half mile across the pond and retrieved the hiking contingent now known as Team Trek.

Following a frosty clear night, the objective for the next day was more intimidating. Delivering Team Trek back to the railroad tracks, their intent was to follow the tracks east for a short distance and then bushwhack over thickly forested Attean Mountain, waxing optimistic they could correctly descend and meet us at a campsite near Holeb Falls on the Moose River. Meanwhile, Bill and I would paddle down Holeb Stream for a mile and connect with the meandering Moose River. From there, we'd canoe about eight miles through Camel Rips to a portage trail around Holeb Falls. An unplanned adversary was a consequential fall storm.

While Bill and I paddled in heavy driving rain, dauntless Team Trek labored through their strenuous mountaineering odyssey in the stormy weather. A testament to their orienteering skills, the thoroughly drenched hikers were waiting for us at the Holeb Falls portage trail. Traveling with just one canoe, the relatively short carry was quickly accomplished. At that time, the campsite at the foot of the falls was adjacent to a dilapidated cabin. Gusting winds and pouring rain convinced our weary band that the wretched hut was preferable to our flimsy tents. The choice was a good one as several large branches and a couple of nearby trees fell during the night.

Prospects appeared good for Bill and me the next morning as there were clearing skies, high water, and a forceful tailwind. Intrepid Team Trek was faced with a dilemma: cross the river immediately and attempt another bushwhack to a possible connector road that led to civilization or follow along the north shore of

Moose River for about six miles and have us meet and transport them across the river to a camp road at Spencer Rips. They chose the latter—a poor decision. While elevated water and a substantial gale propelled us rapidly through Mosquito Rips to Spencer Rips, Team Trek toiled mightily, wallowing through an extensive swamp before reaching the Voyageur ferry service. During lunch, afternoon itineraries were finalized. Weary Team Trek contrived to trudge out the camp road for about four miles and then follow Hardscrabble Road east for another ten miles to US Route 201 near Lake Parlin. Bill and I would guide the cumbersome canoe for seven miles to Attean Pond followed by a three-mile crossing to the landing.

The strong current provided exciting descents on two rapids called Attean Falls immediately before entering the pond. Once we navigated north on open water, the powerful tailwind became a challenging broadside. For the remaining three miles, large breaking waves battered us from port side adding copious amounts of water to our already heavily laden vessel. Sighting the bright blue LUV truck at the landing was a welcome relief.

By the time we arrived at Lake Parlin, exhausted and hypothermic Team Trek was thrilled to see the overloaded LUV truck hurtling down the highway. Acknowledging Mike's considerable contribution to the endeavor, truck bed duty was alternated on the return trip to Augusta.

A few years later, my wife Nancy and our youngest son Adam again completed the bow trip. Paddling across Holeb Pond, eight-year-old Adam caught numerous brook trout and repeated that success at the foot of Holeb Falls. When we awoke after camping at the falls, Adam was suffering with intense stomach pain. Concerned he might have a serious medical ailment, we hurriedly paddled to Attean Landing. While unpacking, the source of his discomfort was determined. Not a fan of fried fish, he'd consumed our entire supply of green apples.

I've completed the Moose River Bow Trip about a dozen times over forty years. Until recently, the expedition had always been called the bow trip. Apparently, the popularity of beginning on Holeb Pond hence avoiding the long portage has resulted in a name change. Now, some sources designate the excursion from Holeb Pond Landing to the Attean Pond Landing the bow trip and the former bow trip is called the loop trip. Not me. There is only one bow trip and it begins and ends at Attean Pond Landing. The other outing is the "sissy" trip.

However, the portage should not be underestimated. About 1.2 miles in length, it's always a rocky, muddy, hilly, demanding undertaking. The ramshackle cabin at Holeb Falls has been replaced by a new improved shelter. The cabin and all campsites are first-come first-served.

THINGS TO KNOW

Location: Somerset County, northwestern Maine
Length: 34 miles
Difficulty rating: Class I & II with a strenuous portage
Water levels: Since the Moose River Bow Trip is primarily a flat-water expedition, it can be completed from ice out in the spring to late fall. In low water, the rapids may need to be portaged or lined.
Scouting and portages: Camel Rips, Mosquito Rips, Spencer Rips, and two rapids called Attean Falls should be scouted. A long portage is required between Attean and Holeb Ponds and Holeb Falls must be carried.
Unique potential hazards: There are several Class II rapids. Paddlers should have Class II skills or be prepared to portage them. Dangerous swims are a risk and injury or death is a real possibility. Trippers should have sufficient fitness levels to carry all boats and gear on the 1.2-mile portage. This usually requires at least two trips (unless your party consists of four people with one canoe). A popular trip, weekends and holidays may be crowded and vacant tent sites scarce.
Approach to Holeb Falls: The approach to Holeb Falls is confusing. About 4 miles after Camel Rips, high ledges on the

right and huge boulders in the river indicate the falls are close. Shortly after, take a left turn into a narrow channel and then an immediate right turn. The second left turn is a dead end. Paddle about a half mile through a couple of easy drops and turn left. The portage trail begins there. Take the time to ensure you've made the right choice as the falls are very dangerous.

Directions: Follow the directions in Chapter 26 to West Forks. Continue north on Route 201 for 21 miles to an intersection with Routes 6 and 15 on the right and Attean Pond Road on the left. Follow Attean Pond Road for about 2.5 miles to the end where Attean Pond Boat Landing is located and parking is available.

Alternative Trips:

Holeb Pond to Attean Pond: This trip is not recommended. How will you explain the decision to your grandchildren?

Attean Pond and Attean Mountain Surf & Turf: Paddle to campsites located on the southwestern shore of Attean Pond. A two-mile trail leads to one of the Attean Mountain peaks with excellent views. If this is done in conjunction with the bow trip, give yourself an additional day. A bushwhack over Attean Mountain from Holeb Pond is not recommended.

A young paddler lands a fish on the Moose River. (Photo – Ken Gordon)

Chapter 46 - Webster Stream and East Branch of Penobscot

Following Thoreau

A canoe trip down legendary Webster Stream and East Branch of the Penobscot River is the quintessential Maine river adventure. The exciting and intriguing endeavor offers a unique opportunity to paddle the same waterways the venerable author, poet, and philosopher Henry David Thoreau explored over a century and a half ago. Challenging whitewater rapids, magnificent waterfalls, scenic lakes, demanding portages, and almost continuous spectacular views punctuate this four- to six-day canoe trip. It all takes place in the shadows of the majestic peaks of Baxter State Park.

Thoreau and his Penobscot Indian guide, Joe Polis, traveled the region in the mid-1800s. Part of their journey in 1857 included the very same route that constitutes the present-day Webster Stream and East Branch canoe trip. While possible to paddle an abbreviated version, many canoe tripping purists insist on a longer choice that embodies their feat and more closely duplicates Thoreau's experiences. That excursion begins on Telos Lake in the Allagash Wilderness Waterway ending downriver at one of the egress points on the lower East Branch.

Over the years, members of the Penobscot Paddle and Chowder Society (PPCS) have completed several trips on Webster Stream and the East Branch. Most have begun at Chamberlain Bridge which spans a narrow waterway connecting Chamberlain and Telos Lakes northwest of Baxter State Park. Usually ending at Whetstone Falls near Stacyville, the expedition is about sixty miles in length with seven partial or complete portages required. Since the drive from Stacyville around the park to Chamberlain Bridge is a lengthy one that includes significant logging road travel, hiring a shuttle service is far more time efficient than running your own. Fortuitously, accomplished Maine Guide Dan Pelletier is a PPCS member.

Fall is an ideal time for a canoe trip on Webster Stream and the East Branch. Dam operators at the outlets of Telos and Grand Matagamon Lakes normally draw the lakes down between mid-September and mid-October. A favorable reliable water level is generally available during that timeframe. Important factors for me: black fly season has ended and the cool autumn air has ushered in the brilliant colors of the changing seasons.

On the most recent PPCS trip, a group of five Chowderheads met at Dan Pelletier's business in Alton on the preceding night. Our team consisted of five solo canoeists: Eggman DeCoster, Doug Field, Helen Hess, Kim Perkins, and an old geezer (that would be me).

The following morning, Dan followed us in his van and boat trailer to the East Branch. West of Stacyville the first obstacle of the journey was encountered, the road to Whetstone Falls was closed. After some discussion, the consensus was to change the takeout to a small landing about two miles upriver. Leaving vehicles at that location, we endured the seemingly endless four-hour drive to Chamberlain Bridge and arrived at Round Pond early afternoon. Also the embarking point for the Allagash Wilderness Waterway, Round Pond is essentially the northwest arm of Telos Lake, as the two are one connected body of water.

The Telos Lake area has a captivating history. During the logging wars of the early and mid-nineteenth century, sawmills and communities along the Saint John and Penobscot Rivers competed for valuable lumber originating in the region. In 1841, dams were built on Chamberlain and Telos Lakes and a canal excavated below the dam at the eastern end of Telos. Logs that would have otherwise been floated north on the Allagash River were diverted south onto the Penobscot.

Partly sunny weather and light winds facilitated an uneventful seven-mile paddle across Telos Lake to the dam where a Maine Forest Service Campsite is located. A short portage was accomplished by carrying our heavy loaded boats around the dam on

Chapter 46 - Webster Stream and East Branch of Penobscot

river right. A feisty descent ensued through shallow fast-moving Telos Cut to a campsite at the finish on the western shore of Webster Lake.

The northwestern boundary of Baxter State Park was intersected about halfway through three-mile Webster Lake the following morning. Camping inside the park must be arranged and paid for in advance. Webster Stream began at the outlet. After about four miles of almost continuous entertaining whitewater, a park lean-to was passed on river right.

The excitement began just downriver. First was Indian Carry Rapid. The twisting passage has a sticky hydraulic that will flip a loaded canoe and should be carefully scouted or portaged on the left. Once scouted, our group completed the complex maneuver without incident. Two miles beyond is Grand Pitch, a two-stage waterfall mandating a portage on the right. Just below are several difficult ledge drops, all potentially hazardous. The arduous half mile portage trail was used to transport gear. After carefully scouting and setting up safety, we successfully negotiated all the complicated ledge descents.

Shortly after, we arrived at Northwest Cove campsite. At this location a few years prior, an uninvited guest joined us for lunch. Clearly attracted by the smell of sardines, a small bear cub warily approached. An experienced hunter in the group surmised his mother had died and he was starving. The little fellow didn't get any sardines, but we left him a supply of apples when departing.

Our intrepid band was hoping for a strong northwest tailwind when leaving the picturesque campsite on the western end of sizeable Grand Lake Matagamon the following morning. On an earlier trip, four canoes had been lashed together, a large tarp elevated, and the flotilla sailed east for several miles. Alas, a headwind was endured for our nine-mile voyage through the eastern boundary of Baxter State Park to Grand Lake Dam.

Completing the laborious portage around the dam on the right and steeply down the bank to the river below, our expedition on the East Branch began. Canoeing a short distance in easy rapids to Matagamon Wilderness Campground, a campsite along the river had been reserved for the night. That evening, supplies were replenished at the campground store and fellow Chowderhead Paul Plumer joined us for the remainder of the excursion.

The next morning began with five miles of quick water and flat water to Stairs Falls. Easier than the name implies, a succession of elongated ledges was run on the left.

Four significant cataracts are confronted in the next five miles. All must be scouted and normally portaged. The first is Haskell Pitch with a half mile portage trail on the right. Beginning with a steep river-wide pitch, a long Class III runout continues for some distance turning left and then right before ending at the bottom of the portage trail. Our resolute group carried gear while simultaneously carefully scouting the intimidating plunge at the beginning. Identifying a complex constricted descent tight right, everyone guided their craft through the challenging route and finished the entire rapid with one minor swim.

Pond Pitch was next. A possible route was discerned center left but the risk of filling up and broaching was too great. Everyone completed the short carry left. Disaster was avoided when an empty runaway canoe was corralled just before tumbling over the edge.

Less than a mile below, the most spectacular and intimidating falls on the journey commenced, Grand Pitch. While run by expert kayakers at some levels, the vertical eighteen-foot drop with a difficult complex approach is not navigable in a tripping canoe. A portage trail on the left passes through an exceptional campsite overlooking the falls. Tenting next to the roar of the falls was the ideal setting for our last night on the river.

The final day began with the fourth cataract, Hulling Machine. Named by early river drivers, the falls begins with a precipitous boulder-strewn pitch followed by a lengthy Class II/III rapid. The choice is a long portage trail on the right or a short steep carry left allowing paddlers to negotiate the lower portion. As usual, our undaunted group chose to paddle rather than endure the lengthy carry.

Chapter 46 - Webster Stream and East Branch of Penobscot

Below Hulling Machine, about ten miles of easy rapids and flat water ensued to the confluence with Seboeis River in a swampy area. Another four miles of quick water brought us to the prearranged takeout two miles above Whetstone Falls. The plan to leave all vehicles was a fortuitous one. Dry clothes were waiting and no time-consuming shuttle was necessary prior to the drive home. Thoreau never had it so good.

THINGS TO KNOW

Location: Piscataquis and Penobscot Counties, northern Maine
Length: Approximately 60 miles for the described trip
Difficulty rating: Class II, III, and IV with several strenuous portages
Determining water level: Visit Matagamon Lake Association website for current dam release information: http://www.katahdinoutdoors.com/dam/flowdata.html. Telos Dam releases in the range of 300 to 500 cubic feet per second (CFS) for Webster Stream and 700 to 1500 CFS from Grand Lake Dam for the East Branch are recommended for the described trip.
Scouting and portages: Indian Carry Rapid, Ledge Drops below Grand Pitch on Webster Stream, Stairs Falls, Haskell Pitch, and Pond Pitch should be scouted. Portage Telos Dam, Grand Pitch on Webster Stream, Grand Lake Dam, Grand Pitch on East Branch, and Hulling Machine. Consider portages on Indian Carry, Ledge Drops on Webster, Haskell Pitch, and Pond Pitch.
Shuttle services: Dan Pelletier, Maine Guiding Wilderness Adventures: http://maineguiding.com/ and Katahdin Region Wilderness Guide Service: http://www.katahdinoutdoors.com/guiding/

Camping:
  Baxter State Park campsites:
  https://baxterstatepark.org/

Matagamon Wilderness Campground:
https://matagamon.com/

Unique potential hazards: There are many challenging whitewater rapids including Indian Carry Rapid, Ledge Drops below Grand Pitch on Webster Stream, Stairs Falls, Haskell Pitch, and Pond Pitch that rise to the Class III/IV level. Paddlers should have solid Class III whitewater paddling skills. Dangerous swims are a risk and injury or death is a real possibility. Extreme caution should be used when approaching Grand Pitch on Webster Stream and Grand Pitch on East Branch. Inexperienced canoe trippers should consider hiring a guide.

Directions:

Chamberlain Bridge: See directions in Chapter 41.

Whetstone Falls: From the junction of Interstate 95 and Maine Route 11 in Sherman Station, follow Route 11 south for about 5 miles to a right turn on Old Matagamon Tote Road in Stacyville. Drive about 7 miles west on Old Matagamon Tote Road to the bridge over Whetstone Falls.

Alternative Trip: The Seboeis River is a nearby alternative canoe trip. Located east of the East Branch, the recommended starting point is on Grand Lake Road about 10 miles east of Matagamon Wilderness Campground. The Class I/II 35-mile trip to Whetstone Falls on the East Branch has one mandatory portage. While possible to begin farther north, there are several miles of continuous Class III/IV whitewater immediately above Grand Lake Road that would be very difficult to navigate in a loaded tripping canoe.

Chapter 46 - Webster Stream and East Branch of Penobscot

Canoeists below Hulling Machine on the East Branch of the Penobscot. (Photo – Ron chase)

SECTION IX. BACKPACK TRIPS

Backpackers hike a section of the Appalachian Trail. (Photo – Ron Chase)

Chapter 47 - Appalachian Trail over Saddleback Range

Traversing Saddleback with the Boys

When my sons were growing up, mountain hiking was one of our favorite outdoor activities. Perhaps typical of Maine hiking families, trekking the entire Appalachian Trail was often a topic of conversation. At various times, Eric, Adam, and I discussed the possibility of attempting the two-thousand-mile test of endurance together.

Time passed, the boys matured to young men, their lives became more complicated, and I grew old. Just getting us together in Maine for a few days was a challenge. Eventually, it became apparent arranging for the three of us to be on the trail as a team for four months was not a realistic goal. A less time-consuming alternative was explored.

Completing a portion of the fabled Appalachian Trail remained an objective. My research and a prior backpacking experience convinced me that all things considered, the Saddleback Range is the most spectacular section of the Appalachian Trail in Maine. The 21.6-mile expedition from Route 4 near Madrid to the Caribou Valley Road in Carrabassett Valley links five peaks. Four of the summits are four thousand footers, and 4,250-foot Sugarloaf is the second tallest mountain and third highest peak in Maine. While not always the case, on this issue "the boys" agreed with Dad.

Remarkably, an idyllic three-day August forecast was predicted when all three of us were available. Packs, tents, and gear were assembled and meals planned. A shuttle vehicle was delivered to the Caribou Valley Road where the Appalachian Trail crosses adjacent to the South Branch of the Carrabassett River. From there, we drove north through Stratton, followed Route 16 west to Rangeley, and then traveled south on Route 4 to a parking area on the right where the Appalachian Trail intersects.

Weighed down with overloaded packs, we immediately began the trek by negotiating the upper Sandy River. After intersecting a logging road, hiking was easy for about a mile to a side trail on the left leading to Piazza Rock. Discarding our hefty packs near the Piazza Rock Lean-to, climbing the immense overhanging boulder was an imperative. Shortly after, another trail on the left led to a location called The Caves. Actually narrow passageways formed by huge boulders, the unique caverns also merited exploration.

Leaving the Piazza Rock area, the trail steepened while passing Ethel and Mud Ponds. Continuing to Eddy Pond on the left at about mile three, an excellent tent site was located near the picturesque tarn. Anticipating the following day would be an arduous one with significant elevation gain, the consensus was to establish camp early. Reducing the weight in our packs by consuming the substantial evening meal was an added incentive.

The next morning, the trail began climbing abruptly in a conifer forest shortly after departing from Eddy Pond. Adam moved ahead while Eric and I maintained a steady more gradual pace. After about a mile, we emerged onto a bluff in sparse scrub growth. High above, Adam could be seen advancing towards the summit of Saddleback Mountain. Shortly after, an approaching hiker anxiously announced, "There's a kid up there running with a full pack." The name of the sprinting backpacker was no mystery to us.

After ascending the exposed western slope of Saddleback in hot steamy weather, we found the 360-degree views at the top where Adam awaited were spectacular. The elongated ridge extending northeasterly provides one of the most magnificent mountain vistas in Maine. Impressive 4,041-foot Saddleback Horn dominated in the distance. Following a precipitous descent into an attenuated col, we scaled the alpine-like peak.

Persevering northeasterly in rugged terrain, we negotiated open Saddleback Junior before arriving at Poplar Ridge Campsite for lunch. Plummeting steeply to Orbeton Stream, we stopped for a relaxing cool down in the chilly water. Passing an old logging road soon after, the trail rose gradually to the top of forested Lone

Chapter 47 - Appalachian Trail over Saddleback Range

Mountain. A side trail to Mount Abraham was encountered in the saddle below. Climbing steadily on the shoulder of Spaulding Mountain, we culminated our demanding day of mountaineering at Spaulding Mountain Campsite, a little short of the summit. A bug-infested location, the Chase Boys prematurely retired to their tents.

After some additional elevation gain early the next day, a spur trail on the right led to the summit of Spaulding. The short climb to the reputedly 4,010-foot summit offered views of another four thousand footer, Mount Abraham. For many years, the elevation for Spaulding was listed as 3,988 feet. While the rest of the Appalachian Range is gradually shrinking, Spaulding is inexplicably growing taller.

Continuing on a hilly wooded ridge for about two miles, we arrived at an ancillary trail to Sugarloaf Mountain on the right. Following a rocky gradual ascent to the open summit of the second highest mountain in Maine, a panoramic view of the entire Bigelow Mountain Range was the reward for our efforts. The iconic Sugarloaf Ski Resort could be observed immediately below.

Returning to the Appalachian Trail, the path descended steeply along precipitous cliffs on the western shoulder of Sugarloaf in a dense stunted conifer forest. The gradient moderated shortly before reaching the South Branch of the Carrabassett River. After fording the shallow mountain stream, our journey ended on the dusty Caribou Valley Road.

While our excursion only encompassed a very small segment of the Appalachian Trail, sharing what is arguably the most impressive expanse of the path in Maine with my sons was a very special experience.

THINGS TO KNOW

Location: Franklin County, western Maine
Length of described trek: 21.6 miles
Difficulty: Strenuous

Unique potential hazards: Extended above tree line exposure to the elements. Several sections require boulder and rock scrambling, increasing the risk of serious falls. High winds and extreme conditions on the Saddleback Ridge are a risk. Carrying a map, compass, and GPS are recommended.

Views: Phenomenal on Saddleback Ridge and from the summit of Sugarloaf Mountain

Directions:

Appalachian Trail on Caribou Valley Road: See Chapter 14 for directions to Carrabassett Valley Airport in Carrabassett Valley. From there, continue north on Routes 27/16 for about 7.5 miles to the Caribou Valley Road on the left. Turn onto the rough dirt road and continue for about 4 miles to the Appalachian Trail. The road may be closed before reaching the AT due to bridge problems.

Appalachian Trail on Route 4 near Madrid: See Chapter 30 for directions to Reeds Mill Road in Madrid. From Reeds Mill Road, continue north on Route 4 for about four miles to where the AT intersects. A parking area is on the left.

A backpacker on the summit of Saddleback Mountain on the Appalachian Trail. (Photo – Ron Chase)

Chapter 48 - Baxter State Park – Nesowadnehunk Field to Roaring Brook

The Mountains are Alive with the Sound of Singing

Arguably, Acadia National Park and Baxter State Park are the two most exceptional outdoor recreation areas in Maine. Choosing one over the other is difficult but an advantage Baxter has is the abundance of several premiere backpacking trips.

After my wife Nancy and our friends John and Diane Stokinger completed an expedition to Chimney Pond, we began studying our park maps for interesting alternatives. An excursion beginning at Nesowadnehunk Field, traveling through the Wassataquoik Lakes region to Russell Pond, up to remote Davis Pond, over Hamlin Peak to Chimney Pond, and out to Roaring Brook was our ambitious choice.

Planning the complicated undertaking was a logistical challenge. Campsite reservations were needed sufficiently spaced to accomplish our mission in the five days and four nights available. Organizing a shuttle to negotiate the time-consuming rough park roads was also a necessity. Traveling from and to our homes in central Maine also had to be factored into the equation.

Our decision was to reserve a lean-to at Roaring Brook for the first night, positioning us to leave a shuttle vehicle and drive to Nesowadnehunk Field to begin our trek on day two. Securing lean-to reservations at Little Wassataquoik Lake, Davis Pond, and Chimney Pond allowed for manageable daily hikes on the twenty-seven-mile exploit.

Arriving at Roaring Brook early afternoon on a sunny August day provided sufficient time for a hike. Our choice was a two-mile climb to the summit of 3,122-foot South Turner Mountain. The rocky open peak provided an extraordinary panoramic view of the Katahdin massif including portions of our upcoming endeavor. A close encounter with a large moose feeding in Sandy Stream Pond on our return completed an exceptional first day in the wilderness paradise.

After negotiating park roads to Nesowadnehunk Field on the far western perimeter of the park, our merry band departed northeasterly under clear blue skies on the Wassataquoik Lake Trail. We eagerly anticipated the 9.3-mile venture to Little Wassataquoik Lake Lean-to. Initially encountering easy hiking following Little Nesowadnehunk Stream on fresh legs, excellent progress was made. As we skirted the shore of Center Pond at about the midway point, outstanding views of North and South Brother Mountains were savored during our lunch break.

When stimulating scenery is lacking, backpacking can sometimes be a tedious boring process. Not so when trekking with John and Diane. Singing, dancing, and uproarious humor are constants. Our version of Dean Martin's hit song *Houston* can often be heard echoing through the hills when we're negotiating demanding wilderness trails. "I'm a face without a name, just walking in the rain. Going back to Houston, Houston, Houston."

No rain was encountered on our way to Little Wassataquoik Lake but water was a problem when progressing through a wet section of trail with several stream crossings. Gentle hiking followed on what appeared to be an ancient logging road to a steep incline. Persisting over the pitch, our destination was accomplished arriving at the lean-to on scenic Little Wassataquoik Lake.

More sunshine greeted us on the second day of our outing. A daunting ten-mile journey to remote Davis Pond was the objective. Progressing along the shore of picturesque Wassataquoik Lake, a spur trail on the right led to captivating Green Falls. A boat landing providing canoe access to an island lean-to was passed at the western end of the lake. A dam separating portions of Six Ponds was negotiated before joining Pogy Notch Trail at bustling Russell Pond Campground.

After lunch at Russell Pond, the crooning ramblers advanced towards Davis Pond on the Northwest Basin Trail. The path climbed gradually and passed North Peaks Trail on the left after about a mile. Paralleling Wassataquoik Stream for a couple of miles while enjoying a forgiving gradient, the boulder-strewn mountain freshet was eventually forded and the trail began to

Chapter 48 - Baxter State Park - Nesowadnehunk Field to Roaring Brook

steepen. "I've got holes in both of my shoes, I'm a walking case of the blues, saw a dollar yesterday but the wind blew it away. Going back to Houston, Houston, Houston."

Our boots held up well but rugged conditions were endured entering isolated Northwest Basin. No one was feeling the blues after passing Lake Cowles and arriving at a large rock formation that afforded exceptional panoramic vistas of the unique mountain region. Shortly beyond, the yodeling rovers arrived at Davis Pond Lean-to. Although a remarkable location, an imperfection was the unwelcome presence of black flies. The consensus was it was too late in the season for the nasty airborne blood suckers.

"I haven't eaten in about a week, I'm so hungry when I walk I squeak." No one went hungry but the dehydrated meals were wearing thin after finishing breakfast the following morning. An arduous precipitous climb up the basin wall to Northwest Plateau followed. "Nobody calls me friend, it's sad the shape I'm in. Going back to Houston, Houston, Houston."

Northwest Plateau was the beginning of a glorious above tree line expanse of high elevation hiking on the Katahdin massif. Persevering southerly, an invigorating ascent was completed to Hamlin Peak, Maine's second highest point. The summit marked the beginning of a steady descent on magnificent Hamlin Ridge. Our strenuous day ended following North Basin Trail and a short section of Chimney Pond Trail to yet another idyllic location, Chimney Pond. The crowded campground was a stark contrast to secluded Davis Pond.

The last of our dehydrated meals was consumed on our final day in one of Maine's most exceptional locations. Lighter packs, a steady descent, and buoyant melodious spirits punctuated the 3.3 mile return to Roaring Brook. "I got a home and big warm bed and a feather pillow for my head. Going back to Houston, Houston, Houston."

THINGS TO KNOW

Location: Piscataquis County, north-central Maine

Length of described trek: 27 miles

Other distances:
Nesowadnehunk Field to Little Wassataquoik Lake: 9.3 miles
    Little Wassataquoik Lake to Davis Pond: 10.1 miles
    Davis Pond to Chimney Pond: 4.3 miles
    Chimney Pond to Roaring Brook: 3.3 miles
    Difficulty: Strenuous
    Unique potential hazards: Extended above tree line exposure to the elements from Davis Pond to Chimney Pond. Several sections require boulder and rock scrambling, increasing the chance of serious falls. High winds and extreme conditions are a risk above tree line. Carrying a map, compass, and GPS are recommended.
    Views: Phenomenal throughout but particularly from Davis Pond to Chimney Pond
    Directions:
        Roaring Brook: Follow directions in Chapter 1 to the left turn on Golden Road. Continue north on Millinocket Road for about 2 miles to Baxter State Park Road on the right. Drive about 2 miles on Baxter State Park Road to Togue Pond Gate and pay fees or confirm reservations. Bear right and follow the Roaring Brook Road for about 7 miles to Roaring Brook Campground.
        Nesowadnehunk Field: Leave Roaring Brook Campground and return to Togue Pond Gate. Turn right before the gate and drive northerly on the Park Perimeter Road for about 14 miles to Nesowadnehunk Field.
    Park Information: Visit their website at https://baxterstatepark.org/

Other Trip Recommendations:
    South Branch to Russell Pond: Out and back
    Roaring Brook to Russell Pond: Out and back
    South Branch to Roaring Brook: Traverse

Chapter 48 - Baxter State Park - Nesowadnehunk Field to Roaring Brook

Trout Brook Farm to Webster Outer Campsite: Out and back
Trout Brook Farm Five Ponds Loop
Roaring Brook to Chimney Pond: Out and back
Russell Pond to Chimney Pond via North Peaks Trail: Can be part of a traverse or loop

Backpackers prepare to descend Hamlin Ridge in Baxter State Park. (Photo – Ron Chase)

SECTION X. DOWNRIVER CANOE AND KAYAK RACES

A practicing racer takes a swim on Souadabscook Stream. (Photo – Ron Chase)

Chapter 49 - Kenduskeag Stream

Embracing the Kenduskeag Stream Canoe Race

The Kenduskeag Stream Canoe Race is the most renowned downriver race in Maine. Many superlatives apply. It's the most popular, oldest, and easily receives the most media coverage. In fact, the race is the largest paddling event in New England and one of the most substantial in the entire country. Some years, as many as 1,500 contestants have participated.

Television crews, radio announcers, newspaper reporters, and scads of onlookers called "river vultures" flock to the bridge below Six Mile Falls to watch the carnage. They're never disappointed because the cataract is the epicenter of chaos. During every race, the complex Class III rapid dumps multitudes of unfortunate paddlers into the frigid frothy waves. Those unable to self-rescue are hauled out by dedicated safety teams. While Six Mile Falls is the preferred vulture hangout, thousands of spectators gather to watch the staggered countdowns in the village of Kenduskeag and the excitement at various other locations along the race course.

The race was founded by Ed "Sonny" Colburn and Lew Gilman in May 1967. The first competition had 34 contestants and only 25 finished. Since then, almost 29,000 paddlers have participated in the annual event. Sponsored by the Bangor Department of Parks and Recreation, the race begins in the tiny town of Kenduskeag and travels 16.5 miles downstream, ending in Bangor just before joining the Penobscot River. Each year, the contest is convened on the third weekend in April.

The 51st Kenduskeag Stream Canoe Race held in 2017 was not the first rodeo for Carolyn Welch. At age 80, she was back for her 23rd event. Beginning in 1992, Carolyn had participated in the competition with three different tandem canoe partners. This year, she had a new paddling companion, sixty-eight-year-old Bud Gilbert.

As had been her tradition, Carolyn met Bud the day before the race for a trial run. Since they had never been in a canoe together, a warmup paddle was particularly important this year. Listed at 8.75 feet on the USGS Kenduskeag gauge, the water was high. They were worried about their safety canoeing alone, but attempts to recruit other paddling teams had been unsuccessful.

Confident about the easy first ten miles, they launched a short distance above Six Mile Falls, and halted to scout the intimidating rapid on river right. The waves were enormous in the preferred left channel. While watching, two canoes capsized. An alternative passage in the center was partially obstructed by a tree branch. When additional boats flipped attempting that route, a portage was their cautious choice.

During their paddle to the first mandatory portage at Flour Mill Dam, the current was swift, gusty headwinds challenging, and the usually easy rapids more difficult than Carolyn had previously experienced. After investigating the portage routes around Flour Mill and Maxwell Mill Dams, there was some disagreement on whether to carry right or left at Maxwell. As a precaution, Carolyn stashed her canoe wheels on river right cabled to a tree. Reconnoitering Shopping Cart Rapid immediately below Maxwell, both agreed the large waves and a complex maneuver required to avoid a huge boulder would present significant complications during the race.

While Bud returned home, Carolyn followed her usual routine. First was a visit to the local Gifford's Ice Cream stand. Enjoying a delicious ice cream cone was her reward for a busy, active day. Her final stop was a favorite local motel.

Race day began early for Carolyn and Bud. The temperature was a chilly 33 degrees when they met at the takeout in Bangor at 6:15 a.m. After leaving Bud's vehicle to shuttle them and their boat after the race, they drove to Six Mile Falls for a final reconnaissance. The water level had dropped about a foot and the daunting descent appeared easier than the previous day.

Chapter 49 - Kenduskeag Stream

Proceeding to the village of Kenduskeag, Carolyn found a parking space while Bud paid the fee and obtained a race packet. Registered in the C-2 Mixed Experienced class, their assigned number was 109. Due to some preparation delays, they missed their scheduled start time. Instead, the determined racers departed with the 141 to 145 group, beginning seven minutes late.

As anticipated, the first part of the race was uneventful with high water propelling them rapidly downstream. About a mile above Six Mile Falls, greetings were exchanged with their friend and race icon Zip Kellogg who stands in his canoe during the event. A crowd and media favorite, as usual Zip was stylishly dressed, this year wearing a white suit and hat.

Approaching the top of Six Mile Falls, a decision was made to attempt the left channel. As they plunged through the consequential waves, copious amounts of icy water cascaded over the bow partially filling their craft. Powering ashore on a tiny island, they quickly emptied the heavy vessel. The remaining descent through the falls was deftly completed without incident. Numerous overturned boats were passed at the bottom as Carolyn and Bud began their sprint through easier rapids towards the Flour Mill portage.

Both fatigued when arriving at the portage trail, Bud dragged the canoe while Carolyn did her best to assist. After negotiating a minor rapid, the Maxwell Mill portage was next. A last-minute choice was to attempt the portage on river left. The trail was muddy and slippery and that resulted in a long, exhausting haul. Using Carolyn's portage wheels concealed on the opposite side of the stream would likely have been preferable.

Progressing through surging waves in Shopping Cart Rapid, they were turned sideways attempting to move right rendering them on a collision course with a huge boulder. As they straightened their canoe at the last second, the hazardous obstacle was barely avoided and they were then launched into a substantial wave train with another canoe following immediately to their left. While the two tandem teams desperately attempted to remain upright in perilous curlers, the other vessel momentarily crashed over the top of their stern deck. Amazingly, both boats remained upright while many others capsized. Swiftly dumping their water laden craft, the intrepid duo paddled through the finish line to the takeout.

Finishing 11th in their class with a time of 3:34:08, it's doubtful any other tandem team had a combined age as high as 148 years. While loading the boat on Carolyn's car after completing the shuttle, a microburst tore the canoe from her hands, dumping it to the ground. She suffered two broken fingers.

If you think this was the end of Carolyn's Kenduskeag racing career, you're wrong. She and Bud were back for her 24th race in 2019 and were planning a 25th when the race was cancelled due to the pandemic in 2020.

THINGS TO KNOW

Location: Penobscot County, Central Maine
Length: 16.5 miles
Difficulty: Moderate
Scouting and required portages: Recommend scouting Six Mile Falls before the race. Paddlers should have an advance plan. There is an optional portage on the right. Near the end of the race, Flour Mill Dam and Maxwell Mill Dam are mandatory portages. Portage Flour Mill on the left and carry Maxwell either right or left. Just below, Shopping Cart Rapid should be scouted from river right.
Water levels: There is a USGS Kenduskeag gauge. Five feet is low and over eight high. Consult the following link for the level: https://waerdata.usgs.gov/me/nwis/uv/?site_no=01037000&PARAmeter_cd=00065,00060.
Race information: http://kenduskeagstreamcanoerace.com/
Directions:
Six Mile Falls: From the junction of Interstate 95 (Exit 186) and Route 15 (Broadway) in Bangor, drive about 4 miles westerly on Route 15 to a bridge over Kenduskeag Stream.
Put-in: From Six Mile Falls, continue about 6.5 miles west on 15 to the Stetson Road on the left in the Town of Kenduskeag.

Chapter 49 - Kenduskeag Stream

Turn left onto Stetson Road and cross the bridge over Kenduskeag Stream to the put-in.

Takeout: The takeout location has changed in recent years. Recommend consulting with race officials in advance.

Racers on Kenduskeag Stream. (Photo - Tammy Kelley)

Chapter 50 - Souadabscook Stream

An Icy Rite of Spring

If Kenduskeag Stream is the big enchilada of the Maine down-river racing circuit, Souadabscook Stream is the hot tamale. A narrow, twisting Class III whitewater gem, Souadabscook consists of challenging rapids, steep descents, sticky holes, and a demanding portage. While racing skills are important, the ability to maneuver through complex rapids is a corresponding necessity. Normally the third competition of the spring racing season, it's usually scheduled for the second Saturday of April. The water temperature is frequently in the thirties, snow and ice shelves sometimes line the banks, a swim means an instantaneous "ice cream headache," and ice floes are occasionally an adversary.

While the racing sector of the stream is located in Hampden, the source is a collection of small ponds in Hermon and Carmel. The first portion of the 7.3-mile race course is primarily flatwater while the rapids are concentrated in the last half. The American Whitewater Association rates Souadabscook Class III+ when the water is high. Due to the difficulty level, helmets are required.

A large field of participants assembled in calm water above Bog Road Bridge in Hampden for my first Sou race in April 1990. Accompanied by my eleven-year-old son, Adam, testing our skills in the Junior/Senior class was the intent. Our racing vessel was a now discontinued 16-foot Old Town Kennebec. An adequate whitewater canoe when designed and manufactured, the Kennebec had two less than redeeming racing qualities: it was heavy and slow.

Race conditions were ideal with sunny weather and a medium water level. Competitors were organized into staggered brackets of four, most in the same class. Our quartet of Junior/Seniors lined up beside one another immediately above the bridge as a

Chapter 50 - Souadabscook Stream

race official commenced the countdown. The opposition appeared daunting. When the start was announced, the four tandem boats advanced downriver in a flurry of racing strokes.

Two teams quickly moved ahead of us shortly after entering Hammond Pond. Reassuring ourselves we'd catch them in the rapids with our theoretically superior whitewater canoe, Team Slug plodded along, meandering circuitously in flat water for a long three miles to the first significant rapid, Class II/III Manning Mill. We missed our intended line on the left and large waves broke over the bow, adding unwanted ballast to our already heavy boat.

Another Junior/Senior team passed us while approaching a ledge drop called Boy Scout Rapid. Substantial waves and a pour over on the right seemed guaranteed to add more weight to the Kennebec, so bouncing down a rock-filled channel close to the left shore was our gamble instead. Despite the bumpy ride, our durable vessel handled it cleanly.

The next rapid was intimidating Emerson Mill Falls. Having scouted the Class III descent in advance of the race, the plan was to ferry right to left across the top of the falls followed by a hard right turn once a narrow sloping tongue was located far left. Reminding Adam he needed to execute an effective cross draw when entering the slot, Team Slug glided through while avoiding additional water accumulation.

Just before reaching a ledge drop called Great Expectations, another Junior/Senior team darted by on our right. Amassing water over the gunnels at the bottom, the most difficult and complex rapid in the race was next. Dismissing the notion to stop and dump, Adam bailed while I paddled as our weighty ark advanced towards Class III Crawford's.

Entry into upper Crawford's was problem free. Turning left, exploding surf could be observed below a menacing river-wide horizon line. The center is an impassable boulder garden so the choice is hard right or hard left. Left was our decision. Taking more water while angling through breaking waves, we progressed within a few feet of an impressive rock formation on river left.

Turning immediately left below the outcropping and running parallel with the pitch, the intent was to quickly identify an abrupt right turn that facilitates a smooth slide down the ledge. Although we recognized the sweet spot, our water-laden barge couldn't be turned quickly enough, tumbling through a rock pile farther left instead. This time the Kennebec was an asset as we plowed downriver just missing a Junior/Senior team broached on a ledge below.

We then completed Crawford's with several more inches of accumulated water and one more rapid remained before the portage. Adam bailed as I steered into Papermill Rapid. Unable to sustain a narrow route on river right, a monster wave dumped more water into what was essentially a floating bathtub.

Persevering to the left bank with a boat filled to the gunnels, the portage was next. While struggling to empty our ponderous craft, another team of competitors in our class overtook us. Adam was too short to help with the boat portage, so he carried the paddles. Deflating the center air bag, I lifted the burdensome Kennebec onto my shoulders. The exhausting quarter mile portage seemed much longer.

Quick water followed for a long mile to a Class II rapid below a snowmobile bridge that was skirted tight left. A precise maneuver left to right was required to navigate through a more technical passage just below. The approach to an S-Turn Rapid was confusing. Beginning extreme left, the choice was a difficult ferry to the right or a plunging over two rocky ledges far left. Selecting the latter, the lumbering Kennebec endured more abuse.

Easy rapids continued to the finish on river right just above a dangerous descent called Hell's Gate. Team Slug had overestimated their abilities. A fifth-place finish left us in the middle of the pack. The demanding endeavor had proven a humbling experience.

In addition to being a premiere racing venue, Souadabscook Stream is one of Maine's most popular early spring whitewater runs. Since formation of the Penobscot Paddle and Chowder Society (PPCS) in 1969, challenging the Sou has been a rite of spring

Chapter 50 - Souadabscook Stream

for many Chowderheads. A coastal stream, it's usually one of the first waterways to experience ice out. Club members often schedule an "icebreaker" exploratory in late February or early March. Besides furnishing numerous race participants, the PPCS has provided race safety for many years.

A mandatory portage during the race, Great Falls is the most substantial rapid on the Stream. A precipitous Class IV+ descent, the consequences of swimming are substantial. The falls can be portaged on the right or left. The runout below called Rec Center is an entertaining Class III.

THINGS TO KNOW

Location: Penobscot County, Central Maine
Length: 7.3 miles
Difficulty: The Sou is the most technically difficult downriver race in Maine. A mandatory portage in the race, Great Falls should be considered very difficult.
Scouting and required portages: Recommend scouting Emerson Mills, Crawford's, and Great Falls. Great Falls is a mandatory portage in the race. Hell's Gate has been run by experts. However, it is a tidal falls and there is a life threatening hydraulic at some levels. The vast majority of paddlers avoid the potential dangers and takeout above.
Water levels: If the USGS gauge level for the Kenduskeag Stream is above 5.0, there is usually enough water to run the Sou. There is a painted gauge on the left bridge abutment below Emerson Mill Rapid. The Sou can be run from minus .5 to over 3 feet. Higher levels become more difficult.
Race Information:
https://inmemoryofeliot.wixsite.com/souadabscookrace
Directions:
   Race Takeout: From the junction of Exit 180 on Interstate 95 and Cold Brook Road in Hampden, follow Cold Brook Road easterly for about 2.5 miles to US Route 1A. Turn right on

1A, cross the bridge over Souadabscook Stream to the Hampden Water District on the immediate right. Historically, the water district has permitted use of their property for the race takeout.

Race Put-in: From the junction of Exit 180 on Interstate 95 and Cold Brook Road in Hampden, follow Cold Brook Road westerly for about 2 miles to Bog Road on the left. Turn onto Bog Road and travel about 3 miles to the Bog Road Bridge.

A canoeist runs Emerson Mill Falls on Souadabscook Stream. (Photo – Nancy Chase)

About the Author

A Maine native, Ron Chase currently resides in Topsham, Maine, with his wife Nancy. They have two grown sons, a daughter-in-law, and two granddaughters. He has been an avid outdoor enthusiast for over 45 years, participating in adventures throughout the United States, Canada, Scotland, France, Switzerland, Costa Rica, and New Zealand. When not writing or engaged in outdoor escapades, he operates a tax consulting business.

The author of the mountain guidebook, *Mountains for Mortals – New England*, and *The Great Mars Hill Bank Robbery*, a biography of Vietnam War hero and bank robber Bernard Patterson, Ron has written an outdoor column for a regional newspaper and contributed articles to several magazines. He currently writes columns for four newspapers, articles for *Maine Seniors* magazine, and blogs for the *Bangor Daily News* blog network, all entitled "Seniors Not Acting Their Age."

Ron is a graduate of the University of Maine and retired from the Internal Revenue Service. He is a U.S. Army veteran who served in Korea and Alaska and is a member of the VFW. Formerly a Registered Maine Guide, he was active in the Appalachian Mountain Club (AMC) as canoe chair and a trip leader. Currently, he is treasurer of the Penobscot Paddle and Chowder Society (PPCS) and a frequent trip coordinator. In 1997, he was the 38th person certified by the AMC Four Thousand Footer Committee as having climbed the 100 highest peaks in New England in the winter. He has led more than 300 whitewater, hiking, winter mountaineering, cycling, skiing, canoeing, and sea kayaking trips for the AMC, PPCS, and as a Maine Guide.

www.ingramcontent.com/pod-product-compliance
Lightning Source LLC
Chambersburg PA
CBHW042131160426
43199CB00021B/2875